THE WELFARE OF FOOD

The Welfare of Food

The Rights and Responsibilities in a Changing World

Edited by
Elizabeth Dowler and Catherine Jones Finer

Blackwell
Publishing

© 2003 by Blackwell Publishers Ltd,
A Blackwell Publishing Company

First published as a special issue of *Social Policy and Administration*, 2002

350 Main Street, Malden, MA 02148-5018, USA
108 Cowley Road, Oxford OX4 1JF, UK
550 Swanston Street, Carlton South, Melbourne, Victoria 3053, Australia
Kurfürstendamm 57, 10707 Berlin, Germany

First published 2003 by Blackwell Publishing Ltd

Library of Congress Cataloging-in-Publication Data has been applied for

ISBN 1-4051-0245-X
A catalogue record for this title is available from the British Library.

Set by Graphicraft Typesetters Ltd, Hong Kong

For further information on
Blackwell Publishing, visit our website:
http://www.blackwellpublishing.com

Contents

Notes on Contributors

David Barling is Senior Lecturer in Food Policy at the Institute of Health Sciences, City University, London.

Martin Caraher is Reader in Food Policy at the Institute of Health Sciences, City University, London.

Elizabeth Dowler is Senior Lecturer in Social Policy and Food, in the Department of Sociology, University of Warwick.

Alizon Draper is Senior Lecturer at the School of Integrated Health at the University of Westminster.

Judith Green is Senior Lecturer in Sociology, HSRU, at the London School of Hygiene & Tropical Medicine.

Ulla Gustafsson is Senior Lecturer in the School of Sociology and Social Policy, University of Surrey, Roehampton.

Karim Hussein is now Senior Agricultural Economist at the OECD, Paris. He was formerly Research Fellow and Manager of the ODI Food Security Technical Support Facility, Overseas Development Institute, UK.

Anne Itto Leonardo is coordinator for NGO activities, USAID in New (South) Sudan.

Margaret Itto Leonardo is Director of the New (South) Sudan Council of Churches, Uganda Branch.

Tim Lang is Professor of Food Policy at the Institute of Health Sciences, City University, London.

Erik Millstone is Reader in Science and Technology Policy in the Science and Technology Policy Research Unit (SPRU), University of Sussex.

Elizabeth Ojaba is a freelance consultant on nutrition and food emergencies, currently working as nutritionist and food security adviser for Oxfam UK in Afghanistan. She and the Itto Leonardos are sisters.

Graham Riches is Director of the School of Social Work and Family Studies at the University of British Columbia.

Geoff Tansey is an independent writer and consultant.

Patrick van Zwanenberg is a Research Fellow at the Science Policy Research Unit of the University of Sussex, and has a specialist interest in the role of science in BSE policy-making.

Preface

"Broadening perspectives on social policy" involves more than encouraging mainstream social policy specialists to broaden their ideas—as well as paying attention to neglected aspects of the subject as presently defined. A key object has been to persuade specialists in potentially related fields to contribute to what is hoped will be an ever-widening social policy debate, to everyone's advantage. This has, of course, produced a variety of challenges, to the authors of papers in the present as well as in previous collections and possibly to readers.

Each venture in the series so far has turned out to be truly innovatory; we hope this volume continues what is becoming a tradition. Nevertheless, on the one hand, many of the contributors in the present issue, as in earlier like issues, are being invited to address the concerns of an audience more or less unfamiliar to them. On the other hand, social policy audiences are being asked to respond to visions of the world and its priorities which may differ markedly from those to which they have been accustomed, some of which come from activists and practitioners rather than academics.

Certainly, issues of "field-distance"—whether between specialisms within social policy or in respect of apparently distinct disciplinary areas bearing upon it—are never simple or unidimensional. The very fact of selection as a topic for this series implies, in practice, that the area chosen is already possessed of at least some social policy-conscious specialists, whose work is known to at least an interested coterie of social policy mainstreamers.

Earlier issues in this series have focused either on a particular related disciplinary area—such as criminology (issue 31.5, 1997) or environmentalism (issue 35.5, 2001)—or else on hitherto neglected aspects of social policy specialists' own range of activities—namely "Transnational Social Policy" (issue 32.5, 1998), "New Risks, New Welfare" (issue 33.5, 1999), "The Business of Research" (issue 34.5, 2000). In comparison to all of which, the present choice of "Food" is different again.

Food is not, so far, a defined specialism in its own right: on the contrary, many disciplines claim an interest, from economists (for whom "consumption" refers to purchase) to nutritionists (for whom "consumption" means eating) via sociologists, anthropologists, agriculturalists, political scientists, food technologists, historians, epidemiologists, health promotion . . . the list could go on! Many of these disciplines are represented by authors in the present volume. In short, "food" is a topic of abiding concern, to both peoples and their governments, right around the world, for a kaleidoscopic range of reasons. So multidisciplinarity, in this case, is to be matched by a multiplicity of perspectives.

Specifically, the choice of Food as this year's special field of interest was based on the following set of considerations, hard to resist:

- food is a subject of urgent topical concern within the UK, the EU and the world in general;
- it has hitherto been conspicuously under-documented, from social policy points of view;
- it is a multifaceted subject area with numerous potential linkages to social policy concerns;
- it boasts a no-less multifarious network of specialists, some of whom are already members of the international academic social policy community in their own right.

Even so, it was a daunting prospect for us as editors to decide how to approach so broad a topic, and deal with it so as to reflect at least some of the diversity of current research and concerns. "Food" could potentially relate to virtually every aspect of all our lives. Obviously, we have had to be selective in our choice of topics and contributors.

The object has been, quite simply, to range over as many aspects of the subject as possible, within the span of social policy import and importance: from "food patenting", food safety, food security, food aid and regulated food provision via individual choice and collective responsibility. We have tried to take in the global aspects too, including concerns of the international community, the private as well as the public sector, and the voices of those often excluded. We face the challenge of definitions and language: how to describe different parts of the world in ways which reflect their economic, political and social realities. In the past, the term "third world" was used to denote non-industrialized countries (i.e. not the "first world") which were also not part of the so-called communist block ("second world"). These terms are hardly appropriate today, and the use of "developed" and "developing" countries is misleading also. The latest (equally confusing) term "North" is used to refer to rich, industrialized countries, and "South" to refer to everywhere else. In the present case, we have not imposed any terminology on the authors.

The opening paper sums up both the problems and possibilities of the subject: "Joined-up Food Policy" being a challenge whose implications this impressive team does its best to expose to detailed examination. This is nicely balanced by Tansey's paper on "Patenting our Food Future", which unpacks the notion of a "food system", and explores the tortuous but critical international ramifications of intellectual property rights in this arena. These scene-setting papers are in turn succeeded by two very different approaches to aspects of food safety: Millstone and van Zwanenberg address food safety institutions in the UK and EU, and Draper and Green look at consumer constructions of choice and risk, largely from a UK perspective.

We enter a different order of reality again, with Hussein's piece on global issues of food security and the response by the international community to its present challenges, coupled with the papers from Riches on food banks in Canada, and from Ojaba and her sisters Itto Leonardo, on the humanitarian uses of food aid in "complex emergencies", specifically in South Sudan. Taken together, these papers demonstrate the inadequacy of crude "North–South" (or for that matter first–third world) distinctions in matters of food insecurity. They also raise critical issues of human rights—and of state, institutional and agency capacities and willingness to respond to food security and entitlement failures.

Rights and responsibilities are also the themes of the final two papers, which return to focus primarily on issues in the UK. Gustafsson's observations on the implications of school meals policies addresses and questions the benefits for society and for children; Dowler's concluding observations on the relationship between poverty, participation and (hence) access to food choice, complete the story.

To paraphrase Alan Berg when he was in the World Bank: "food and nutrition are everybody's business but nobody's responsibility". Many have examined why food and nutrition, clearly so central and important, remain "weak issues" in policy terms. Those whose food access or nutritional status is compromised are usually poor and marginalized in society, with little political "clout". Consumers, while fashionable participants in policy activities, do not yet wield real power in most countries. The policy agenda is being set by the bigger actors, so that food concerns can all too easily be reduced to the private, the domestic—the hidden; and thus out of sight (and site) of social policy and out of mind of otherwise leading social actors. We hope this collection of papers will go some way towards challenging that relegation.

Our thanks, as ever, are due to those who agreed and then contrived to deliver, to editorial order, on a tight schedule. We hope the results will prove to have been more than worth all our efforts.

Elizabeth Dowler
Catherine Jones Finer
Editors

1

Joined-up Food Policy? The Trials of Governance, Public Policy and the Food System

David Barling, Tim Lang and Martin Caraher

Introduction: The Challenge of an Integrated Food Policy

Food policy offers a substantial challenge to governments as it reaches across a number of policy areas, demanding responses across these different policy sectors. In recent decades food policy in the United Kingdom has been malfunctioning across a number of these policy sectors including agriculture, health, environment, social and competition policy (Lang *et al.* 2001). In an era of multi-level governance such policy integration is not only required horizontally across policy sectors, but also vertically through different levels of governance. The UK is not alone in this policy challenge. There have been major debates about policy failure in other developed European countries, such as France, Belgium, Ireland, Spain and Germany, often following public outcry about perceived failings in food quality or health control. But the UK does, as ever, make an interesting case study, partly because it was the first industrial nation, and thus the first to sever the links between the urban majority and the land, and partly because of its peculiarities of imperial and national history, today struggling to meld with regional and global integration, on, if not a more equal, then certainly a less colonial footing.

Food policy in the UK is shaped by European Union policy, not just the Common Agricultural Policy (CAP), but also by the regulatory legislation that has buttressed the drive to the single market. The promotion of international trade liberalization and the extension of a rule-based trading system to include agriculture and food have extended regulatory governance to the World Trade Organization (WTO) and the global level. The reform of subnational governance in the UK provides a further evolution in the extension of multi-level governance to the regional, local and community levels. Within the UK, the structure of subnational governance and the allocation of policy responsibilities continue to evolve through an ongoing process of reform, providing a variable geometry for governance.

The governance of food stretches beyond the formal governmental sectors, however, and embraces the private governance of food, notably through the

David Barling, Tim Lang and Martin Caraher

introduction of systems of standards and grading of food products (Marsden *et al.* 2000). Within the food system as a whole change—such as corporate concentration—continues to take place, causing shifts in resource dependencies and power along the food chain (Lang *et al.* 2001). Key corporate players in the food chain have become important in the governance of food in the market economy, leading to the incorporation of these private interests into public systems of regulation (Flynn *et al.* 1999). This mix of public and private governance adds further to the complexity that marks the shift to multi-level governance and a multi-level polity (Gamble 2002).

To address the policy malfunctions of the recent past and present, food policy needs to link policy areas that in the past have too often been dealt with in a disparate manner. There are models being advanced which offer an evidence-based approach to providing both an integrated and sustainable food policy. For example, the 51 nation state members of the World Health Organization Europe (WHO-E) regional committee agreed on a more integrated approach to food policy in September 2000. A three-year process of consultation and debate preceded this landmark resolution. And a five-year process was proposed to upgrade food policies to give equal weight to nutrition, food safety and sustainable food supply (WHO-E 2000). These three policy priorities were configured as the three pillars holding up the roof of health for all. The sustainable food supply approach recognizes the need to include social policy objectives such as reducing health inequalities. A refined version of this approach has been conceptualized as an ecological public health model, adding a fourth pillar which addresses food consumption and cultural dimensions (Lang *et al.* 2001), drawing upon a more complex multipillared approach to food and health (Waltner-Toews and Lang 2000).

Integrating Food Policy in the UK: Institutional and Policy Initiatives and Policy Paradigms

A coherent and sustainable food policy clearly demands policy integration across discrete sectors. But, to what extent is there a joined-up food policy emerging in the UK? To what extent are institutional reforms and new policy initiatives in food policy, of which there have been several in recent years, signalling joined-up thinking? How far does this joined-up thinking go? Within which policy frames and by which interests are these recent initiatives being shaped and delivered? Also, in what ways is UK food policy recognizing and adjusting to complexities of multi-level governance? Are national reforms, such as the establishment of a Food Standards Agency (FSA), occurring at a historical juncture when such responsibilities are being moved more to intergovernmental levels such as the new European Food Safety Authority (EFSA) and the joint FAO/WHO Codex Alimentarius Commission (Codex)? Some much-needed rethinking may slowly be emerging from policy-makers at all levels, but is it sufficient? To what extent does the emergent food policy suggest a joining up of nutrition, food safety, sustainable food supply and consumption? To what extent do the reforms focus on the social policy dimensions of food?

Achieving policy integration across policy sectors and departmental boundaries has proven a generic problem for governments. Departmentalism is entrenched in government, leading to turf mentalities and sustaining policy communities with client interest groups that can insulate officials from outside thinking on policy priorities. An awareness of these kinds of problems led the incoming Blair government in 1997 to promise "joined-up solutions for joined-up problems". Within the core executive of UK government, the main mechanisms for policy coordination have become the prime minister's own office and the Cabinet Office—as opposed to the full Cabinet—as well as the more traditional institution of the Treasury (Holliday 2002; Richards and Smith 2001). Under the Blair–Brown axis the Treasury's Comprehensive Spending Review, with its three-year horizon, has become a centralized auditing of departmental policy performance and promise. The extent to which such centralization can also offer a basis for policy integration across different policy sectors remains uncertain, however. Consequently, other processes have been instituted to try to bridge departmental divides and produce policy innovation. The most favoured under Blair has been the "taskforce" approach, setting up *ad hoc* committees (which run into their hundreds), involving both public and private sector people, to address specific problems (Richards and Smith 2001). A feature of these taskforces has been the involvement of leading corporate executives, including executives from 28 of the leading FTSE-100 companies (Holliday 2002: 103). The more important of the taskforces have been designated Units, and located within the Cabinet Office. One example of these, the Social Exclusion Unit (SEU), is discussed more fully in the next section.

An instructive example of the difficulties of achieving effective policy integration, at least to date, has been the so-called "greening of government initiative" under Labour. The Labour government inherited a range of institutional devices and forums from the previous Conservative government, including: a cabinet committee on the environment, a committee of green ministers and a cross-departmental Sustainable Development Unit. Labour updated the remit of the latter, and added in other institutional reforms—including toughening the remit of the House of Commons' select committees. Yet, the ability of these processes to adjust other departments' policy-making approaches and thinking so as to prioritize environmental issues remains unfulfilled (Jordan 2002). Sustainable development was itself hived off into the new DEFRA in June 2001. Similarly, the integration of environmental policy priorities across and into other policy sectors had proved a difficult task at the EU level, bringing with it the conundrum of trying to operationalize policy along both horizontal and vertical policy dimensions in a multi-level polity. The EU's Fifth Environmental Action Programme "Towards Sustainability" prioritized such integration across five policy sectors. But a review of this programme concluded that "the commitment by other sectors and by Member States to the Programme is partial" (CEC 1999: 3).

The ecological public health model suggests the need for a significant shift in thinking about food policy, arguably a paradigm shift (McMichael 2001). Current UK agricultural policy can be characterized as struggling within an

3

industrialized "productionist" model that emerged after the Second World War. The aim of postwar agricultural policy was to achieve greater self-sufficiency of food production (partly for balance of trade reasons) within a Commonwealth based on a post-colonial preferential trading system. The entry of the UK into the European Community relocated the "production-ist" model within the Common Agricultural Policy (CAP) that sought wider (and contradictory) goals including the maintenance of a rural infrastructure in western Europe and support for both agricultural production and food processing industries. The UK embraced the international neo-liberal trade agenda, within the boundaries of the CAP, with the signing of the GATT Agreement on Agriculture (Barling, in press).

Contemporary UK food policy can thus be placed within a dominant policy paradigm of national wealth creation through international economic competitiveness. Large food manufacturing industries and large farm pro-ducers are encouraged to compete successfully as export competitors in the neo-liberal trading system (notwithstanding the market distortions of the CAP and other national agricultural and food processing support mechanisms). National science and technology policy is geared to supporting these goals, both in agriculture and food technology (Barling and Henderson 2000). Other policy goals such as public health improvements through dietary change, or environmental improvements to the farmed landscape and its biodiversity, are pursued within this paradigm. The dominant paradigm offers a privileged place to certain private interests, notably the large corporate players in the food sys-tem. The shifting resource dependencies of the food system can also engender dispute, as witnessed by that between farmers' groups and the corporate retailers. The importance of the marketplace also allows for the public as consumers to have a voice, although the extent to which the consuming public is being heard or listened to as "food citizens" in policy-making, is less clear.

The dominant paradigm as presented is of course a contested one and so sits uneasily astride UK food policy. There is scope for social agency to generate policy change, be this through consumer activism (Gabriel and Lang 1995, ch. 9), the demonstration of global contradictions (Goodman and Watts 1997) or cultural change (Warde 1997). The rhetorical challenge to the productionist model of the 1980s was promoted strongly from the non-governmental sector in both developed and developing worlds. Their arguments shifted the focus from food production to issues such as: the environmental impacts of food production, the shedding of labour in agriculture, and food consumption, nutrition and its health impacts (Lang 1996). Environmental costs and diet-related health costs (Pretty 1998; Lang et al. 2001), as well as food safety crises, have evidenced contradictions in the dominant paradigm. The public health implications of food safety crises have engendered institu-tional reform, as with the creation of the FSA in the UK. At the EU level, food safety responsibilities have been shifted within the European Commis-sion to the newly formed DG-SANCO (Health and Consumer Protection), followed by the creation of the EFSA.

Yet the CAP's internal contradictions persist—notably in high interven-tion costs and the subsidized "dumping" of surpluses on developing countries and world markets (Watkins 2002). Nevertheless, a direction for reform has been signalled with the intent to shift supports from production ones to non-production rural policy actions, including agri-environment protection and conservation measures, the so-called second pillar of the CAP. In the UK, the replacement of the Ministry for Agriculture, Fisheries and Food (MAFF) with the Department for Food, Rural Affairs and the Environment (DEFRA) in June 2001 signalled a similar shift in intent for agricultural policy. The new department added sustainable development as a clear goal of food and agriculture policy which, while welcome, only seemed to underline further the contradictory goals requiring resolution within UK food policy.

Sustainability in the food supply chain should have a clear social dimension, yet there remain areas of relative food poverty, relative nutritional deprivation and food deserts in the midst of plenty in the UK. In response, the Government's SEU included access to shops among its cross-sectoral action areas. However, at the grassroots level there is being fashioned a range of alternative approaches to food supply, such as local food projects, often involving public bodies (Sustain 2002a). They are providing alternatives to established ways of managing the food supply chain, and achieving greater social inclusion at community levels. Yet what is missing, it can be argued, is a more strategic approach to such policy interventions. Within the rapidly evolving structure of subnational government, new elements such as the devolved assemblies and the English regional development agencies might offer a more "whole supply chain" approach to local food provision.

The institutional reforms do suggest new opportunities for more joined-up food policy at the European level and, within the UK, at national and subnational levels. Indeed there are attempts to introduce both new and joined-up policy initiatives in relation to food at all levels of governance. However, an initial analysis of some of these reforms and initiatives, as presented in this paper, suggests gaps and discontinuities in this policy integration. The policy frames within which such initiatives and reforms are being shaped are recognizing only a partial or bounded integration of food policy, not going as far as either the WHO-E's three-pillar model or the ecological public health model. Furthermore, policy integration initiatives can be relatively short-lived, to be followed by the subsequent hiving-off of specific policies into specific policy sectors, a process described here as "policy confinement". Such confinement will lead policy solutions into established patterns of response, going down established policy paths. The opportunity for framing the policy response in a more progressive way is lost. The contention is that such institutional processes are likely to reflect the realities of power relationships within the food system as a whole and work within the dominant policy paradigm.

The bounded nature of current food policy thinking is reflected in a closer examination of the remits of the new institutions, the FSA and DEFRA. The vertical demands of the multi-level polity are also illustrated with the introduction of the EFSA. The process by which policy integration initiatives slip into policy confinement is here illustrated by using two recent attempts at joined-up thinking on food policy as case studies:

David Barling, Tim Lang and Martin Caraher

1. The SEU's access to shops initiative.
2. The proposals regarding closer integration of different actors, or "recon-
   necting", in the food supply chain put forward by the Policy Commission
   on the Future of Farming and Food (called the Curry Commission) as
   initiated and subsequently carried on by DEFRA.

(PCFFF 2002: 114)

Exogenous shock(s) to the policy system, such as food safety crises, may
bring about some policy change, but such policy change is likely to be incremental. For the UK government to meet the aims of the WHO-E's current
food policy aspirations, further policy integration will be necessary. Further
institutional forms need be put in place that can allow for the evidence base
to lead to more joined-up policy. The setting up of a national food policy council
predicated on the experience of the nutrition councils set up by the Nordic
countries is here proposed as one possible way forward.

Institutionalizing a Bounded Policy Integration: The FSA and DEFRA

The reform of the departmental responsibilities for the environment, in 2001,
was part of the final dismantling of MAFF in response to crises in food safety
and farming. The setting up of DEFRA and the earlier separation of food
standards and safety responsibilities to the FSA have been the two main
institutional reforms in food policy at UK national level in recent years.
These institutional reforms were also an effort to bring in fresh approaches
to food policy and hence to a more integrated policy. But how joined-up has
been the policy advice (in the case of the FSA) and the policy-making (by
DEFRA) on food? Both institutions are relatively young, but some initial
assessment can be attempted and placed within the context of the broader
reach of food policy being sought by the WHO-E.

The main aim of the FSA as set out in the enabling legislation in 1999
was: "to protect public health from risks which may arise in connection with
the consumption of food (including risks caused by the way in which it is
produced or supplied) and otherwise protect the interests of consumers in
relation to food" (FSA 2001). Unlike its predecessor unit in MAFF, the FSA
could claim to be free from the direct sponsorship of any food industry
sector, and is answerable to the minister for public health. The scope of the
FSA's remit offers potential for joined-up policy thinking along the whole
food chain, but it has been interpreted in fairly bounded terms. In practice,
its rationale remains rooted in the dominant paradigm. As the initial gate-
keeper and communicator of scientific advice and of health-related food risk
(in coordination with its scientific advisory committees), it has adopted a role
as defender (rather than independent arbiter) of conventional agriculture and
farming practice and industrialized food manufacturing. The FSA has
adopted a consumerist, market-based approach to many issues of food safety
advice, often stressing the role of individual preference and choice. To this
extent there has been an open, transparent and consultative approach with
a wide range of interests, including consumer groups. What remains unclear,

also, is where and how the public health remit will integrate with health strategies at the Department of Health (DoH) and at regional, local and community levels, notably on diet and nutrition. It is clear that an ecological approach to health is not so far being pursued in the policy advice coming from the FSA.

In March 2002 the FSA advised that it was no longer necessary for consumers to wash and peel fruit and vegetables as a protection against pesticide residues (FSA 2002a). The rationale given was that, since all pesticides had been approved as safe for use within specified residue limits, then their presence on foods was safe. This decision explicitly overturned the interpretation widely held of a previous release from the Chief Medical Officer from 1997. Friends of the Earth highlighted that the FSA had also been concerned that misinterpretation of the CMO's 1997 advice could imply that only organic fruit should be supplied to the National School Fruit Scheme (FOE 2002). The FSA declared that its concern was simply that some consumers were being put off eating fruit and vegetables, because they thought these were not safe to eat unless washed first—in conflict with health promotion strategies to include their consumption as part of a healthy diet (FSA 2002b). However, just three days before, the FSA had issued a press release revealing that the "Consumer Attitudes to Food Standards" survey showed that there had been a rise in the number of people eating more fruit and vegetables in the past year (FSA 2002c). Not included in this release was that the survey also showed a significant proportion of consumers held concerns about the use of pesticides on food (50 per cent), when prompted. This concern ranked equal third with livestock feed, coming after food poisoning (59 per cent) and BSE (55 per cent) as major concerns (FSA 2002d: 59). As Lang has suggested, a joined-up indicator for food policy, signifying both environmental and public health protection, should be that consumers are able to eat unpeeled (but washed) carrots and fruit (Lang 1997). However, the FSA effectively passed over any opportunity for a fresh debate regarding the health impacts of pesticides and their use in conventional agriculture. In short, the agro-chemical status quo was retrieved and joined-up thinking avoided.[1]

In the wake of an Advertising Standards Authority ruling on the accuracy of health claims made by organic food producers in 2000, the FSA issued a position paper on organic foods. It stated that it "considers that there is not enough information available at present to be able to say that organic foods are significantly different in terms of their safety and nutritional content to those produced by conventional farming" (FSA 2000). The paper provided scant evidence, one way or the other. The FSA could have provided an opportunity to launch an appeal for much-needed research into finding if there were any comparative nutritional and safety differences, and offered seed funding from its own research budget. No such opportunity was taken, defence of the status quo was seen as sufficient.

The consumerist approach of the agency was reflected in the submission it made to the DEFRA-sponsored Curry Commission on the future of food and farming. Based on its own consumer survey evidence, it grouped consumer concerns on shopping for food into primary concerns (price, time and convenience) and secondary concerns (intensity of production, animal welfare, and environmental) (FSA 2001). However, no discussion was made of the implications of the secondary concerns (which go beyond the moment of shopping) for the nature of the food system and consumers' concerns regarding the dominant production methods of conventional agriculture. Rather the importance of maintaining regulatory control systems through the food chain was seen as the key to addressing these "secondary concerns". In sum, the agency's potential for an advisory role, adopting a wider and more integrated approach to food policy, has not been taken. Rather, it has adopted a conservative and relatively narrow approach to its remit of protecting the consumer against "risks caused by the way in which it [food] is produced or supplied" effecting a defence of conventional agriculture and food production. To this extent it has been willing to take a more activist role: not exactly policy-making, but certainly effective policy promotion, as the few examples given above illustrate.

The FSA was one of several national food agencies either set up or promised in EU member states in the late 1990s and early 2000s. The EU introduced its own agency, the EFSA, in January 2002. The EFSA's mission is to "provide scientific advice and scientific and technical support for the Community's legislation and policy in all fields which have a direct or indirect impact on food and feed safety. It shall provide independent information . . . and communicate on risks" (CEC 2002). The remit reaches along the whole food chain and feed supply chains, but the scientific opinions are limited to food safety only. The scope of the Authority does include scientific advice on human nutrition in relation to Community legislation, and assistance on communication on nutritional issues within the Community's health programme, but only at the request of the Commission. The remit is clearly bounded. The proliferation of national food agencies will also pose a significant challenge to harmony in the multi-level European polity (Barling and Lang 2002).

The Authority also has the role of "promot[ing] and coordinat[ing] the development of uniform risk assessment methodologies in the fields falling within its mission" (CEC 2002: 13). In the case of GM crops (part of its remit) the boundaries and methodologies for risk assessment have been highly disputed by member states, sometimes in conflict with the EU's own scientific committees (Levidow et al. 2000). The enabling legislation for the Authority recognized that other legitimate factors may have to be included in a risk assessment (societal, economic, traditional, ethical and environmental) (CEC 2002: 2). This was included to fall in line with ongoing discussion concerning the scope of other legitimate factors in risk assessment at the Codex Alimentarius Commission. Codex has the role of advisory body to the WTO on what are legitimate technical standards for food safety (and therefore comply with the trade rules) under the Sanitary and Phytosanitary Agreements. In this case multi-level governance reaches up to the global level of intergovernmental negotiations.

Meanwhile, the reorganization of the ministries for agriculture and environment into a new merged ministry covering Environment, Food and Rural Affairs, in the UK in June 2001, signalled the promotion of an integrated rural policy. The aims and objectives of DEFRA acknowledge the environmental impacts of agriculture, and promise a more protective management of biodiversity, natural resources and the countryside (DEFRA 2002a). The European Commission's intent to reform the CAP through a shifting of subsidies to the second pillar of the rural development programme is endorsed (DEFRA 2002a). Under the Agenda 2000 CAP reform process, a policy known as "modulation" is the current means for member states to accelerate such a shift. Under modulation an individual member state is allowed to transfer up to 20 per cent of current CAP subsidies from direct production supports to rural development programmes, but the member states must provide matched funding (an equal amount) from their own national budgets. The extent to which the UK Treasury will sign up to this solution is, at the time of writing, unclear, since its political priority may be to reduce the costs of CAP as budget expenditure rather than to rearrange and further support it via endorsement modulation.

The place of food in DEFRA's strategy is also evolving. The presence of the word "food" in the department's title is believed to have been a last-minute inclusion. The objective for the food supply chain includes sustainable, safe and competitive—a challenging combination. Health protection is linked to adverse environmental impacts and to food safety along the supply chain; but there is no recognition of the public health link of diet in the aims and objectives (DEFRA 2002a). DEFRA's sustainable development strategy addresses public health in relation to environmental protection (ignoring the pollution consequences of food miles). It places diet and nutrition in the context of the food chain, promising "an assessment of programmes to improve diet and nutrition across government, to see where work can be joined up and focused more effectively on improving health and reducing inequalities" (DEFRA 2002b: 29). It fails to grasp the link between public health and a sustainable food supply chain.

In the wake of the foot-and-mouth crisis the Cabinet Office launched the Curry Commission to look at the future of food and farming. DEFRA was charged with the role of formulating the policy follow-up to that Commission's recommendations. The Curry Commission's remit was bounded within the international trade paradigm, to advise the government "consistent with . . . increased trade liberalisation" (PCFFF 2002: 2). While this remit compromised the nature of the recommendations (Fairlie 2002), these were nonetheless wide-ranging. DEFRA's initial consultation response to the recommendations gives a fuller sense of how the department's thinking is evolving with regard to food policy (DEFRA 2002c).

Joined-up Policy Initiatives: The Slippery Slope from Policy Integration to Policy Confinement

Recent institutional reforms have seen the joining-up of some aspects of food policy, albeit in an incremental and somewhat muddled manner. Beyond these bounded reforms further efforts to address aspects of food policy in a more joined-up and innovative perspective have been launched. Two examples are the Social Exclusion Unit set up by the Cabinet Office and their Policy Action Team (PAT) 13 on access to shops, and the Curry Commission that

David Barling, Tim Lang and Martin Caraher

reported to the Cabinet Office and is "owned" by DEFRA. Each case illustrates the difficulties of achieving a subsequent, sustained joined-up follow-through.

In the case of the PAT 13 recommendations to the DoH, the only tangible outcome has been the follow-up of an economic small business dimension located in the Department of Trade and Industry (DTI). The wider needs of policy action on food poverty seem to have stalled. Meanwhile, one of the key areas for policy action arising from the Curry Commission report was to provide a more integrated approach to the food supply chain. However, the recommendation that a new food chain centre be located at the Institute of Grocery Distribution (IGD), a food industry research body, suggests a joined-up solution that favours the already dominant interests of the large retailers in the food supply chain—in the pursuit of economic efficiency. Policy initiatives that start as joined-up and cross-sectoral may lose that characteristic by being relocated to more distinct policy sectors dominated by a particular department or agency (complete with a bias towards their entrenched client interests). In such cases policy integration slips into a form of "policy confinement". Also, the incorporation of corporate interests into the regulatory process for food may result in the allocation of the policy solution to established interests within the contemporary food system, who support the dominant policy paradigm.

The Social Exclusion Unit, based in the Cabinet Office, was a prime example of the Blair government's efforts to produce joined-up thinking and joined-up policy solutions. The PAT 13 focused on access to shops, in response to the mounting evidence that there are structural determinants to food poverty and poor access, that had been slowly acknowledged in central government (HM Government 1992; DoH 1996; Acheson 1998). Issues such as poor planning, housing without shops, a decline in rural and urban transport, unsafe streets, differential pricing, a decline in small and local shops and sheer lack of disposable income have been evidenced as having an impact (Ambrose and MacDonald 2001; Carley et al. 2001; Cranbrook 1998; Ellaway and Mcintyre 2000; Piachaud and Webb 1996; Pickering et al. 1998; Dowler et al. 2001a). Such factors are beyond the control of any individual household or even neighbourhood to control.

A study of Sandwell, an area which is ranked the seventh worst for ill-health in England, where a third of households had gross incomes below £5,500 a year and where a third do not have a car, has shown that, while there may be shops apparently within "range", there are large networks of streets and estates within Sandwell where no shops selling fresh fruit and/or vegetables exist (Dowler et al. 2001b). Moreover, where such shops do exist, they are often expensive. The low incomes are no incentive for supermarkets to site there. The PAT 13 report's suggestions for "joined-up" policy on access to shops required action on siting, transport, planning, urban and rural regeneration (DoH 1999). But the only visible action, up until June 2002, was the relocation of this policy initiative to the DTI and their small business strategy (DTI 2002). An opportunity for a wider engagement of local participants in food issues, for example through local retail forums linked to neighbourhood management strategies as recommended by PAT 13, was thus lost (DoH 1999: 33–4).

The Curry Commission produced a plethora of recommendations, several of which focused on the food supply chain. DEFRA are charged with taking the report's recommendations forward in policy terms, invoking a further framing of priorities, a key aim being a joined-up food chain (DEFRA 2002c: 6). The Food Chain Centre is to operate at the national level, and assumes that the deficiency in current farming and food policy can be framed in terms of competitiveness and efficiency such as promoting and implementing the managerial strategy known as efficient consumer response (ECR). DEFRA's initial priority for the food supply chain is to ensure safety in the red meat chain, an initiative aimed at securing consumers' purchasing confidence post-BSE and foot-and-mouth, coordinated by a Red Meat Industry Forum and the new Food Chain Centre (DEFRA 2002c: 8).

Curry also called on the Regional Development Agencies (RDAs) to devise a regional food component for their economic strategy, and to be coordinated with the industry-centred "Food from Britain" and its regional groups, in order to maximize marketing promotion in overseas markets. Farmers and growers are encouraged to organize "post-farm gate" in order to get a share of value added from the food chain, with DEFRA suggesting a new Agricultural Development Scheme to help improve their marketing and consumer reach (DEFRA 2002c: 8). In the past dairy farmers' arrangements to gain value added "post-farm gate" fell foul of the government's competition authorities with the break-up of the Milk Marketing Board. Conversely, farmers' and growers' complaints of unfair practices by the large retailers in respect of food supply contracts merely precipitated a voluntary code of activity (for retailers). Although Curry recommended some improvements to the operation of this code, there is no challenge proposed to the dominant power relationships in the conventional food supply chains. The Curry Commission did call on RDAs to consider aiding local food initiatives in terms of processing, distributing, planning, networking, and linking them with established businesses (PCFFF 2002: 3–48). But the paradigm was that of an import–export trade model of efficiency, rather than a localist, diverse supply chain. To that extent, by pursuing a conventional notion of market efficiency, the government looks set to promote a food supply chain which continues to externalize its environmental costs, lengthening supply chains and use of non-renewable energy (Jones 2001). Conventional trade thereby is accorded a higher priority than environmental protection.

What is also largely missing from these Curry recommendations is recognition of the social dimension to the food supply chain. A sustainable food supply chain should deliver social as well as economic and environmental benefits (Pretty 1998). But social and environmental sustainability are not being addressed in a joined-up manner. Rather, economic sustainability is at the forefront. DEFRA's initial follow-up document does recognize Curry's limited recommendations regarding the role of food and farming in public health, wanting "to identify and make changes to food and farming which contribute to improving nutrition and reducing diet related ill health" (DEFRA 2002b: 7). It identifies that consumers "need easy access to an affordable, healthy diet" and commends efforts to promote a healthy diet. However, the consumerist mind-set prevails, with the key question "How can the supply of healthier produce and product lines be increased to drive changes in consumer demand?" (DEFRA 2002b: 17). Public health is viewed in the market terms of the needs of individual consumers rather than the needs of populations, whereas what should be being asked is how might farming increase fruit and vegetable production and the food chain increase accessibility of supply to all sections of the population?

There is thus hesitant progress being made towards an integrated food policy, but bounded remits and the confinement of policy initiatives into more narrow departmental channels remain stumbling blocks. The pre-eminence of the market and economic competitiveness restrict attempts at joined-up thinking progressing to a more integrated food policy.

Moving to an Ecological Public Health Model for Food Policy? A National Food Policy Council and Regional/Local Supply Chain Strategies

A socially responsive and sustainable food policy necessitates political mechanisms and processes that can frame policy options in a broader and more integrated fashion than has been achieved to date. Wider and more inclusive social agencies need to be incorporated also, extending beyond the seats at the table reserved for large players in the food economy. Recent reforms and initiatives in the UK have been hesitant and incomplete in this regard. The Nordic countries, notably Norway and Finland, have pioneered a more joined-up food policy around the integration of a public health dimension into their food supply in an attempt to reduce food-related ill health.

A key feature in Norway has been a food and nutrition policy that is integrated with agricultural, fishery, price, consumer and trade policy and has had the support of many of the food producers (Helsing 1987; Milio 1990; Oshaug 1992; RNMA 1975). However, this has been a contested process. For example, Norway's nutrition policy has come under attack from counter-experts, funded by the dairy industry, who sought to counter evidence on the fat-related risks of coronary heart disease (Norum 1997). Meanwhile, Finland pioneered a grassroots process of reform through the North Karelia project from the 1970s. The project targeted smoking, blood pressure control and diet, and started preventive activities throughout the country. Over 20 years, the dietary intake of Finns has been monitored and vegetable consumption has doubled. Fruit and berry consumption—the latter being culturally important within Finland—also increased. The proportion of saturated fats in total fat consumption declined, while fish consumption rose. The health agencies worked with the food industry to alter the food supply, thereby linking the push of supply with the pull of demand. The result is a culture that encourages Finns to eat for life, not a premature grave. A 55 per cent decline in male mortality in North Karelia from coronary heart disease, for example, has been recorded in the period 1972–92 (Pietinen 1996). A key strategy has been close integration between health and other agencies. For instance, dietary guidelines were designed for schools, other mass catering institutions and other social groups including old people and the armed forces.

Institutional coordinators for an integrated approach to policy advice on food supply and public health have been the National Nutrition Councils of Norway and Finland. These councils have a long history, and have broadened their role to expand into the wider dimensions of food policy. In the case of Norway, the Nutrition Council is relatively weak in terms of political power and its main success has been in the presentation of the nutritional and dietary evidence (Tansey and Worsley 1995: 219; Norum 1997: 198). To this extent the Council has driven a process of policy learning to which other institutions and actors have responded. The UK needs to find an equivalent mechanism for reaching across the policy sector barriers plaguing governmental organization and impeding efforts at more joined-up thinking, thus providing an agency for driving policy change. A national food policy council could be one such mechanism. The UK's implementation of the International Conference on Nutrition action plan took the form of two taskforces (on nutrition and breastfeeding) and the inclusion of nutrition in the 1992 Health of the Nation plan (WHO-E 1995). While these were not insignificant steps, they fell short of a framework for the new millennium, and of the type of institutional reform envisaged by the WHO-E, who endorsed the example of the national nutrition councils as good practice (WHO-E 1995: 2).

A national food policy Council for the UK could be a mechanism for integrating overall policy thinking and for providing ministers with a channel for specialist advice. The advice would draw from all of the WHO-E's pillars of food policy, promoting an integration of evidence across these areas to inform policy-makers. Its advisory role would fit within the Whitehall tradition. With the demise of the Committee on Medical Aspects of Food Policy (COMA) and its replacement by the Scientific Advisory Committee on Nutrition (SACN), expert advice on specific areas of scientific value has been retained, but there is no longer any wide-ranging source of advice on overall policy implications. Important avenues of thinking and research have therefore been unnecessarily restricted. The remit of the Council would have to be sufficiently broad and inclusive, and not repeat the bounded approach of the Food Standards Agency. Membership of the Council would need to be multi-disciplinary and to cover the reach of the ecological public health approach. Such a Council would not be a magic bullet reform, any more than the introduction of the FSA has been, but it could provide a platform for the advance of an ecological public health model of food and for the evidence upon which it is based. It would also provide a potential driver for the national-level adoption of the WHO-E's food and nutrition action plan in the UK. However, such policy advance would in turn depend on the response of the lead institutions, DEFRA, DoH and the FSA—plus the government itself within the core executive—and their willingness to move from within the current confines of the dominant paradigm.

The picture at the local level in the UK is one of islands of policy innovation, rethinking and challenge to the dominant paradigms of food policy. At the grassroots levels across the UK, local food initiatives are attempting to set up their own solutions to food access and supply problems (Sustain 2002a). These are important developments in food policy. Local food projects provide a form of empowerment and learning for participants, but are often fairly isolated initiatives, lacking continuity of funding and permanence (McGlone *et al.* 1999). Also, short-term, unsupported actions at a local level, while offering policy alternatives, may be unhelpful to the extent that they can generate a sense of a problem's being "solved", thus removing the pressure for more sustained action around the issue of food supply (Caraher *et al.* 2001). A more structural and strategic level of intervention at local and regional levels of governance is also needed.

The formulation of regional strategies for food supply, below the national-level chains, should be predicated upon social and environmental sustain-ability, rather than merely location branding and external marketing. The evolving reform of subnational government in the UK is setting in train a variable geometry of regional and local agencies. These range from: devolved assemblies in Scotland and Wales and an assembly for London, to regional development agencies (and possible assemblies) and revised regional government offices (incorporating the old MAFF regional offices), to restructured local authorities and the regional and local restructuring of the NHS. Within this mosaic lies the potential for policy innovation, but also an awkward geography of regional and local bodies covering differing spatial boundaries.

In England the new RDAs may provide a potential platform for such strategic intervention, but it is not clear to what extent their role will go beyond an economic approach to food policy. The sustainability criterion in their role is relatively weak, calling on them merely to contribute to sustainable devel-opment "where it is relevant in their area to do so" (HM Government 1998: part 1.4). The RDAs' responsibility covers rural areas and there is scope for a more integrated and sustainable local food production policy to be drawn up with DEFRA and its rural director in each regional government office (with the exception of London) (DEFRA 2002a: 34–5). An initial study of the English RDAs' policies in relation to stimulating local food economies concluded: "there has been too much emphasis placed on regional locality foods for export rather than local foods for meeting the needs of commun-ities in the regions" (Sustain 2002b). This branding and export marketing approach was reflected in the recommendations of the Curry Commission.

Public procurement, such as through public sector catering contracts, offers a potential lever for engendering a more sustainable food supply. The NHS is the largest single purchaser of food in the country, spending £500 million a year on meals for patients, staff and visitors (DoH 2000: 4.16). As a food purchaser, the NHS could play a vital role in sending important messages along the food supply chain by their food procurement policy (UK SDC 2002). But EU and national laws governing public sector procurement provide constraints to the scope for such a role. EU competition legisla-tion prohibits territorial preferences being specified in public purchasing contracts (such as local foods). To be sure, there is scope for the imaginative interpretation of quality criteria when applied to contracts for food supply, such as applying sustainability criteria (Sustain 2002c). Yet local government legislation in the UK demands that local authorities obtain "best value" in securing contracts and prohibits the use of non-economic criteria. Initial efforts by the Welsh Development Agency and the Welsh Assembly to get their local authorities to focus on local sourcing for all their contracts were rebuffed by the Welsh Local Government Association as being prohibited under national and EU competition legislation (Pickard 2002). However, Belfast City Council has managed to introduce an environmental purchasing policy to inform its contracting (Sustain 2002d).

In addition, public sector authorities can help and advise small and medium businesses, such as farmers and growers, on how to prepare bids for their contracts (UK SDC 2002). The UK Cabinet has set up a Sustainable Procurement Group to make recommendations on a policy framework for joined-up government objectives on procurement and sustainable development (due to report in July 2002), although food was not high on its agenda. The scope for such policy innovation within the multi-level governance of public procurement is still unclear and is unfolding. Nonetheless, it provides a potentially powerful complement to the more grassroots-based local food projects that have already emerged.

Conclusions

A joined-up food policy remains a substantial challenge for the UK, and the extent of joined-up thinking applied to food policy remains bounded. The UK government has signed up to the commitment to the WHO-E's three-pillar model of food and health, but the extent to which it is aware of this commitment, beyond the DoH, remains unclear. It will need to broaden its thinking on food policy in order to engage successfully (rather than merely rhetorically) with the WHO-E's model, and so move towards an ecological public health approach. The steps towards a more integrated approach have been hesitant, and confined within the dominant paradigm that informs food policy. The multi-level governance of food is also located within this national economic competitiveness/international trade liberalization paradigm. Multi-level governance at the supranational level is a consequence of the priorities of the world trade rules and of the internal European market, although this is not always a harmonious process, as reflected by the disputes over the role of CAP in a liberalizing world trade system. These international drivers serve to narrow the breadth of the national government vision. The Curry Commission, a potentially far-reaching platform for policy change, was curtailed by its remit to observe the government's commitment to trade liberalization.

And yet, the contradictions of the contemporary food system are providing the external shocks to the system of governance to provoke policy change. Food safety has returned as an issue of public health and created widespread institutional change. The need to manage and ameliorate the environmental impacts of intensive agriculture is also being recognized by institutional and policy reform. The diet-related costs to public health of the operation of the contemporary food system are being recognized but have yet to be addressed properly, as have the structural causes of food poverty in the midst of affluence and plenty. Countries such as Norway and Finland have found their own routes to develop a more integrated approach to food, the environment and

David Barling, Tim Lang and Martin Caraher

public health, and offer models for more joined-up thinking and potential institutional means (such as a national food policy council). The role of a sustainable food supply chain in addressing the social and public health problems of food policy have yet to be grasped by UK policy-makers. However, at the local and community levels there is a change stirring as local food initiatives act as policy innovators in making new links in the supply and consumption of food. It remains to be seen if local and regional governments can provide the structural platforms to promote this new thinking on a widespread basis. It also remains to be seen if the national government can significantly shift its own thinking, in turn.

Note

1. We are grateful to Barbara Baker, an MA food policy student at Thames Valley University for drawing our attention to this example.

References

Acheson, D. (1998), *Independent Inquiry into Inequalities in Health Report*, London: HMSO.
Ambrose, P. and MacDonald, D. (2001), *For Richer, For Poorer? Counting the Costs of Regeneration in Stepney*, Brighton: Health and Social Policy Research Centre, University of Brighton.
Barling, D. (in press), Impact of international policies (CAP) and agreements (WTO) on the development of organic farming. In F. den Hond, P. Groenewegen and N. van Straalen (eds), *Pesticides: Problems, Improvements, Alternatives*, Oxford: Blackwell Science.
Barling, D. and Henderson, R. (2000), *Safety First? A Map of Public Sector Research into GM Food and Food Crops in the UK*, Centre for Food Policy Discussion Paper, 12, London: Thames Valley University.
Barling, D. and Lang, T. (2002), Food agencies: an effective response to a consumer crisis? Paper presented to the Theoretical Approaches to Food Quality Workshop, ESRC Centre for Research on Innovation and Competition, UMIST, Manchester, 10–11 January.
Caraher, M., Hewitt, G., and Dowler, E. (2001), *Food Action Projects in London: A Report to the Food Action Network*, London: London Regional Office NHS.
Carley, M., Kirk, K. and McIntosh, S. (2001), *Retailing, Sustainability and Neighbourhood Regeneration*, York: Joseph Rowntree Foundation.
CEC (1999), *Europe's Environment: What Directions for the Future? The Global Assessment of the European Community Programme of Policy and Action in Relation to the Environment and Sustainable Development, "Towards Sustainability"*, COM 13598/99, Brussels: Commission of the European Communities.
CEC (2002), Regulation (EC)No. 178/2002 of the European Parliament and of the Council of 28 January 2002 laying down the general principles and requirements of food law, establishing the European Food Safety Authority and laying down procedures in matters of food safety, *Official Journal of the European Communities*, February, L31/1–L31/24.
Cranbrook, C. (1998), *Food Webs: A Report on Local Food Networks in East Suffolk which Demonstrates the Importance of Local Shops and Services to Rural Communities*, London: Council for the Preservation of Rural England.
DEFRA (2002a), *Working for the Essentials of Life*, March, London: Department for Environment, Food and Rural Affairs.

DEFRA (2002b), *Foundations for Our Future—DEFRA's Sustainable Development Strategy*, June, London: Department for Environment, Food and Rural Affairs.

DEFRA (2002c), *Sustainable Food and Farming—Working Together*, March, London: Department for Environment, Food and Rural Affairs.

DoH (1996), *Low Income, Food, Nutrition and Health: Strategies for Improvement. Report by the Low Income Project Team for the Nutrition Taskforce*, London: Department of Health.

DoH (1999), *Improving Shopping Access for People Living in Deprived Neighbourhoods: a Paper for Discussion. Policy Action Team: 13*, London: Department of Health for the Cabinet Office Social Exclusion Unit.

DoH (2000), *The NHS Plan: a Plan for Investment; a Plan for Reform*, London: Stationery Office.

Dowler, E., Turner, S. with Dobson, B. (2001a), *Poverty Bites: Food, Health and Poor Families*, London: Child Poverty Action Group.

Dowler, E., Blair, A., Donkin, A., Rex, D. and Grundy, C. (2001b), *Measuring Access to Healthy Food in Sandwell*, Final Report, August, Sandwell: Sandwell Health Authority/Health Action Zone.

DTI (2002), *Speakers' Notes from Small Retail Service Seminar, 15 February 2002 held at the DTI Conference Centre, London SW1*, London: Department of Trade and Industry.

Ellaway, A. and Macintyre, S. (2000), Shopping for food in socially contrasting localities, *British Food Journal*, 102, 1: 52–9.

Fairlie, S. (2002), Commissioning consensus, *Ecos*, 23, 1: 52–7.

Flynn, A., Marsden, T. and Harrison, M. (1999), The regulation of food in Britain in the 1990s, *Policy and Politics*, 27, 4: 435–46.

FOE (2002), *Pesticide Safety Advice for Children to be Withdrawn*, Press Release, 26 March, London: Friends of the Earth.

FSA (2000), *The Food Standards Agency's View on Organic Food—A Position Paper*, August, London: Food Standards Agency.

FSA (2001), *Submission from the Food Standards Agency to the Policy Commission on Farming and Food for England*, London: Food Standards Agency.

FSA (2002a), *Food Standards Agency Advice on Washing or Peeling Fruit and Vegetables*, Press Release, 26 March, London: Food Standards Agency.

FSA (2002b), *Scientists Issue Pesticide Advice*, Press Release, 26 March, London: Food Standards Agency.

FSA (2000c), *Public Getting More Food-savvy*, Press Release, 22 March, London: Food Standards Agency.

FSA (2000d), *Consumer Attitudes to Food Standards—United Kingdom*, February, London: Food Standards Agency.

Gabriel, Y. and Lang, T. (1995), *The Unmanageable Consumer*, London: Sage.

Gamble, A. (2002), Policy agendas in a multi-level polity. In P. Dunleavy, A. Gamble, R. Heffernan, I. Holliday and G. Peele, *Developments in British Politics 6*, rev. edn, Basingstoke: Palgrave, pp. 290–307.

Goodman, D. and Watts, M. J. (eds) (1997), *Globalising Food: Agrarian Questions and Global Restructuring*, London: Routledge.

Helsing, E. (1987), *Norwegian Nutrition Policy in 1987: What Works and Why?* Report from a research seminar, Vettre, Norway, 27–28 April, Copenhagen: WHO Regional Office for Europe.

HM Government (1992), *Health of the Nation*, London: HMSO.

HM Government (1998), *The Regional Development Agencies Act*, London: HMSO.

Holliday, I. (2002), Executives and administrations. In P. Dunleavy, A. Gamble, R. Heffernan, I. Holliday and G. Peele, *Developments in British Politics 6*, rev. edn, Basingstoke: Palgrave, pp. 88–107.

Jones, A. (2001), *Eating Oil*, London: Sustain.

David Barling, Tim Lang and Martin Caraher

Jordan, A. (2002), Environmental policy. In P. Dunleavy, A. Gamble, R. Heffernan, I. Holliday and G. Peele, *Developments in British Politics 6*, rev. edn, Basingstoke: Palgrave, pp. 257–75.

Lang, T. (1996), Going public: food campaigns during the 1980s and 1990s. In D. F. Smith (ed.), *Nutrition in Britain: Science, Scientists and Politics in the Twentieth Century*, London: Routledge, pp. 238–60.

Lang, T. (1997), *Food for the 21st Century: Can it Be both Radical and Reasonable?* Centre for Food Policy Discussion Paper, 4, London: Thames Valley University.

Lang, T., Barling, D., and Caraher, M. (2001), Food, social policy and the environment: towards a new model, *Social Policy and Administration*, 35, 5: 538–58.

Lang, T. and Rayner, G. (eds) (2002), *Why Health is the Key to Farming and Food*, London: Chartered Institute of Environmental Health, Faculty of Public Health Medicine of the Royal Colleges of Physicians, National Heart Forum, UK Public Health Association, Health Development Agency.

Levidow, L., Carr, S. and Wield, D. (2000), Genetically modified crops in the European Union: regulatory conflicts as precautionary opportunities, *Journal of Risk Research*, 3, 3: 189–200.

McGlone, P., Dobson, B., Dowler, E. and Nelson, M. (1999), *Food Projects and how They Work*, York: York Publishing/Joseph Rowntree Foundation.

McMichael, A. J. (2001), *Human Frontiers, Environments and Disease*, Cambridge: Cambridge University Press.

Marsden, T., Flynn, A. and Harrison, M. (2000), *Consuming Interests*, London: UCL Press.

Milio, N. (1990), *An Analysis of the Implementation of Norwegian Nutrition Policy 1981–1987*, First European Conference on Food and Nutrition Policy, Budapest, 1–5 October, Copenhagen: WHO Regional Office for Europe, EUR/ICP/NUT 133/BD/1.

Norum, K. (1997), Some aspects of Norwegian nutrition and food policy. In P. Shetty, and K. McPherson (eds), *Diet, Nutrition and Chronic Disease: Lessons from Contrasting Worlds*, Chichester: J Wiley, pp. 195–206.

Oshaug, A. (1992), *Towards Nutrition Security*, Country Paper for Norway, International Conference on Nutrition, Oslo: Nordic School of Nutrition, University of Oslo.

PCFFF (2002), *Farming and Food: a Sustainable Future*, January, London: Policy Commission on the Future of Farming and Food.

Piachaud, D. and Webb, J. (1996), *The Price of Food: Missing out on Mass Consumption*, London: London School of Economics STICERD.

Pickard, J. (2002), Welsh council chiefs reject "buy local" plan, *Financial Times*, 9 April: 3.

Pickering, J., Greene, F. and Cockerill, T. (1998), *The Future of the Neighbourhood Store*, Durham Reports on Retail Futures 1, Durham: Durham University Business School.

Pietinen, P. (1996), Trends in nutrition and its consequences in Europe: the Finnish experience. In P. Pietinen, C. Nishida and N. Khaltaev (eds), *Nutrition and Quality of Life: Health Issues for the 21st Century*, Geneva: World Health Organization, pp. 67–71.

Pretty, J. (1998), *The Living Land*, London: Earthscan.

Richards, D. and Smith, M. J. (2001), New Labour, the Constitution and reforming the state. In S. Ludlem and M. J. Smith (eds), *New Labour in Government*, Basingstoke: Palgrave, pp. 145–66.

RNMA (1975), *On Norwegian Nutrition and Food Policy*, Report no. 32 to the Storting, Oslo: Royal Norwegian Ministry of Agriculture.

SEU (1999), *Improving Shopping Access for People Living in Deprived Neighbourhoods. Report of Policy Action Team 13 of the Social Exclusion Unit*, London: Department of Health for the Social Exclusion Unit/Cabinet Office.

Sustain (2002a), *Local Food: Benefits, Obstacles and Opportunities*, Sustainable Food Chains Briefing Paper 1, London: Sustain.

Sustain (2002b), *The English Regional Development Agencies: What Are they Doing to Support Sustainable Food Economies?* Sustainable Food Chains Briefing Paper 4, London: Sustain.

Sustain (2002c), *Public Sector Catering: Opportunities and Issues relating to Sustainable Food Procurement*, Sustainable Food Chains, Briefing Paper 2, London: Sustain.

Sustain (2002d), *Public Procurement of Sustainable Food: Current, Planned, and Related Initiatives*, Sustainable Food Chains Briefing Paper 3, London: Sustain.

Tansey, G. and Worsley, T. (1995), *The Food System*, London: Earthscan.

UK SDC (2002), *Food Procurement for Health and Sustainable Development*, May, UK Sustainable Development Commission: London.

Waltner-Toews, D. and Lang, T. (2000), A new conceptual base for food and agriculture: the emerging model of links between agriculture, food, health, environment and society, *Global Change and Human Health*, 1, 2: 116–30.

Warde, A. (1997), *Consumption, Food and Taste*, London: Sage.

Watkins, K. (2002), *Rigged Rules and Double Standards: Trade, Globalisation, and the Fight against Poverty*, Oxford: Oxfam International.

WHO-E (1995), *Nutrition Policy in WHO European Member States: Progress Report following the 1992 International Conference on Nutrition*, June, Copenhagen: World Health Organization.

WHO-E (2000), *World Health Organization Regional Committee for Europe. Resolution: The impact of food and nutrition on public health*, 50th Session, EUR/RC50/R8, 14 September, Copenhagen: World Health Organization.

2

Patenting Our Food Future: Intellectual Property Rights and the Global Food System

Geoff Tansey

Since the early 1990s the international rules affecting the most basic part of the food system—the plants and animals grown by farmers—have been changing. This paper sketches out some of those changes. The processes by which the rules governing intellectual property rights (IPRs), such as patents, copyright, trademarks and trade secrets, are made is highlighted, along with their potential impact on our food future.

IPRs matter because they underpin the new knowledge economy—their ownership and control will affect the distribution of wealth and power. IPRs allow creators and inventors to exclude others from copying or using their work or invention without permission. The justifications used for strong IPRs globally are that they provide the necessary incentive, proper reward and required security for investment in R & D to produce life-improving innovations (May 2000). James Boyle, professor of law at Duke Law School, argues that their effects will be widespread, but not as beneficial as their proponents suggest: "The blandishments of the international information industries notwithstanding, more intellectual property rights may actually mean *less* innovation, less heterogeneity in culture and environment and a less informed world of public debate" (Boyle 1996: 197). IPRs, he argues, are being used as part of a new round of enclosures in what were the global commons—including genetic information encoded in the genes of people, plants, animals and micro-organisms (Boyle 2001).

Others see stronger, global, IPRs as helping to bring about a new form of feudalism. They will alter social relations in ways that mean individuals never "own" things like software, seeds or sounds. Instead, purchasers are only licensed by their corporate rights holders to use them in very limited ways and are excluded from acts normally associated with real property, i.e. the ability to lend, share, give away or sell it (Drahos 2002).

So where does food come into this? It is at the heart of these changes because of the links between IPRs, biotechnology and marketing. First, I want to outline a view of the food system as background, before looking at the relevant international rules. Then I will consider the current changes and some ideas for how to respond to rule-making processes that have, to date, proceeded with very little input apart from the vested interests in whose advantage the new rules are.

A Food System Overview

Pressures for change in the food system come from the overfed, industrialized world. Within this system, there is a struggle going on between various actors—farmers, input suppliers, traders, manufacturers/processors, distributors, caterers and consumers—for *power* and *control* over the future supplies of food, and how the *benefits* and *risks* arising from different activities will be distributed (Tansey and Worsley 1995).

There is not space here to discuss these key groups of actors but no set is homogeneous and there are differences of interests within any group, e.g. between small and large farmers, or retailers and manufacturers. The struggle between actors is fuelled by a changing market structure in which there is a growing economic *concentration* of power within any sector of the food system. In their home markets, industrialized-country actors face a fundamental constraint, which may seem strange in a world where around 800 million people go hungry, of limited demand. In developed-country agriculture the key problem is overproduction, with decreasing returns to producers. Food processors and retailers face overfed customers who spend, on average, a declining percentage of their disposable income on food. For while people can have two cars and three or four TVs they cannot increase their food consumption two-, three- or four-fold and survive for long without major health problems. Indeed, some developed countries' food systems are becoming dysfunctional and producing nations with growing levels of obesity as the pressures grow on people to overeat. Yet food poverty is still a reality in rich countries, for some.

The limited demand we have for food—healthy diets are possible from a relatively limited range and amount of basic ingredients—means that the main actors in the food system face pressures identified over 30 years ago by the OECD:

- of increased competition for the money spent on food,
- to increase use of technology to generate greater returns to investment,
- to seek increased productivity from the labour and capital employed, and also
- to diversify their activities.

(OECD 1971)

It also leads them to look beyond their saturated markets and expand into global markets and to seek ever-better tools for control over their activities—tools like biotechnology and patents.

A complex web

The food system is a complex web connecting various components which are:

Biological. The living processes used to produce food and their ecological sustainability. We rely on a well-functioning biosphere. Human activity,

Geoff Tansey

however, is having an increasing impact on the biosphere and "there are broad areas of the Earth, in both industrial and developing nations, where increases in food production are undermining the base for future production" (World Commission on Environment and Development 1987).

Economic and political. Today's food system has a *history*: it has resulted from the interplay of different political and economic forces over time. Globalization —of useful plants and animals—has taken place over thousands of years, but especially since the European conquests. Today, the rules are being globalized.

Social and cultural. Our *human needs* and wants, physiological and psychological, social and cultural. These needs are complex, many-sided and interact and are not simply for nutrients. To satisfy these fundamental needs people have to be actively involved in meeting them.

The prevailing norms and laws governing activities in the system result from the way particular interests are able to shape the legal framework governing the relationships.

Tools for control

The various actors use whatever tools they can to control their operations and cope with the pressures they face, including:

Science and technology. Historically, technological developments have not necessarily depended on a correct scientific understanding of why something works. Trial-and-error invention produced many new technologies before the science behind them was understood, especially in agriculture. It is still the basis of much innovation. Those who are the first to introduce innovations stand to gain the most benefit. However, advances in scientific understanding may underpin development of new technologies as, for example, in nuclear power and biotechnology. Modern biotechnology (see below) offers a new tool with a transforming power in technological control capacities. In agricultural biotechnology research and development, led largely by the private sector, patents are of great importance. In commercial plant breeding another form of IPR (plant breeders' rights) is important.

Information. The ability to monitor, use and control information is one key to success for the different actors in today's food system—from weather conditions and market prices to consumer profiles and concerns. Consumers and farmers tend to rely on publicly available information while larger actors, such as traders, manufacturers and retailers, use more private sources. Some they produce themselves, others they buy in from outside. This information may be in the form of R & D results, market research or expert advice. The capacity of these actors to gather, interpret and use information is much greater than that of a farmer or consumer. The spread of global media, broadcasting similar images across the world, helps fuel product

22

globalization and reinforces brand images (usually protected by trademarks or copyright).

Management. The technologies and understanding of people's behaviour developed in the past 100 years have affected the way production is organized and processes and people managed. Today in the USA there are moves to patent business methods.

Laws, rules, and regulations. The challenge for societies, and for consumers acting as citizens through political processes, is to set the framework within which these actors work and how they use these tools. The various actors make use of a range of IPRs—patents, trade secrets, trademarks and copyright. Laws themselves can also be tools that benefit actors differentially. Some actors have been created by other laws, e.g. limited liability companies, which reduce the risk of those involved, and have been given rights as judicial persons. Some of these laws were developed rapidly during the industrial revolution to promote investment and innovation but may not deal with responsibility for adverse consequences of innovation. Other laws and rules that set the framework in which the actors operate are hammered out in international fora like the World Trade Organization (WTO), the Convention on Biological Diversity (CBD) and the UN's Food and Agriculture Organization (FAO).

Modern biotechnology and intellectual property

Modern biotechnology encompasses a number of different areas of varying controversy including:

- *cloning*: the process of producing genetically identical individuals from part of an organism;
- *marker-assisted breeding*: the use of DNA markers, rather than characters or traits, to speed up the process of selective breeding of plants or animals for agricultural use;
- *genetic engineering (transgenics)*: the broad term given to all the techniques which are used to isolate specific genetic material (DNA) from one organism and introduce it into another.

Modern biotechnology stems from a revolution in the history of the biological sciences about the way in which living organisms operate. For the scientists involved it is exciting, cutting-edge work, as Daniel Charles's account of the development of agricultural biotech illustrates (Charles 2001). It is also seen, often, as an inevitable part of progress.

Whatever the controversies surrounding modern biotechnology—in particular genetic engineering—for many actors in the food system it provides new tools to further their particular interests. Its potential to open up new market opportunities all over the world lay behind the relatively recent expansion of private-sector interest in agricultural research in developed countries. Re-engineering crops offers the prospects of linking their structure and properties more closely to the interests of food processors as well as to proprietary chemicals that might be used to trigger specific traits or be used without damaging the crops. Thus, the basic inputs into agriculture—plants and animals—are in the process of being transformed. The transformation is not just scientific and technological, however, but in the structure of the seed and input industries and in the rules governing the system.

New players were attracted into the business of seed production, largely from the chemical and pharmaceutical industries. They have invested billions of dollars over the past two decades in agricultural biotechnology research and development (R & D) and want to see returns on this investment. These corporations have a long history of using patents as business tools and require some form of control over their rights both to their research tools and to prevent reuse of their products, such as seeds, without permission or further payment. Industry, led by the pharmaceutical, recording, software and film industries, pushed for changes in the IPRs rules internationally and to allow for patenting of living organisms (Drahos 1995, 2002).

Changing the Rules

Companies naturally want to stop others from copying—or buyers reproducing—new products if they can. This can be done in two ways. One is by legal means, through IPRs where such rights can be enforced. The other is through attempting to develop technologies that will stop seeds germinating or specific traits being activated without a purchased input—these are projected genetic use restriction technologies (GURTs) also dubbed 'terminator' and 'traitor' technologies.

IPRs are closely linked to biotechnological innovation and have clearly contributed to its development (Barton 1999). The IPRs regime is important because of the role it plays in underpinning private-sector-led innovation and establishing and maintaining market power. The most important change in the global regulatory framework comes from the Agreement on the Trade-related Aspects of Intellectual Property Rights (TRIPS). This was one of the agreements that made up the package of measures agreed at the end of the Uruguay Round of trade talks under the General Agreement on Tariffs and Trade (GATT) and led to the setting up of the World Trade Organization in 1995. TRIPS means developed- and developing-country members of the WTO must adopt the same minimum levels of intellectual property protection—including in agriculture.

The TRIPS Agreement

The TRIPS Agreement specifically protects private, not public, interests. It:

- creates minimum standards of intellectual protection that all WTO members must recognize in seven areas, including patents, copyright and trademarks;
- ensures that states make available to rights-holders institutional procedures to enforce their IPRs; and

- provides a procedure for regulating disputes between states concerning their obligations under the agreement, backed up by sanctions for non-compliance.

Higher levels of protection are allowed, but not lower ones. This is like saying everyone must take a minimum size 7 shoe—larger ones are permitted but not smaller ones. A minimum one size must fit all, with patents on any process or product having to last a minimum of 20 years, for example. This is the most wide-ranging expansion of IPRs in history and stops developing countries doing what most developed countries did, i.e. copy others' technology to catch up, only adopting IPRs when it suited them and choosing the level of protection (Thurow 1997).

The new IPRs rules raise two issues. One concerns the way we make global rules—and illustrates the unbalanced nature of this process. The other issue is whether the content is appropriate—and illustrates the difficulties and dangers of trying to cover very different societies and circumstances with the same rules. To take the first point, these rules were developed with very little public involvement and introduced into the WTO against strong, but in the end futile, opposition from developing countries. TRIPS originated from a small number of major business interests with a handful of corporations and lobbyists responsible for crafting its terms and pushing, via various developed-country governments, the agreement through the Uruguay Round and into the WTO (Drahos 1995, 2002). Most notable among these was the USA where debate about strengthening the IPRs regime was couched in terms of ensuring and maintaining "its competitive advantage in the global system" (May 2000: 119). Most developing countries played little part in the negotiations and opposed the introduction of IPRs into the GATT negotiations.

Thus the current international IPRs regime, unlike, for example, that in the environmental arena, has been developed by a narrow set of actors with relatively little involvement from civil society. These actors have been drawn mostly from the legal and industrial fields and, as "epistemic communities", are very influential in shaping the global regulatory framework (Braithwaite and Drahos 2000). Such communities are "composed of professionals (usually recruited from several disciplines) who share a commitment to a common causal model and a common set of political values. They are united by a belief in the truth of their model and by a commitment to translate this truth into public policy, in the conviction that human welfare will be enhanced as a result" (Haas 1990: 40–1). This relatively small group represents powerful corporate interests and professionals and this has not produced balanced policies.

Towards the end of the negotiations on TRIPS, as a result of strong resistance from a few developing countries, various modifications were made to provide some degree of flexibility in its implementation. These apparent flexibilities include the lack of definition of any terms and exclusions to the all-encompassing patent requirements of Article 27. This requires that "patents shall be available for any inventions, whether products or processes, in all fields of technology, provided that they are new, involve an inventive step and are capable of industrial application".

Geoff Tansey

As a result of considerable opposition to this, some exceptions are allowed. Article 27.3(b) permits WTO members to exclude from patentability:

> plants and animals other than micro-organisms, and essentially biological processes for the production of plants or animals other than non-biological and microbiological processes. However, Members shall provide for the protection of plant varieties either by patents or by an effective *sui generis* system or by any combination thereof. The provisions of this subparagraph shall be reviewed four years after the date of entry into force of the WTO Agreement.

The language of this exception is deliberately complex—described as "constructive ambiguity" by some negotiators—and continues to be subject to interpretation and legal argument over its meaning (Tansey 1999). The requirement to introduce patents or some other form of plant variety protection (PVP) requires considerable change in many developing countries and extends IPRs into agriculture often for the first time there.

Despite the review called for in 1999, four years after the agreement came into force, there has been little progress with a wide range of views on what should happen and whether specific interpretations or amendments are needed. Many proposals have been put on the table, mostly from developing countries. They include

- the extension of exclusions from patentability to all lifeforms;
- extension of the timetable for implementation;
- prevention of biopiracy;
- respecting use of traditional knowledge and farmers' rights;
- amendment in the light of the Convention on Biological Diversity (CBD) and International Understanding (now Treaty, see below) on Plant Genetic Resources for Food and Agriculture;
- developing new types of *sui generis* systems of plant variety protection; and
- calls for deletion of the exclusion and no lowering of standards of protection.

(Correa 2001, table 1)

Although TRIPS provisions on patents and plant variety protection impinge most directly on food, through their direct effect on agriculture, other provisions, such as those on trademarks and geographical indications, may also have a bearing in so far as they affect poor people's livelihoods and affect access to food.

A confusion of fora

TRIPS is not the only Agreement concerned with IPRs and food; others in a number of other international fora are also relevant. All of which makes for a very confusing and difficult-to-follow set of negotiations affecting food. Two major international agreements—the Convention on Biological Diversity (CBD) agreed at the Rio Earth Summit in 1992 and the International

Treaty on Plant Genetic Resources for Food and Agriculture (ITPGRFA) finally agreed in November 2001 after seven years of difficult negotiations—as well as two other bodies, the International Union for the Protection of New Varieties of Plants (UPOV after its French title) and the World Intellectual Property Organization (WIPO), also are relevant (Tansey 2002).

Different ministries and interests are involved in negotiating at these different fora and there is considerable difficulty in achieving coherence between them—or at least avoiding outright conflicts or contradiction. This was highlighted in an aptly titled report *Why Governments Can't Make Policy: The Case of Plant Genetic Resources in the International Arena*. It reviewed decision-making in Brazil, France, Germany, India, Kenya, the Philippines, Sweden and the USA, and found it to be a problem in all countries. It said: "The combination of a complex international negotiation process and a complex set of issues with tremendous long term social, economic and political impact is the perfect setting for a breakdown of international consensus on the issues of genetic resources" (Petit *et al.* 2001). This is made more difficult as major players such as the USA use "forum shifting" as a negotiating tactic—moving discussions from one place to another in an attempt to reach their overall policy goals (Braithwaite and Drahos 2000, ch. 24).

Impacts on our Food Future

The changing IPRs regime will affect the balance of power between actors in the food system and alter the risk/benefit relationships in it. The impact of these changes may be felt through their effects on the direction of research and development, market concentration, control of food supplies, and effects on poor farmers and consumers. The proponents of a stronger IPRs regime globally argue it is necessary and will be beneficial by stimulating R & D and promoting investment by private enterprises in improving food production. The impact of IPRs on development are far from clear-cut, however, and may adversely affect the poorest (Dutfield 2002).

Many effects of these global rules changes are subtle, or indirect and multifaceted, and the nature and use of specific IPRs may change market, social and cultural relationships. Those most involved in product manufacture make the most use of patents, plant variety protection, trade secrets and trademarks. Those closest to the consuming public make greater use of trademarks, and increasingly of databases, while some specialist producers use geographical indications. As the reach of the market, increasingly globalizing, goes further into developing countries so too will the major actors make use of IPRs there as part of their business strategies.

Balancing public and private interests

The right to food is recognized by the human rights regime (Article 25 of the Universal Declaration of Human Rights and Article 11 of the International Covenant on Economic, Social and Cultural Rights) and global intellectual property regulation must take account of these fundamental and binding human rights obligations. Per Pinstrup-Andersen, Director-General of the

International Food Policy Research Institute, argues that, "[w]here national governments fail to take appropriate action, food security fails. Hunger persists largely because of governance and policy failure at the national level" (Pinstrup-Anderson 2001: 15).

Already there is debate in the developed countries that levels of IPRs protection may be too high:

> There are legitimate reasons to be concerned about the highly protective standards that have emerged recently in the United States and the European Union. These laws and judicial interpretations provide broad patent protection for software and biotechnological inventions. They also promote extensive rights in the formulation of databases, which could have a negative effect on scientific research. It remains to be seen whether such standards tilt the balance within those jurisdictions toward the private rights of inventors and away from the needs of competitors and users. It is not too early to claim that they are inappropriate for developing economies and net technology importers. (Maskus 2000: 237–8)

In strengthening these private rights, a key question is whether they support the social and economic welfare of the poor in developed and developing countries and whether they will assist in meeting the development goals to which most states are committed. To make them do so requires strong states to deal with any ill effects and strong judicial systems, both of which may be lacking. It may also require clear national and international liability regimes, competition policy that prevents monopolistic practices and other complementary policies. Most of these are lacking in many developing countries.

Agricultural research and development

The trend to proprietary science, which makes much use of IPRs—mainly patents and plant breeders' rights—is raising major questions about the nature of R & D. This includes its effects on the exchange not just of germplasm (e.g. seeds) but also of ideas, experience and techniques which researchers use to spark off other ideas. The restrictions on the sharing of information may be as profound as the effects on germplasm flow. Basically, lawyers hate scientists talking together at conferences, potentially "giving away" potentially valuable knowledge: ". . . if the legal staff had had its way, the scientists would have published as little as possible" (Charles 2001). Science on the other hand has flourished in an open, transparent, sharing cultural environment. The use of confidentiality agreements in universities and research institutions, which are also doing more and more commissioned research, is further eroding the openness to sharing of knowledge. Claims to confidentiality in data supplied to regulators for approvals, e.g. for new crops, may also be increasingly challenged.

Farmers sharing knowledge—and seeds—gained from empirical experience has been behind innovation and development in agriculture for millennia. That experience has been supplemented and expanded by an organized, state-supported, science-based research effort for about 150 years. Agricultural research has been carried out by public bodies nationally and internationally—and spread to farmers—largely as a public good, since those needing its results lack the capacity to do the research itself, and the benefits flowing from improved agriculture go to society as a whole. Recently, the private sector has taken a growing role in the industrialized countries with their small farming populations and wholly commercial farming systems. However, it focuses on areas where it can best ensure returns on its investment.

Joseph Stiglitz, when he was chief economist at the World Bank, pointed out two issues to consider when there is a shift in R & D to the private sector. One is that "relying on the private sector for agricultural research is likely to result in under investment from the point of view of society" and the other is that this applied research relies on continued publicly funded basic research and has greatly benefited from past university and other public sector research (Pinstrup-Andersen 2001). In other words, the public has subsidized, and continues to subsidize, private R & D.

The further publicly financed research moves away from that usable by farmers, the more the only people who can capture its benefits are those geared up to do further research to turn fundamental research ideas into applied research. They can then produce new practices and products of use to farmers. If this is left to the private sector, it will focus on processes and produce products it can take out IPRs on and serve markets that can absorb those products and services. The new biotech-based agricultural firms strongly favour the use of patents to ensure exclusive use of their developments. They may also try to obtain broadly defined patents on key processes, or enough patents to achieve what those in the patent business call "clustering"—building enough patents, preferably interlocking, around a product to prevent others getting into the field. Another tactic is "bracketing"—surrounding a competitor's patent with so many of one's own that it cannot be commercialized (Granstrand 1999).

Competing in the patent game requires considerable resources—both to take out and to maintain patents—and legal expertise to defend them. Unless patent-holders are able to defend them, at least in the major markets, they are useless. According to Blakeney, "a single patent application, carried to completion in key markets, costs an estimated $200,000. Defending a patent application costs at least this amount again" (Blakeney 2001/2, fn 60). Most small players look for larger companies to license their inventions or buy them out.

National patent practices are still in a state of flux; the least-developed countries are not obliged to follow or implement TRIPS until 2006 and may seek extensions to this deadline. Patents are national and only apply in territories where they are taken out. Companies may not apply for them in small markets. Also, what may be allowed in some jurisdictions, such as the USA, may not be allowed in some other jurisdictions which exclude plants and animals or apply very strict definitions in patent procedures, e.g. on inventive step.

Seed provision

The IPRs regime will affect the nature of seed provision. Formal seed production systems linking public and private R & D and breeding companies dominate seed provision in industrialized countries, where most farmers buy their seeds. More informal seed production systems with production largely by a mixture of farmers and public institutions exist in many developing countries, where most farmers save their own seeds. In most jurisdictions except the USA, plant varieties cannot be patented, although the position in the EU has changed recently to be more like that in the USA. Originally, European countries developed an alternative to patents for plant varieties, plant breeders' rights (PBRs), which became embodied in UPOV (see p. 27) (Dhar 2002). These place fewer restrictions on the use of new varieties than patents.

Most developed countries want UPOV adopted as the *sui generis* system of plant variety protection required in TRIPS, but many developing countries do not. Industry argues that PBRs will enable it to undertake breeding work and also bring in foreign material to developing countries. However, "[t]here is not one ideal *sui generis* system that will suit the needs of all countries" (IPGRI 1999).

The key questions to ask about a new regime, argues Rangnekar in a background study for the UK's Commission on Intellectual Property Rights, are "has the access to foreign bred genetic material enhanced national capacity in plant breeding and what is the impact on food security? Existing literature on Kenya does not provide encouraging evidence on either of these two issues" (Rangnekar 2002: 7). After examining the economic impact of PVP he concludes:

- research conducted in the private and the public sector are non-substitutable as they are targeted at different farming groups. The shrinking resource base of the public sector and the low possibility of cost recovery, place ever greater demand for external revenues.
- closer institutional linkages between the public and the private sector raise public welfare questions in terms of accountability and transparency.
- the spread of proprietary control in research tools and uncertainty in the limits of ownership make the conduct of agricultural research all the more difficult by requiring complicated negotiations.

(Rangnekar 2002: 6)

Dhar argues that adopting the plant variety systems developed by the industrialized countries and embodied in UPOV is not adequate and suggests approaches that take into account farmers' rights and allow seeds bred by farmers to be reused by them (Dhar 2002). Under patent law, there is no farmers' exemption to allow the use of farm-saved seed as allowed for in UPOV. The International Plant Genetic Resources Institute (IPGRI) notes that "breeders and modern biotechnology companies often perceive the farmers' exemption as potentially reducing the profit, or the expectation of profit. Consequently, there may be strong opposition on the part of breeders and modern biotechnology companies to this exemption in countries where patent-like protection for plant varieties is being considered" (IPGRI 1999).

There is pressure now for patents to be extended to plant varieties and for PBRs to become more patent-like in their conditions. Even those on both sides of the argument about the use of PVP tend to be more concerned about its replacement by patents—expecting such an outcome to lead to a few major companies controlling seed production for all major commercially important crops within a few years. In part, this is because PVP legislation allows further research on PVP varieties and commercialization of that research, but patenting does not. Though there is normally a research exemption, commercialization of anything developed requires permission of the patent-holder—which can be a considerable disincentive to further work and block its use. It is a major problem with public goods research since the objective is to develop new products and methods and give them away.

Rethinking the rules

The variety of concerns has led to different views about the extension of patents into the biological sphere since the 1980s. Suggestions, which would require the current international rules agreed in TRIPS to be changed, include:

- To remove all biological materials, including micro-organisms, from patentability and seek other reward systems to encourage innovations. This is a major task and requires considerable development, both of the policies required and coalitions to achieve it.
- To amend the terms and conditions for patentability to facilitate agricultural research for development. For example, Ismail Serageldin argued at the Global Forum on Agricultural Research (GFAR) that a number of options be considered:
    - patent length on research processes should be restricted to 5–6 years, by which time often new processes had been developed anyway, and which gave companies a head start (Serageldin 2000);
    - set a flat fee for use of the patented process after a fixed time so users cannot be held hostage by monopoly rights holders;
    - develop a clip-art-like toolkit of patented technologies (i.e. free for public use and easily obtainable) that would be freely available to public good national and international R & D in specific countries or for specific poor people's crops; or
    - declare certain regions as a kind of "conservation area" where the rights of patent-holders are restricted or overridden for the greater public good.
- To exclude basic processes, e.g. N-fixation or gene sequences (somewhat like allowing a software company to patent use of the letter E or the word "the") from patentability.

None of these will happen easily. They require substantial political effort to be achieved. And all have implications for the way TRIPS is implemented, interpreted and possibly amended in the future.

Geoff Tansey

Rural Opportunities and Market Structures

Other concerns about the impact of IPRs focus less on the implications for market structure than on opportunities in rural and urban areas. The work of Amartya Sen and others has shown that simply increasing food production does not necessarily end food insecurity for the poor. The market and social structure of food and farming matter, as well as lower prices and more food production. The growing economic concentration of firms in agricultural development, especially in biotechnology, suggest the market structure in which private R & D operates will be particularly important. Professor John Barton identifies a number of concerns—both static and dynamic—to arise from IPRs in agriculture for developing countries:

- Effects on seed prices, which he expects to be increased in the tens of percentage points not hundreds. However, this is a reason why public seed provision will be needed in countries with oligopolistic seed markets.
- Use of trademarks, patents and PVP to protect major developed-world markets from competition and likely to increase the use of lawyers.
- Use of patent portfolios to restrict follow-on research by potential competitors and public sector bodies. This requires countries to ensure developing-world researchers have a legal right to use such research.
- The need to counter oligopolistic tendencies through competition and anti-trust measures—as IPRs help underpin mergers and acquisitions activities.
- The need to restrict broad patent claims and patents on fundamental innovations.

He argues that the "impact of intellectual property on the international industrial structure will, in the long run, be far more important than any more static rent flow associated with prices for products containing intellectual property" (Barton forthcoming). More bluntly, what will be the effect of a handful of companies controlling the production of the basic plant and animal inputs into farming globally?

Any moves to counter the expected effects of IPRs, however, assume that providing support to small farmers is a policy goal. In many states there are *de facto* policies which aim or tend to reduce the number of small farmers, a process which some feel the more private-sector, IPR-based approach in the future will exacerbate. If small farmers are squeezed out, as has historically been the case in the industrialized countries, the key issue is the existence of alternative livelihoods through which they can maintain their food security. Given the vast differences between countries, with farming populations varying from a considerable majority of the population to a small minority, a range of policy options will be needed to ensure food security during such changes. As Tripp points out, these need different approaches from enabling some households to leave farming, others to have technologies to improve their efficiency and protect natural resources they manage, and others to become fully commercial farmers—depending upon the livelihood strategy (Tripp 2001: 485).

Environmental Aspects

Two areas of environmental concern link our food future, biotechnology and IPRs. One is whether the balance of rights and obligations achieved in the current IPRs regime is such as to minimize any accidental damage (e.g. unforeseen consequences of biological innovations on ecosystem viability). This is related to risk management, adequate trials, monitoring and evaluation, constraints on over-rapid deployment of technology without an adequate biosafety regime and a sufficiently robust liability regime to compensate for (or provide mechanisms to ensure food available to do so) any such effects. In a world threatened with increasingly variable and extreme weather events such as storms, floods and droughts, linked to climatic change, could widespread application of IPRs-protected, less diverse crops affect the sustainability of farming systems as well as farmers' and researchers' efforts to adapt to climatic changes? Already, "the main cause of genetic erosion in crops, as reported by almost all countries, is the replacement of local varieties by improved or exotic varieties and species" (FAO 1998: 33). Will there be sufficient flexibility for both farmers and researchers when IP and contract law could reduce it?

Another concern is over the deliberate use of biotech weapons aimed at disrupting agricultural production of specific groups or regions. To avoid this requires conflict prevention, non-use of such weapons, systems to prevent their development and use, and means of verification. It is in the verification area that questions have arisen over how far industry concerns over protection of their IP could impede controls to prevent the intentional use of biotechnology to inflict damage through the development and use of biological weapons by either states or terrorists (Meier 2002).

Trademarks, Trade Secrets and Geographical Indications

Although patents and PVP are likely to have the most direct effects on the shape of food production through their impact on farming, other IPRs may also affect food. This will depend upon how far their use advantages or disadvantages different groups, local or national industries versus transnational industries, prices, market structures and access to food, especially by poor people, and the ability of traditional communities to market local products.

Many companies make strong use of trademarks, and a focus on brands and substantial marketing investment to secure their markets. The use of trademarks is often linked to other tools for control such as brand advertising. Greater efforts to protect brands and increase market share are increasingly likely. For example, in 1993, the chairmen of Unilever, the Anglo-Dutch multinational, called brand equities "the most valuable items in our stewardship" and saw "the power of our brands as the engine of long-term growth". During that year, the company spent almost 12 per cent of turnover (£3,284 million) on advertising and promotional investment. More recently they said: "We are focused increasingly on driving the growth of our leading brands and dealing with other brands in ways which create value for shareholders" (Burgmans and Fitzgerald 2002).

There has been a spate of mergers and acquisitions in the food industry over the past decade, which is still continuing, as firms gear up to serve global markets and also to counter the growing power of multiple retailers. Brands still remain a crucial part of their strategy, although Unilever announced in 2000 plans to cut out three-quarters of its 1,600 brands to focus on 400 around the world.

For some products, a combination of widely advertised branded [trademark] products and trade secrets—Coca-Cola being the most famous—can be used. Others may develop certification schemes to show that those people supplying the goods have followed a particular practice, e.g. organic production or artisanal methods. The ability of small producers to find markets for their often unadvertised products is very different from the ability of those whose supply chains lead into globally promoted branded products.

In urban areas the replacement of the indigenous street foods activities in many developing countries—often linked to local supplies—with trademarked franchises of global fast food chains could also put poor people's ability to access adequate diets at risk (FAO 1992: 16–17). Such a switch to fast food could also have wide-ranging social and economic implications and be more expensive (Schlosser 2002).

For other groups of producers, making a product in a particular way or region as designated by a name, linked to the region and method of production, provides a marketing tool that allows them to capitalize on their uniqueness (think of e.g. Roquefort cheese, Parma ham). Such designations normally come out of a well-established activity that has national recognition and produces things sought after by consumers. In a study of these issues and of five case studies of essentially niche products (kava, Rooibos tea, quinoa, basmati rice, and neem) David Downes and others concluded: "Both geographical indications and trademarks show the greatest potential [to benefit local producers] where traditional small-scale production is still present, on the supply side, and where end-use products are marketed directly to consumers. In other words, they are less likely to be appropriate when the product is a commodity traded primarily in bulk" (Downes et al. 1999).

There is considerable disagreement among developing countries about the economic benefits of extending stronger protection to geographical indications of foodstuffs. Some, such as India, favour this, believing they will gain from having protection for a range of products such as basmati rice. Others, such as Argentina, with a large segment of the population tracing their roots back to Europe and with tastes for European-type foodstuffs, fear that production of the local version of many products will become much more difficult if they are prevented from using terms associated with the foodstuff, which are likely to be reserved to products, such as cheeses, from Europe.

There is also the problem of the misappropriation of traditional knowledge of food crops, and the lack of systems for ensuring benefit sharing with traditional and indigenous communities (Correa 2001). Other kinds of instruments than IPRs may be needed to protect their knowledge, as well as excluding plants and animals from patentability as allowed in TRIPS. Moreover, if indigenous crops such as quinoa, or nuna or yellow beans are patented in developed countries, in what is now called biopiracy, this may foreclose export markets there—since patent-holders can prevent the import of products that infringe their rights, or which are produced by processes they hold rights on. Or if other crops have look-alikes which are produced and trade-marked and widely marketed this may also undermine the potential markets for developing-country crops.

Prospects for Better Policy-making

Clearly this is a complex area. Although there is much more detail available (see References), to date far too little attention has been paid to the impact of IPRs on our food future. It requires more people with a wide range of interests to engage with both the implications of IPRs and the policy-making that surrounds them. Both the processes that go on to make them need rebalancing—to give a greater voice to those affected by the rules in developed and developing countries—and some of the rules themselves need changing. There has been a significant growth in interest in this area in the last few years with a range of development bodies such as Oxfam and Action Aid and the UK Food Group's Agrobiodiversity coalition highlighting some of the IPRs issues.

Some groups, such as the Third World Network, work with developing-country governments and groups to raise concern about these issues and press for rule changes. Other organizations, such as the Quaker UN office in Geneva (QUNO), work where negotiations go on to help make them more just and balanced processes. QUNO has worked to strengthen the capacity of developing-country negotiators to deal with these issues and have a more effective dialogue with the developed countries pushing for stronger IPRs (Tansey 2001).

Our global food future is linked to the working of these rules. We must broaden the interests involved in making these seemingly esoteric and complex rules, and we must monitor how they affect our food future. And we must make, or negotiate, changes to these rules if they undermine food security for people today or tomorrow.

Notes

Geoff Tansey is an independent writer and consultant. This paper draws heavily on work done for the Quaker UN Office in Geneva in the preparation of a longer discussion paper entitled "Food security, biotechnology and intellectual property—Unpacking some issues around TRIPS" available on *www.quno.org.ch*, click on Geneva pages.

References

Barton, J. (1999), *Intellectual Property Management, 2020 Vision, Focus 2—Biotechnology for Developing-Country Agriculture: Problems and Opportunities*, Brief 7 of 10, Rome: IGPRI, October.

Geoff Tansey

Barton, J. (forthcoming), Intellectual property, biotechnology, and international trade: two examples. In T. Cottier, P. C. Mavroidis and M. Panizzon (eds), *Intellectual Property: Trade, Competition, and Sustainable Development the World Trade Forum*, vol. 3, Ann Arbor: University of Michigan Press.

Blakeney, M. (2001/2), Intellectual property rights and food security, *Bio-Science Law Review*, 4, 5: 1–13.

Boyle, J. (1996), *Shamans, Software and Spleens—Law and the Construction of the Information Society*, Cambridge, MA: Harvard University Press.

Boyle, J. (2001), The second enclosure movement and the construction of the public domain. Paper presented at Conference on the Public Domain, Duke University School of Law, 9–11 November. *www.law.duke.edu/pd*

Braithwaite, J. and Drahos, P. (2000), *Global Business Regulation*, Cambridge: Cambridge University Press.

Burgmans, A. and Fitzgerald, N. (2002), *Annual Report*, Unilever, London: Unilever.

Charles, D. (2001), *Lords of the Harvest—Biotech, Big Money, and the Future of Food*, Cambridge, MA: Perseus Publishing.

Correa, C. M. (2001), *Traditional Knowledge and Intellectual Property: Issues and Options Surrounding the Protection of Traditional Knowledge*, Geneva: Quaker UN Office, November. Available on *www.quno.org* (Geneva pages) and GRAIN at *http://www.grain.org/publications/trips-countrypos-en.cfm*

Dhar, B. (2002), *Sui Generis Systems for Plant Variety Protection: Options under TRIPS*, Geneva: Quaker UN Office, April. Available on *www.quno.org* (Geneva pages).

Downes, D. R., Laird, S. A. *et al.* (1999), Innovative mechanisms for sharing benefits of biodiversity and related knowledge: case studies on geographical indications and trademarks. Paper prepared for UNCTAD Biotrade Initiative, Geneva.

Drahos, P. (1995), Global property rights in information: the story of TRIPS at the GATT, *Prometheus*, 13: 6–19.

Drahos, P., with Braithwaite, J. (2002), *Information Feudalism: Who Owns the Knowledge Economy*, London: Earthscan.

Dutfield, G. (2002), Literature survey on intellectual property rights and sustainable human development, February 2002, available at *http://www.ictsd.org/unctad-ictsd/doc/bioblipr.pdf*

FAO (1992), Street foods. In *Food and Nutrition: Creating a Well-fed World*, Rome: FAO, pp. 16–17.

FAO (1998), *The State of the World's Plant Genetic Resources for Food and Agriculture*, Rome: FAO.

Granstrand, O. (1999), *The Economics and Management of Intellectual Property: Towards Intellectual Capitalism*, Cheltenham and Northampton: Edward Elgar.

Haas, E. B. (1990), *When Knowledge Is Power: Three Models of Change in International Organizations*, Berkeley and Los Angeles: University of California Press.

IPGRI (1999), *Key Questions for Decision Makers: Protection of Plant Varieties under the WTO Agreement on Trade-related Aspects of Intellectual Property Rights*, Rome: IPGRI.

Maskus, K. E. (2000), *Intellectual Property Rights in the Global Economy*, Washington, DC: Institute for International Economics, pp. 237–8.

May, C. (2000), *A Global Political Economy of Intellectual Property Rights: The New Enclosures?* London: Routledge.

Meier, O. (2002), Verification of the Biological Weapons Convention: what is needed next? *Medicine, Conflict and Survival*, 18, 2: 175–93, and other articles in this special issue.

OECD (1971), *Food Policy*, Paris: OECD.

Petit, M. *et al.* (2001), *Why Governments Can't Make Policy: The Case of Plant Genetic Resources in the International Arena*, Lima: International Potato Centre (CIP), October.

Pinstrup-Andersen, P. (2001), Achieving sustainable food security for all: required policy action. Paper prepared for Mansholt Lecture, Wageningen University, The Netherlands, 14 November. See *www.ifpri.org*

Rangnekar, D. (2002), Access to genetic resources, gene-based inventions and agriculture, study paper 3a, Commission on Intellectual Property Rights. *http://www.iprcommission.org/documents/Rangnekar_study.doc*

Schlosser, E. (2002), *Fast Food Nation*, London: Penguin.

Serageldin, I. (2000), *International cooperation for the public good: agricultural research in the new century*. GFAR, Dresden, 21–23 May. Available at *http://www.egfar.org*

Tansey, G. (1999), *Trade, Intellectual Property, Food and Biodiversity: Key Issues and Options for the 1999 Review of Article 27.3(b) of the TRIPS Agreement*, London: Quaker Peace and Service. Available on *www.quno.org*

Tansey, G. (2001), IPRs, food and biodiversity: Quaker UN Office work and concerns identified there. Paper presented at World Bank NGO Agricultural Science and Technology Roundtable Discussion, 16 April. Washington DC. Available on *www.quno.org*

Tansey, G. (2002), *Food Security, Biotechnology and IPRs: Unpacking Some Issues around TRIPS*, Geneva: Quaker UN Office. Available on *www.quno.org*

Tansey, G. and Worsley, T. (1995), *The Food System: A Guide*, London: Earthscan.

Thurow, L. C. (1997), Needed: a new system of intellectual property rights, *Harvard Business Review*, September-October.

Tripp, R. (2001), Agricultural technology policies for rural development, *Development Policy Review*, 19, 4: 479–89.

World Commission on Environment and Development (1987), *Our Common Future*, Oxford: Oxford University Press.

3

The Evolution of Food Safety Policy-making Institutions in the UK, EU and Codex Alimentarius

Erik Millstone and Patrick van Zwanenberg

Introduction

Ever since the British government announced on 20 March 1996 that a novel fatal disease in humans (now called variant Creutzfeldt-Jakob disease or vCJD) had emerged and was almost certainly caused by consuming BSE-contaminated food, the UK and the European Commission (and other EU member states) have been struggling to deal with the consequences of a serious loss of public confidence in the safety of foods and in food safety policy-making institutions. Those crises have not only provoked reform within the EU, the reverberations have also spread to the Codex Alimentarius Commission (and its joint UN-FAO and WHO expert advisory committees) that, under the rules of the World Trade Organization, sets benchmarks for global safety standards for internationally traded food products. BSE was not, however, an isolated problem. It was just the most challenging of a lengthy series of food safety scares and crises concerning food chemical and microbiological safety that had arisen since the early 1980s.

One of the main ways in which the authorities have responded to those challenges has been by initiating a broad range of structural and procedural reforms to the ways in which public policies are decided, legitimated and communicated. In this paper, we outline some of the more important respects in which national and international authorities have changed the ways in which they assess and manage the risks to human consumers of food-borne hazards. The focus is on developments in the UK, the EU and, at the global level, the Codex Alimentarius Commission, and the period covered runs from the late 1960s until the present day.

The *Ancien Régime*

If we go back to the *status quo ante* (i.e. the period from the 1960s up to about the mid-1990s) the key structural and procedural features of the food safety policy-making system included the following:

- UK, European and Codex institutions with responsibility for setting consumer protection standards were also responsible for industrial sponsorship of the food and agriculture industries and/or for the promotion of trade.

- The regulatory regimes operated under conditions of official secrecy and lacked proper mechanisms of accountability, some even relying on non-statutory bodies and procedures.
- Policy decisions were taken on the advice of small closed groups of scientific experts including many drawn from industries and the firms whose products were being regulated.
- Policy decisions were typically misrepresented as having been based on "sound science" with almost all the conflicting policy objectives, implicit framings, uncertainties, and residual risks concealed.
- Policy-makers (both public officials and elected representatives) were typically able, and keen, to hide behind their expert scientific advisors. Scientific advisors were often expected to take decisions about which risks were acceptable and how they should be managed, even though those decisions necessitated political rather than purely scientific judgements.

Taken together, those arrangements entailed *inter alia* that decisions could be, and were, taken to advance commercial and political ends as distinct from the ostensible policy goal, namely the protection of consumers and public health, and they allowed those commercial and political influences to be exercised discreetly and so to remain substantially concealed.

Institutions with primary responsibility for consumer protection were also responsible for industrial sponsorship and/or the promotion of trade

The global benchmark standard-setting institution, namely the Codex Alimentarius Commission, has an ambiguous remit, being responsible for facilitating trade and, within that context, providing an acceptable level of safety for consumers (Codex Alimentarius 2002). At Codex meetings decisions are taken by national delegations, but those delegations have sometimes been headed by trade promotion officials rather than food safety officials and national delegations often include large numbers of representatives of the commercial sector, with direct interests in the decisions they take (Avery *et al.* 1993; Suppan and Leonard 2002).

Within the European Commission responsibility for regulating food safety was, for many years, located in Directorate-General III (DG-III), which initially had responsibility for promoting the interests of European industry. It was subsequently redesignated as having responsibility for the EU's internal market and enterprise.

In the UK the remit of the Ministry of Agriculture, Fisheries and Food (MAFF) included responsibility for the promotion of the economic interests of UK farmers and the food industry as well as responsibility for almost all aspects of food-related consumer protection policy. (The only exceptions were that the Department of Health was responsible for the microbiological aspects of food safety and for nutrition policy, but even on those issues MAFF and through it the food industry exerted considerable influence.) Prior to the autumn of 1989 there was, moreover, no systematic separation within MAFF of those contrary responsibilities.

At all three levels of governance, the empirical evidence strongly indicates that the practice of locating within a single institution responsibility both for promoting the interests of trade and/or particular industrial sectors and at the same time for regulating those sectors has meant that consumer and health interests have been routinely subordinated to the objectives of furthering the commercial interests of farming and the food industry. Policy-makers at the national, regional and global levels of governance have typically insisted, however, that there was either no conflict of interest between promotion and regulation of the food sector, or that policy fully reconciled both sets of objectives. In part that pretence was maintained by representing food safety regulation as a purely scientific and administrative operation (see below).

Several aspects of the regulatory regimes operated on non-statutory bases

The Codex Alimentarius is a voluntary agreement among member states, and the Codex decision-making bodies have no statutory basis whatsoever. The joint expert committees of the Food and Agriculture Organization (FAO) and World Health Organization (WHO) are, in effect, entirely *ad hoc*. They have neither statutory responsibilities nor any lines of accountability. Codex does not legislate standards for international trade, but since the creation of the World Trade Organization in 1994, if a country imposes a standard more restrictive than that set by Codex that may be *prima facie* grounds for a complaint under the rules of the WTO by a country wishing to sell into that country's market.

In the UK, pesticide regulation prior to 1985, for example, took the form of a voluntary agreement between government and pesticide manufacturers and distributors. Food contact materials, such as plastic packaging were similarly subject to a voluntary agreement until 1992. In the UK the main expert advisory committees, including the Food Advisory Committee, the Committee on Toxicity and the Advisory Committee on Pesticides had no statutory bases. Ministers could establish or abolish them at will, and follow or disregard their advice as they saw fit.

Voluntary regimes facilitated negotiated, flexible and discretionary forms of decision-making. Although that meant that relatively few resources were needed to operate the regulatory regimes, their non-statutory bases militated against effective oversight.

Furthermore, at a national level, government relied on trade associations to ensure that industrial members abided by voluntary controls, and thus relatively harmonious relations between regulators and industry were vital. Industry could always refuse to comply and this added pressure on regulators to ensure that their proposals and interventions were acceptable to industry. As one senior official in MAFF's pesticide safety division noted in 1978: "[u]nreasonable demands [for product and toxicological data] could lead to a break in the *essential mutual trust* between government and industry" (Bates 1978: 174; emphasis added).

Flexibility and discretion were facilitated and fostered by official secrecy

Under British and European legislation it was often unlawful for the public to know what evidence was taken into account, or how decisions were reached. WHO-FAO committees kept scientific data confidential but they had no statutory authority for doing so. Expert advisory committees, at all levels of governance, often judged dossiers of information that were mainly or entirely assembled by the companies whose products were being judged. Much of the information was the property of the companies concerned, and if the companies chose not to publish it, then the UK, EU and global authorities would not require disclosure. None of the scientific analyses undertaken by expert committees in MAFF, the EU or the WHO-FAO committees were subject to peer review. In the UK, the publication of the advice from expert advisory committees to ministers was entirely at the discretion of the ministers. Under the *ancien régime*, ministers did not always accept the advice of their experts, but when they did not do so, hardly anyone, other than the firms concerned, knew what had happened. In general, it was simply not possible for independent analysts or scholars to know, even less to document, how regulatory decisions were made. The types of negotiations and conflicts that occurred, both within expert committees and between advisory scientists, civil servants, ministers and firms were not available for scrutiny by the public, the media, independent scientists, the legislature or the judiciary. Expert committees lacked transparency and public accountability, proceedings were often not published and the committees were not subject to requirements of due process.

Policy decisions were typically taken on the advice of small closed groups of scientific experts selected through entirely opaque processes

In all three jurisdictions, experts have been drawn from government, academia and industry, though not from organizations representing consumers. In many cases industrial scientists have been drawn from the same industries and firms whose products were being regulated. Members of the expert advisory committees who were not directly employed by industry could, and often did, act as paid consultants to the companies whose products they were evaluating, even though those links were often not disclosed.

Codex sets standards by reference to advice from joint UN FAO and WHO bodies such as the Joint Meeting on Pesticide Residues (JMPR) and the Joint Expert Committee on Food Additives (JECFA) (Millstone 2001). Not only have some members of those committees acted as paid consultants to the companies whose products they have evaluated, but some of the World Health Organization's retired scientific staff members have returned to work for JMPR as consultants while also working on behalf of private companies in order to help influence JMPR's conclusions, but concealing those activities from both the WHO and the members of the committees (Zeltner *et al.* 2000).

At the European Commission, members of expert advisory committees were never required to reveal any conflicts of interest until 2000, and the provisions introduced then were quite limited. Even though committee members are now required to disclose to the Commission if they have commercial links, the Commission will not disclose that information unless the individual gives explicit consent. The information that the Commission discloses is not available in public documents or on a website, but can only be obtained in response to an explicit written request.

In the UK there was no requirement for declarations of interest by members of expert advisory committees to committee secretariats, fellow committee members or the general public until after the 1989 salmonella crisis, and even then such declarations were only partial. Since the early 1990s members of UK expert advisory committees have been required to indicate whether or not they have either direct or indirect interests in relevant firms, but the scale and intensity of those links remain undisclosed and have often been difficult to ascertain. In 1987, however, the *Guardian* reported an interview conducted with Francis Roe, a senior advisor to the UK government on chemical safety (Erlichman 1987). Roe was a member of the Committee on Toxicity (CoT) but he also acted as a paid consultant to many of the companies whose products the CoT was evaluating. Erlichman explained that Roe argued that he was not beholden to any of the companies because he took money from all of them. "At any one time I am involved with 30 to 40 companies. I don't feel I need to defend one, to be truthful." When asked why he did not step aside when a topic on which he had an interest arose on the agenda he replied: "I asked the chairman whether he wanted me to leave the room or not, but the fact is that on many occasions with the CoT I would have to declare an interest on every item on the agenda" (*ibid.*). The WHO's expert toxicologist advising the JMPR was paid approximately $50,000 a year for three years to advise the tobacco industry on how to respond to evidence that the ethylene bisdithiocarbamate fungicides that are used extensively on tobacco plants may be seriously toxic (Zeltner *et al.* 2000).

Policy decisions on food safety in the UK and at the European Commission were typically misrepresented by policy-makers as having been based on, and only on, "sound science"

The practice of representing food safety standards as based on, and only on, "sound science" had a number of important dimensions and repercussions. First it meant that policy judgements were represented as if they were concerned only with risks to public health. In practice, however, those decisions also typically took into account information and/or assumptions about the supposed benefits of, or need for, such products or processes. A decision to permit a food additive or pesticide involved judgements in which trade-offs were made as between risks and benefits, but those judgements were often misrepresented as if they were solely based on a "scientific risk assessment".

The UK's Food Advisory Committee (or FAC) (and before it the Food Additives and Contaminants Committee [FACC]) juxtaposed evidence of the possible risks posed by food additives against considerations of the "need" for those additives, but the FAC did not interpret the concept of "need" in terms of what consumers might "need", but in terms of what was useful to producers or to the trade. For example, the FAC judged that there was a "need" for food colourings because they helped the manufacturers and retailers to sell products that might not otherwise be saleable (FACC 1979).

At the European Commission, the Scientific Committee for Food was given responsibility for making judgements about "safety", with issues of "need" or "utility" being either taken for granted or left to the marketplace—in other words, if consumers buy it or products containing it, it is "needed". Even when "need" was explicitly addressed, it was often treated relatively superficially. For example, there is some evidence that several artificial sweeteners might pose a toxic hazard (Millstone 1988). Those compounds have been deemed acceptable in part because it has been officially assumed that they provide significant benefits by substituting for sugar consumption and helping consumers to control or even diminish their body weight, and that those benefits outweigh the putative risks. The evidence of benefits was not, however, critically examined. If it had been, greater attention would have been given to the evidence showing that in dietary terms, artificial sweeteners are supplementing sugar consumption rather than substituting for it, and that in relation to weight control they are at best ineffective, and possibly counterproductive (Stellman and Garfinkel 1986; Blundell and Hill 1986).

Many of the Codex's, the European Commission's and the UK's advisory committees have in practice provided not just scientific advice but rather policy advice and specific policy recommendations. The contrast is an important one. If their advice had been strictly scientific it would have been confined to indicating what was, and was not, known about the possible consequences of adopting a range of alternative policy options, leaving it to risk-managers and policy-makers to choose among those options in the light of that information. The advice from the committees has, however, typically been monolithic and prescriptive, recommending the adoption of particular options. Scientific considerations on their own, especially uncertain ones, cannot entail unique policy judgements. It therefore follows that political judgements about the acceptability of uncertainties and risks were being made by ostensibly scientific fora. The Codex, the Commission and the UK authorities have repeatedly represented decisions as having been based on, and solely on, "sound science" while in practice they were based on implicit and covert economic and political considerations and judgements.

Another important consequence of the appeal to "sound science" was that scientific uncertainties were typically understated, glossed over or concealed, even though decisions were in practice typically based on incomplete, uncertain and equivocal evidence. A significant convergence of interests obtained in which ministers, civil servants and members of expert advisory committees had a shared interest in representing the judgements of expert advisors as if they were far more robustly grounded and constructed than was the case. On the rare occasions when uncertainties were highlighted they were typically those that surrounded judgements that policy-makers and their advisors were choosing to reject. The uncertainties that qualified the policy conclusions adopted were almost invariably concealed.

An example of highly selective interpretations of uncertainty concerns the assessment of the toxicity of a group of fungicides known as ethylene bisdithiocarbamates or EBDCs. In a review of the EBDCs, the UK's Advisory

Erik Millstone and Patrick van Zwanenberg

Committee on Pesticides (ACP) subjected a long-term mouse study which
provided *prima facie* positive evidence of carcinogenicity to numerous criticisms regarding its design, and argued that it was flawed because the
tumours in mice may have occurred by chance. On the other hand, a negative study conducted with rats was taken at face value by the ACP and
deemed to constitute sufficient evidence of the absence of any carcinogenic
effects. In that particular case, however, the probability of a false positive
result in the mouse study was statistically very unlikely, given the incidence
of tumours, the number of animals, and the historical record of background
tumours in the strains of mice concerned. By contrast, the chances of a false
negative result in the rat study were particularly high given the very small
number of rats involved in the experiment (van Zwanenberg and Millstone
2000). Consistently inconsistent ways of selecting and interpreting data in
ways that opportunistically favoured industry, especially from animal toxicological studies, were not uncommon in UK science-based policy-making systems (Abraham 1995).

The appeal to "sound science" also served to support an official approach
to risk communication that the UK Public Inquiry into BSE referred to as
"sedation" and "reassurance" (Phillips *et al.* 2000, vol. 1, para. 1179). Reas-
suring narratives were typically represented as legitimated by, and only by,
reliable and complete scientific knowledge. Not only were uncertainties and
policy decisions about the acceptability of risk concealed, so too were the
existence of such risks as might remain once the regulations had been fully
implemented. The UK government's concern with the economic viability of
the food industry and with the impact of its policy decisions on public
expenditure complicated its interpretation and representation of the risks.
Whenever regulatory decisions were taken, the impression was given that the
food supply was completely and unproblematically safe, and that the authorities were solely concerned with the protection of public health. Because
official risk communication messages represented science as reliable, decisive
and as the sole determining factor in the decision-making process, non-
scientific considerations such as assumptions about benefits and social judgements of acceptability, as well as a concern with the economic interests of
farmers and the food industry were all concealed (Millstone and van
Zwanenberg 2001).

Finally, because decisions about the scope of risk assessments, i.e. which
kinds of effects to deem as risks and which to exclude or discount, and about
the trade-offs between risks and benefits were frequently taken within scientific committees and misrepresented as purely scientific, ministers and
officials could, and did, hide behind the advice of the scientists, displacing
responsibility for policy on to committees of experts (Hood *et al.* 2001).
Although, in some regulatory arenas, scientific committees were obliged
to take responsibility for the policy aspects of their advice, detailed analyses of regulatory decision-making have shown that officials sometimes
set up expert committees in ways that favoured particular policy outcomes,
although scientists' decisions were later construed as if they were purely
scientific and independent judgements. As one MAFF official acknowledged:
"you have to turn to external bodies to try to give some credibility to public

pronouncements, [but] you are very dependent therefore on what the Committees then find . . . Really the key to it is setting up the Committee, who is on it, and the nature of their investigations" (BSE Inquiry Transcript 1998).

In the case of the Veterinary Products Committee's (VPC) evaluation of the genetically modified lactation-promoting hormones known as recombinant bovine somatotropin (or rBST) the minister first announced what policy would be, namely that the use of the product was safe and acceptable, and then asked the committee for its advice. The secretariat tried repeatedly to persuade the VPC to endorse rBST, and when eventually the VPC insisted on advising ministers that it was not satisfied that rBST was acceptably safe, the Department encouraged the company sponsoring rBST to appeal to the Medicines Commission. That appeal was successful, although rBST was never allowed into full commercial use in the UK because of an EU-wide ban.

In the case of the Southwood Working Party, which advised MAFF and the Department of Health on BSE, the MAFF secretariat attempted on several occasions to try to ensure that the committee would produce the advice the officials wanted to receive. For example, MAFF's permanent secretary told the committee that he hoped that any recommendations it made would not lead to an increase in public expenditure (Southwood 1998, para. 25). After MAFF officials had seen a draft recommendation for a ban on the use of ruminant protein from the feed, not only of cattle but of all herbivores, officials and ministers successfully exerted pressure on the committee to drop that particular recommendation because it was uncongenial for non-scientific reasons (Phillips *et al.* 2000, vol. 4, paras 9.21 and 9.25).

In summary, before the late 1990s the Codex, EU and UK food safety regulatory regimes provided classic examples of something closely approximating to "regulatory capture", although the interests of MAFF and DG-III were never identical to those of their commercial and industrial client stakeholders, because as well as seeking to promote their clients' interests they also had their own institutional and political interests (Bernstein 1955; Sabatier 1975).

The Crises that Undermined the *Status Quo* and Provoked a Wave of Institutional Reforms

A lengthy series of food safety scares and crises started in the UK in October 1984 with food additives, to be rapidly followed by, for example, botulism, pesticides, Alar, rBST and other veterinary medicines, salmonella, BSE and *E. coli* 0157 and GM foods. The most serious of those crises concerned BSE, but in the late 1980s it was not obvious that BSE would cause more difficulties than any of the other sets of concerns. In continental Europe there were similar problems with hormones, antibiotics, dioxins in animal feeds, toxic cooking oil in Spain and antifreeze in Austrian wine.

The food safety crises of the late 1980s and early 1990s provoked a few marginal, and token, reforms in the UK. For example, in November 1989, partly in response to public concern about issues of food safety, a Food Safety Directorate was established within MAFF to give at least an appearance of a separation of responsibilities for food safety from food production sponsorship.

A Consumer Panel was also established in 1991, but there is no evidence that it had any effect on policy. Ministers and officials saw it as a forum through which MAFF's messages could be disseminated, rather than as an occasion for listening or engaging substantively with consumer concerns. In the late 1980s and early 1990s, however, there were no significant or even token reforms to either European or the global policy-making institutions. The European Commission was focusing on the completion of the integration of the European Single Market in time by 1992, and Codex was focusing on the increase in its global authority once the WTO was established in 1994.

Several elements of the UK's regulatory regime were given a statutory basis, but that was as much a consequence of EU membership as a political aspiration to advance beyond the *status quo*. Slightly more of the scientific data, upon which regulatory decisions were based, were placed "in the public domain", but the criteria by which those data were selected and interpreted remained obscure. Some of the data used by the Committee on Toxicity were, for example, deposited in the British Library's remote location in Wetherby, North Yorkshire. Initially MAFF's policy was that anyone wishing to inspect those data would have to make an appointment, and then travel to Wetherby. Complaints from consumer representatives persuaded MAFF next to propose that, upon request and with an appointment, documents could be transferred to the British Library in London, and further complaints pressured MAFF to allow photocopies to be obtained, but only at a relatively high cost. Some of the data used by the Advisory Committee on Pesticides were also placed in a MAFF office in London and, on appointment, could be viewed—but only one document at a time! However those arrangements were to be characterized, they hardly counted as "freedom of information".

MAFF also decided to require some partial declarations of interests by members of expert advisory committees. Members of the FAC and CoT, for example, had to disclose, though only in vague and general terms, whether they, or their departments, were in receipt of funding from relevant firms, or if they held shares in those companies. At the European Commission, after March 1996, members of expert advisory committees were expected to disclose such information to the committee secretariat, but not necessarily to other members of their committees or to the general public. Most of those marginal reforms were designed to fend off growing public and political criticism, but they did not fundamentally alter the decision-making practices or the policy outcomes.

The acute BSE crisis that erupted on 20 March 1996 was a defining watershed. The UK government's announcement of a probable link between consuming BSE-contaminated food and the emergence of new variant CJD, after years of repeated assurances that British beef was "perfectly safe", unleashed the most damaging science-based political crisis that has ever occurred in the UK or the EU. The ensuing crisis contributed to the downfall of the Major government, the creation of the Food Standards Agency and, along with foot-and-mouth disease, to the abolition of the Ministry of Agriculture, Fisheries and Food.

A crucial institutional change in the UK has been the creation of the Food Standards Agency (FSA). On his first day as prime minister in May 1997, Tony Blair received the James Report, which recommended the creation of an FSA, answerable to the Department of Health, which would separate regulation from sponsorship, and provide ministers with advice on consumer protection. The FSA was established in April 2000 and took over responsibility for consumer protection and public health aspects of food policy.

The initial idea had been that the FSA would be responsible for the entire food chain—"from the plough to the plate"—but in practice it did not work out like that. For reasons that have never been explained, the government decided that MAFF would retain primary responsibility for veterinary and agricultural aspects of food policy, so that the FSA's responsibility runs only "from the farm gate to the plate". MAFF retained its industrial sponsorship remit, and retained primary responsibility for three key areas of food safety policy, namely BSE, pesticides and veterinary medicine, while the FSA has indirect oversight of those policy domains.

When the FSA was established, it outlined three core values that would guide its work: to put the consumer first, to be open and accessible, and to be an independent voice. Those guidelines represented an abrupt change from the *status quo ante* and reflected an analysis of some of the principal shortcomings in MAFF's approach to policy-making.

Another significant change, prompted eventually by the foot-and-mouth epidemic of 2001, was the abolition of MAFF. MAFF's remaining functions, as well as responsibility for environmental policy formerly located in the Department of the Environment, Transport and the Regions (DETR), were transferred to a new Department for Environment, Food and Rural Affairs (DEFRA) in summer 2001. It remains to be seen what difference DEFRA will make—at the time of writing it is too soon to tell.

A further important development occurred in late 1999 when the UK government effectively acknowledged that public policy on biotechnology could no longer be represented as if it were based solely upon scientific considerations. The response of the British authorities was to establish two new commissions: one called the Agriculture and Environment Biotechnology Commission (AEBC) while the other is called the Human Genetics Commission. These two commissions have rather vague terms of reference, and there is no evidence that ministers have any clear idea about how they will integrate the advice of those commissions with that of their scientific advisors. On the one hand, some members of the AEBC think that they have a role to play in deciding the scope of the risk assessments of releasing GM crops, while on the other hand several members of the Advisory Committee on Releases to the Environment (ACRE) reject that idea entirely, and argue that the AEBC's judgements only become relevant after the scientists have reached their conclusions.

In addition to the institutional changes outlined above, new official guidelines concerning the ways in which scientific advice should be procured and used have been issued by the government's chief scientist (OST 1997). The guidelines emphasize *inter alia* the need to obtain advice from a wide range of sources, and to publish that advice, along with supporting papers. If those recommendations are followed it would constitute a significant step forward.

The UK government also responded to the report of the Phillips Inquiry into BSE, by stipulating that departments should not ask advisory committees to deal with issues beyond their competence, not ask committees to make risk management decisions, not put issues to committees as a way of avoiding urgent action and not be selective in quoting their advice. At the same time the government stated that advisory committees should make clear the uncertainties in their conclusions and make clear what evidence they have reviewed and what they are merely quoting (HMG 2001). Those are eminently sensible recommendations, but as the Ministry of Defence's response to the debate about "Gulf War Syndrome" and the Department of Health's handling of the debate about the triple vaccination for mumps, measles and rubella show, they are not yet being fully implemented.

The BSE crisis, with other food safety scares, has also had a considerable effect on the European Commission. In the late 1990s responsibility for providing scientific advice on food safety was moved away from DG-III to what was then DG-24, and is now called DG-SANCO or the Directorate-General for Health and Consumer Protection. At that stage, however, regulatory authority remained with DG-III. DG-SANCO modified the *ancien régime* by publishing the agendas, opinions and reports of its advisory committees. In the spring of 2000, and in the wake of the crisis over dioxin contamination of animal feeds, the Commission endeavoured to institutionalize a separation of regulation and inspection from sponsorship. The key development was the relocation of responsibility for consumer protection and food safety into DG-SANCO, as well as the creation of a Food and Veterinary Office (based in Dublin) with responsibility for inspecting the member states' implementation of EU regulations and directives. In January 2000, the European Commission published a *White Paper on Food Safety* which proposed the establishment of a new integrated statutory framework covering the EU's entire food chain "from the farm to the fork" and for the creation of a European Food Authority (EFA) to provide authoritative, independent science-based advice to the Commission, and specifically to DG-SANCO (European Commission 2000). That body has subsequently been redefined as the European Food Safety Authority (EFSA) and is scheduled to begin work in the summer of 2002.

In recent years analogous developments have taken place in several other EU member states. The French government has established the Agence Française de la Sécurité Sanitaire des Aliments (AFSSA), the German government has created the Bundesamt für Verbraucherschutz und Lebensmittel Sicherheit and the Irish government created the Food Safety Authority of Ireland, while similar developments are taking place in several other member states. As far as the Codex Alimentarius Commission and the joint expert committees of the WHO and FAO are concerned, reform is proceeding at a glacial pace, although as with an iceberg far more may be moving than is evident from the surface.

A New Rhetoric

At the European Commission and in the governments of many member states, not only have new institutions been created but a new policy rhetoric has also been adopted. The rhetoric asserts that food safety policy should, and will, be made by "independent" agencies advised by "independent scientific experts" and that their procedures should be transparent. Neither the UK government nor the European Commission has, for example, explicitly acknowledged that under the *status quo ante* regulatory capture had occurred, but one of the implicit reasons for creating new institutions, and representing them in terms of their "independence" and "transparency", has been to create conditions in which regulatory capture should be far harder to achieve. Expert advisors are now characterized as being "independent", but we are never told upon whom they may previously have been dependent. One implied message is that they will be independent of commercial interests, but another plausible interpretation is that the scientists should also be independent of political pressures from politicians and officials. If advisory and decision-making processes are genuinely to be entirely transparent then it should be harder than hitherto for policy-makers to hide behind the advice of the scientific experts. On the other hand, by asserting the independence of the experts, it might become easier rather than harder to represent the judgements of the experts as if they were decisive. That will depend on the extent to which the scientists confine their advice to strictly scientific judgements about what is, and is not, known about the likely consequence of adopting a range of possible courses of action, or whether they provide prescriptive monolithic policy recommendations. The most plausible scenario, if more transparent procedures are followed, is one in which both the experts and the policy-makers will try to get the other group to accept as much responsibility as possible for policy outcomes; in other words they will both engage in what Hood and Rothstein refer to as "blame avoidance". At this stage the outcome of that struggle remains unpredictable.

Although the rhetoric may be new, the revised institutional structures have not resolved all of the problems outlined above. For example, the institutional innovations in the UK did not entirely accomplish the separation of regulation from sponsorship. The FSA has to have regard for the costs and impact of regulations on the private sector, and it has accepted a senior member of staff from the retail giant Marks and Spencer to work on "risk management". Furthermore, when MAFF was abolished DEFRA retained responsibility for BSE, veterinary medicines and pesticides, but also took on environmental regulation, including environmental aspects of the regulation of GM crops. It is not obvious that, for example, DEFRA will readily be able to reconcile its responsibility for promoting the interests of British farmers with, at the same time, protecting the British environment from damage from agricultural activities.

Although the new arrangements in the UK promise a clearer separation between the scientific aspects of risk assessment and the political aspects of risk management, ministers continue to avoid overt responsibility for the policy decisions. That was not the original intention when, in January 1998, the government published its White Paper *The Food Standards Agency: A Force for Change* (MAFF 1998). Ministers repeatedly asserted that, once the FSA was in operation, food safety policy in the UK would be decided by democratically accountable ministers and not by unaccountable unelected officials. In practice, however, the board of the FSA has been taking all the policy decisions, with ministers at most applying a rubber stamp to the monolithic and prescriptive advice from the FSA Board. The current arrangements may allow ministers to remain at arms' length from the FSA's decision-making, but they are not necessarily in the long-term interests of the FSA, nor of the consumers whose interests the FSA is supposed to serve.

The role of the EFSA remains similarly ambiguous and indeterminate. The wording of the Commission's proposals is ambiguous as between providing strictly scientific advice on policy options or specific prescriptive policy recommendations, or even decisions. When Commissioner Byrne was challenged on the issue of whether responsibility for policy would lie with DG-SANCO or whether the Commission would hide behind the EFSA, he was unable to provide any answer (Byrne 2001). Similar ambiguity was evident in the remark of a senior DG-SANCO official who said that SANCO wants the EFSA to be "independent but not out of control".

DG-SANCO has also yet to make clear whether it expects the EFSA's scientific advisors to be entirely independent of commercial and industrial interests or whether such links will remain, though more transparently than hitherto. In the UK, the position remains ambiguous. When responsibility for deciding on the environmental release of GM crops lay with the Department for the Environment, Transport and the Regions (DETR), the membership of ACRE was refreshed so that no one on ACRE was employed by, or had a financial interest in, any agricultural biotechnology companies. Perhaps surprisingly, the FSA has not yet removed from membership of the Advisory Committee on Novel Foods and Processes (ACNFP) people who work for or with the biotechnology industry, nor has the FSA ensured that all members of its advisory committees are free of conflicts of interest (ACNFP 2001).

The Food Standards Act 1999, under which the FSA was established, places a duty on the FSA to make public the information on which its decisions are based. In relation to issues such as BSE, for example, the FSA has been far more explicit than MAFF about the uncertainties, the available policy options and the reasons for particular decisions (FSA 2000). The traditional pretence of representing policy as legitimized by, and only by, reliable and complete scientific knowledge is no longer persuasive and therefore new tactics are being adopted. The FSA, and some of its expert advisory committees, has also taken to holding open meetings with stakeholders to take views on needs and priorities and has been encouraging the use of stakeholder groups in the development of policy, including consumer and/or lay representatives in the membership of its advisory committees. It has also started to publish the agendas, papers and minutes of some of its advisory committees.

The FSA has not yet shown how open it will be because, although it has published numerous policy statements, no firm has yet taken the initiative to request authorization for the introduction of a novel product. Several large companies are hoping that one of their competitors will be the first to test the practical content of the FSA's new rhetoric. The FSA Board says that it will be very open, and significantly more open than is required by the Freedom of Information Act, but it remains to be seen quite what that will mean in practice.

The UK's Food Standards Agency has recently published the conclusions of its review of the arrangements under which it received scientific advice (FSA 2002). The FSA report said that "data used as the basis for risk assessments and other committee opinions should be made freely available, within the constraints of confidentiality . . . at as early a stage in the process as possible . . . Whenever time permits, committees should issue a draft opinion for public consultation before offering their final advice" (FSA 2002, paras 64–65).

In relation to confidentiality the FSA report states: "We recommend that each committee should have clear guidelines to define what material can justifiably be regarded as confidential" (FSA 2002, para. 68). Those remarks are hard to interpret. It is not clear why each advisory committee should decide for itself which data it will treat as confidential rather than observing an agency-wide policy of full disclosure in the public interest. Unless all relevant information is in the public domain it is hard to see how the FSA's decisions will be credible or democratically legitimate.

The FSA report also states: "We recommend that all committees should move as quickly as possible to a position where they conduct as much of their business as possible in open sessions" (FSA 2002, para. 66), and that "[c]hairs of advisory committees . . . [should ensure] . . . that no view is ignored or overlooked, and that unorthodox and contrary scientific views are considered . . . [and should ensure] that the proceedings of the committee, if necessary including minority opinions, are properly documented . . . so that there is a clear audit trail showing how the committee reached its decisions . . . We recommend that committee decisions should include an explanation of where differences of opinions have arisen during discussions and why conclusions have been reached, even if alternative opinions were expressed. They should also explain *any* assumptions and uncertainties that are inherent in their conclusions" (FSA 2002, paras 88–89; emphasis added).

If those guidelines were to be strictly observed, it would represent a massive change from traditional practice. Their adoption would reveal, among other things, that the scientific basis of policy-making is far from secure, profoundly uncertain and equivocal. It will also reveal many of the non-scientific considerations that, for the most part, account for disagreements among the scientists.

If expert advisors fully follow those guidelines, it will, moreover, fundamentally transform policy-making regimes into ones in which policy-makers will no longer be able to hide behind their experts. Scientific experts will, moreover, have to restrict their advice to robust conclusions that can be defended without recourse to unsupported claims or assumptions. Making explicit the uncertainties and diversity of scientific opinions would help make the process of risk policy development transparent, and it would help ensure that the different roles of scientific advisors and policy-makers are clearly and appropriately identified and differentiated, and that each group is properly, but separately, accountable for its judgements and decisions.

Erik Millstone and Patrick van Zwanenberg

If those guidelines are followed they should confer greater scientific and political legitimacy on policy-making and reduce, but not eliminate, the difficulties that face both policy-makers and scientific advisors; and it might also result in more precautionary decisions being taken, to the extent that there is democratic support for precaution.

It remains to be seen how far those reforms will also be adopted in other EU member states, by the European Food Safety Authority or at Codex and its expert advisory bodies. Policy-making regimes are in a state of flux. Some, but not all, of the lessons of the food safety scares of the last 20 years have been learnt. Nor have those events and their implications been uniformly interpreted across national, international and global jurisdictions. If policy-making is to be reformed in ways that achieve both scientific and democratic legitimacy, and that genuinely deserve to engender trust among the consuming public, then more rather than less change can be anticipated.

References

Abraham, J. (1995), *Science, Politics and the Pharmaceutical Industry*, London: UCL Press.

ACNFP (2001), *Annual Report 2001*, Appendix 1, London: Food Standards Agency.

Avery, N., Drake, M. and Lang, T. (1993), *Cracking the Codex: an Analysis of Who Sets World Food Standards*, London: National Food Alliance.

Bates, J. A. R. (1978), The control of pesticides in the United Kingdom, *Biotrop, Special Publication*, 7: 165–79.

Bernstein, M. H. (1955), *Regulating Business by Independent Commission*, Princeton, NJ: Princeton University Press.

Blundell, J. E. and Hill, A. J. (1986), Paradoxical effects of intense sweetener (aspartame) on appetite, *Lancet*, Part 1: 1902–3.

BSE Inquiry Transcript (1998), 29 June, p. 79. Available at *http://www.bse.org.uk*

Byrne, D. (2001), Commissioner David Byrne in conversation with Erik Millstone, Bio Vision Conference, Lyon, France, 9 February.

Codex Alimentarius (2002), Preface to *Understanding the Codex Alimentarius*, http://www.fao.org/docrep/w9114e/W9114e01.htm #TopOfPage as of 3 June.

Erlichman, J. (1987), Food watchdog denies conflict of interest, *Guardian*, 20 July: 4.

European Commission (2000), *White Paper on Food Safety in the European Union*, COM(99)719, 12 January, Brussels: European Commission.

FACC (1979), *Interim Report on the Review of the Colouring Matter in Food Regulations*, FAC/REP/29, London: HMSO.

FSA (2000), *Review of BSE Controls*, December, available at *http://www.bsereview.org.uk/data/report.htm* on 4 June 2002.

FSA (2002), *Report on the Review of Scientific Committees*, 15 April, available from *http://www.food.gov.uk/news/newsarchive/58746* on 4 June.

HMG (2001), (Her Majesty's Government, in consultation with the Devolved Administrations,) *Response to the Report of the BSE Inquiry*, Cm 5263, London: Stationery Office.

Hood, C., Rothstein, H. and Baldwin, R. (2001), *The Government of Risk: Understanding Risk Regulation Regimes*, Oxford: Oxford University Press.

MAFF (Ministry of Agriculture, Fisheries and Food) (1998), *The Food Standards Agency: A Force for Change*, Cm 3830, London: HMSO.

Millstone, E. (1988), *Food Additives: a Guide for Everyone*, London: Penguin Books, esp, pp. 179–91.

Millstone, E. (2001), The globalisation of environmental and consumer protection regulation: resources and accountability. In H. Lawton Smith (ed.), *The Regulation of Science and Technology*, Basingstoke: Macmillan.

Millstone, E. and van Zwanenberg, P. (2001), The politics of expert advice: lessons from the early history of the BSE saga, *Science and Public Policy*, 28, 2, April: 99–112.

OST [Office of Science and Technology] (1997), *The Use of Scientific Advice in Policy Making*, see: *http://www.dti.gov.uk/ost/ostbusiness/index_policy_making_old.htm*

Phillips, Lord, Bridgeman, J. and Ferguson-Smith, M. (2000), *The BSE Inquiry*. Volume 1: *Findings and Conclusions*, London: Stationery Office. Available at *http://www.bse.org.uk/*

Sabatier, P. (1975), Social movements and regulatory agencies: toward a more adequate—and less pessimistic—theory of "clientele capture", *Policy Sciences*, 6: 301–42.

Southwood, R. (1998), Witness Statement no. 1 to BSE Inquiry. In Phillips *et al.* (2000) *The BSE Inquiry: Report: evidence and supporting papers of the Inquiry into the emergence and identification of Bovine Spongiform Encephalopathy (BSE) and variant Creutzfeldt-Jakob Disease (vCJD) and the action taken in response to it up to 20 March 1996*, London: Stationery Office.

Stellman, S. D. and Garfinkel, L. (1986), Artificial sweetener use and one-year weight change among women, *Preventative Medicine*, 15: 195–202.

Suppan, S. and Leonard, R. (2002), Comments submitted to the Independent Evaluation of the Codex Alimentarius and other FAO/WHO work on food standards, available at: *http://www.wtowatch.org/library/admin/uploadedfiles/Comments_ Submitted_to_ the_Independent_Evaluati.htm*

van Zwanenberg, P. and Millstone, E. (2000), Beyond sceptical relativism: evaluating the social constructions of expert risk assessments, *Science, Technology & Human Values*, 25, 3, Summer: 259–82.

Zeltner, T., Kessler, D., Martiny, A. and Randerer, F. (2000), *Tobacco Industry Strategies to Undermine Tobacco Control Activities at the World Health Organization*, Report of the Committee of Experts on Tobacco Industry Documents, Geneva: World Health Organization.

4

Food Safety and Consumers: Constructions of Choice and Risk

Alizon Draper and Judith Green

Introduction

This paper examines how risk and choice are and have been constructed in relation to food safety, the public and public policy in the UK. We will trace the shifts in food safety concerns between the early nineteenth century and recent policy initiatives to include consumers in the shaping of food policy. During the last two centuries, the prominence of food safety on the public policy agenda has waxed and waned, suggesting a cyclical interest in the "safety" of food available to the population. However, there have also been sharp discontinuities in the types of risk associated with food and, in relation to policy responses, how "the public", as objects of policy, have been framed.

The history of food safety from the nineteenth century has been shaped by three dominant models of public governance, each constructing particular potential risks from food, and each shaping particular constructions of choice. Early debate around the safety of food constructed a passive and largely ignorant public in need of protection from, first, fraudulence and, by the end of the nineteenth century and increasingly into the twentieth, diseases caused by negligence. By the second half of the twentieth century public policy, aided by a growing social science literature on "lay" decision-making, was addressing a new object: the *consumer*, who could avoid risks through making informed choices. The final shift, at the end of the twentieth century, has been the speculative move towards a more active construction of the public as *citizens*, not only reacting to information about risk but also having an obligation to contribute to policy formation. This paper outlines these shifts by drawing on historical studies of food safety policy and our own empirical research on how contemporary consumers, on the cusp of moving from "consumers" to "citizens", account for their food choices.

Historical Perspectives on the Rise, Fall and Rise of Food Safety as a Public Problem

In the UK, the emergence of issues such as salmonella and BSE as food "scares" (Miller and Reilly 1995) in the 1980s and 1990s implied a prior neutrality of food and food safety, that there was something "new" about concern with the safety of food. Lupton (2000a: 205), for instance, has described "obsession with content and quality of food" as a characteristic of modern Western societies. Anxiety about the quality of food (its provenance, purity or health-promoting properties) has been widely cited as an indicator of contemporary "risk awareness". A study of "expert" views of public concerns in the UK also revealed a perception of the public as being increasingly concerned about a number of food issues, such as BSE, microbiological safety and genetically modified foods (Shaw 1999). Certainly, the media interest in issues of food safety was a relatively new phenomenon in the 1980s and 1990s. As Miller and Reilly note (1995), the last important issue before the salmonella "egg crisis" of 1988 had been an outbreak of typhoid resulting from tinned corned beef in 1964. Until then, they argue, food policy was largely seen as an enterprise orientated towards production rather than quality. Nevertheless, a brief survey of the history of food safety in Britain reveals that it has risen, fallen and risen as an item of both professional and public interest and concern. Furthermore, as the prominence of food safety has risen and fallen as an item of concern, so the nature of public debates and official responses to them has changed and there have been shifts in where the responsibility for ensuring safe food is seen to lie (Collins 1993; Drummond and Wilbraham 1958; Hardy 1999a, 1999b; French and Phillips 1999).

Prior to the mid-nineteenth century, UK national food policy could perhaps be characterized as one of *caveat emptor* in that the burden of risk assessment lay firmly with the public. Food safety, however, began to emerge in the early nineteenth century as issue of public and later governmental concern in relation to food adulteration. The first indications of a concern with the quality and adulteration of food included the work of the German chemist Thomas Accum. Generating considerable popular interest,[1] he revealed some contemporary food adulteration practices, including the addition of large amounts of alum to bread flour and the use of copper and lead salts in beer brewing and boiled sweets (Drummond and Wilbraham 1958). Though Accum was hounded from the country by enraged brewers and others whom he had exposed, his book was followed by other similar exposés such as *Deadly Adulteration and Slow Poisoning: or Disease and Death in the Pot and Bottle* (c. 1830) written by "An enemy of fraud and villainy". Food adulteration continued to attract public concern and research, including a series of articles published in the *Lancet* in the 1850s, detailing the investigations of Dr Arthur Hassall and Henry Lethanby, which led to the appointment of a select parliamentary commission to consider the issue of food adulteration. A number of other interest groups were also involved in campaigning for government action, such as the public analysts, medical officers of health, and the temperance and cooperative movements. Food safety, however, was not a monolithic or uncontested concept, and French and Phillips (1999) argue that each of these groups stressed different aspects of food safety. The temperance movement, for instance, was primarily concerned with "purity", whereas the public analysts were concerned with the composition of foods, adulteration and the prevention of fraud, and the medical officers with health effects.

The Adulteration of Foods Act was passed in 1860 and this is generally seen as the starting point for contemporary legislation and government intervention in the sphere of food and food safety. The Act set forth compositional standards (that is, legal definitions for what constitutes "coffee", "milk" and other basic foodstuffs) for enforcement at local level. Subsequent Acts included the Sale of Foods and Drugs Acts of 1872 (still in force today) and 1899 to prevent adulteration, the 1855 Nuisances Removal Act to prevent "unsoundness" or adulteration, the Margarine Act 1987 which made specific reference to the use of preservatives, the Merchandise Marks Act of 1887, the 1904 and 1908 Public Health (Regulations as to Food) Acts, and the 1927 Sale of Food and Drugs Act. In terms of scope such legislation largely focused on food producers and retailers and the control of their practices, and aimed to prevent chemical adulteration and "unsoundness".

By the late nineteenth century the early concern with adulteration, fraud and food composition had gradually expanded to encompass bacterial contamination and risks of food poisoning (French and Phillips 1999; Hardy 1999a). In the 1880s there were a number of large-scale outbreaks of food poisoning, including an incident at Welbeck Abbey in 1880 during a sale in which 72 cases of illness and 4 deaths were documented among visitors. This was investigated by the local government board and suspicion was focused on the imported American hams that had been served to visitors. Hardy (1999a) considers the handling of this incident significant since, for the first time, a sample of the suspected hams were sent to a microbiologist for examination. He identified the responsible parasite and this episode, according to Hardy, marked not only the beginning of extensive research into the infective organisms found in food and the linking of these with specific illnesses, but also the emergence of "food poisoning" as a public health problem.

An interest in food poisoning meant that existing food safety regulatory frameworks, designed to address the risks of chemical adulteration and fraud due to malfeasance, were extended. Food poisoning risks arose from foods that were not innately dangerous, such as meat or fish, but which had become risky through negligence in their preparation, storage or handling. This posed a significant expansion in responsibilities for food safety and also a need for continued administrative policies to ensure not only pure, but clean food to protect the public in the late nineteenth century. To some extent this move from a regulatory concern with negligence as well as malfeasance reflected broader changes in contract law. Figlio (1985), for instance, discusses the Workmen's Compensation Act of 1897, which established routine procedures for claiming compensation for injuries caused during employment, as a key milestone. Before then, compensation could only be claimed if malicious intent could be proved. By the end of the nineteenth century, acts of negligence were firmly within the scope of public policy.

Much of the responsibility for ensuring clean food was taken on by the public health authorities who incorporated food poisoning within the emerging field of preventive medicine and concern with sanitary science, both of which were premised on a more medical and individualistic perspective. Hardy (1999b) characterizes government action in this late Victorian and Edwardian period as that of liberal interventionism. However, although there was some extension of the power and activities of local government boards and medical officers, the regulatory framework was not extended further, for instance to enhance the control of abattoirs, because of reluctance to interfere with trade and cause price increases. This lack of governmental impetus and unwillingness to intervene persisted into the interwar period and, despite the attempts of the public health officers to awaken the "sanitary conscience" of the British public, was largely matched by public indifference over issues of food safety.

The one exception to this was the debate over the pasteurization of milk, which ran from roughly 1900 to 1945 and aroused not only scientific, but also public interest. The debate arose over whether or not bovine tuberculosis could be transmitted via the consumption of milk and, following this, whether or not the pasteurization of milk as means of controlling bovine tuberculosis should be legally enforced. As Atkins (2000) has shown, the debate reveals conflict over the legitimate role of the state to intervene in the food system, but also differences over the way in which "safety" was framed. The pro-pasteurization lobby drew upon bacteriology and technology, whereas the anti-pasteurization lobby drew on more ideological concerns, such as naturalness, neo-romanticism and resistance to modernization. Although the pasteurization of milk became common practice in the 1950s, the debate over whether it should be compulsory in England and Wales continues.

Following the Second World War national food policy in the UK was focused primarily on food production and the restoration of national food security. Despite the introduction of the notification of food poisoning in 1938—which meant that for the first time it acquired a statistical profile and figures showed an annual increase in the number of food poisoning cases—there was continued reluctance on the part of the government to legislate. The Ministry of Health continued with efforts to educate the public and its position was that of benevolent paternalism, in its desire to provide for and educate a uniformed and sometimes wayward public (often women). The following quote, from Douglas Jay, a British Labour politician in a manifesto called *The Socialist Case* (1939), is perhaps an extreme illustration of this approach:

> Housewives as a whole cannot be trusted to buy all the right things, where nutrition and health are concerned. This is really no more than an extension of the principle according to which the housewife herself would not trust a child of four to select the week's purchases. For in the case of nutrition and health just as in education, the gentlemen of Whitehall really do know better what is good for the people than the people know themselves. (cited by Craig 1970)

It was not only food safety, however, but food generally that lost salience as a consumer concern in the postwar period (Smith 1991). It was arguably only government inertia over rising rates of heart disease, despite recognition of the link with diet, that first put food back on to the agenda as a contested public issue in the 1970s and 1980s (Bufton and Berridge 2000). Many public-interest and consumer groups became involved in campaigning on a number of food issues at this time and, according to Lang (1997), "A new era of public interest in food had been born." In 1988 the furore over salmonella in eggs became labelled as the first "food scare" and food safety became again a salient public and political issue (Smith 1991).

As this brief overview bears out, the position of food safety on the policy agenda, and the risks associated with the consumption of food have shifted over the last 200 years. The issues raised by salmonella and BSE demonstrate some continuities with previous public and policy concerns, in that issues of food quality, bacterial contamination and concern about preserving the "naturalness" of foodstuffs were not new issues. However, the possibilities for policy response have significantly changed since the early nineteenth-century attempts to control production and retail practices. Recent food safety campaigns address the public as potentially knowledgeable, if at times fallible, "consumers", whose role is actively to choose in the light of informed opinion. The proper role of public policy has been debated intensely in the wake of BSE, including via a high-profile public inquiry which criticized the government for a paternalistic approach that belonged, it was argued, to an earlier era, in which the public were not trusted to make rational decisions (Klein 2000).

The Emergence of "Consumers" in Food Policy

That the UK government's handling of the "BSE crisis" was criticized in terms of its assumptions about the nature of the public is perhaps the most overt illustration of a normative model of the "proper" role of public policy by the end of the twentieth century. At the beginning of that century, as professional concerns shifted to bacterial contamination and "clean food", the educational attempts of the sanitarians had framed the public more individualistically, but in need of knowledge to reform their unhygienic behaviours. The public, and the poor in particular, were framed as "ignorant and unwashed" (Hardy 1999a). During the Second World War, UK government policy became directly interventionist with regard to food supply, with the establishment of a Ministry of Food to ensure adequate supplies for the population during the blockade. This is often regarded as a high point in UK government policy regarding food, since it was concerned to ensure not only an adequate but a nutritious diet for all.

However, in the postwar period, food policy became more production-orientated, and arguably was primarily directed towards serving the interests of farmers rather than consumers (Lang 1997; Smith 1991). Yet, in an analysis of the role of the state in structuring consumer food choices via regulation, Flynn et al. (1998) argue that consumer interests were not so much excluded in this postwar period, as framed within the context of collective food security; the role of regulation was to meet the public's interest: namely freedom from want. In the later part of the twentieth century the same authors identify a restructuring of consumer rights, as being framed within food policy and legislation, to a more individualist construction, based on the rights of an individual to consume, the goal of policy being to enhance consumer freedom and choice. This has also been accompanied by a shift of responsibility in the regulatory burden from the public to the private sector (for instance, food retailers now play a central role in enforcing food standards), and to individuals. The rise of the "consumer movement" has reflected a willingness of the part of the public, or at least some of the public, to accept this responsibility, with a growing number of consumer organizations campaigning on food issues from the 1970s (Miller and Reilly 1995).

Gabriel and Lang (1995) have shown how "consumers" have been constructed in various ways, for instance as communicators, as identity-seekers, as rebels and victims—and the concept of "consumer" has been claimed by many different interest groups. The consumer as chooser who actively selects foods in the light of expert opinion (on the safety of beef, or the proper diet to ensure health) was implicit in food safety legislation in the postwar period up until the food scares of the 1980s onwards. Within this construction the public was construed as being in need of more than protection; it also required information, and the skills to apply this information, in respect of food purchasing and preparation decisions. Implicit within this are also the notions of "free choice" and "rational choice".

The culmination of the shift towards consumers as subjects of policy in their own right—i.e. as consumer citizens, having separate interests from those of producers—was perhaps the 1999 Food Standards Act, which established the Food Standards Agency (FSA) as separate from the government ministry responsible for agriculture. The FSA's key remit is to protect the public health by "acting in the consumer's interest in any stage of the food production and supply chain" (FSA 2002). Nutrition education, food labels and dietary guidelines, all popular policy instruments in relation to food, are posited on the notion that the informed individual is one able to make the "right" consumption choice (Duff 1999).

Citizenship and the Individualization of Food Safety

More recently, UK policy has been characterized by tentative moves towards yet more inclusive policy-making processes, not only in relation to food, but also in other arenas, such as health care delivery, policing and housing (see, for example, Cabinet Office 1998). The legitimacy of public involvement in, rather than merely reaction to, food policy is perhaps illustrated by the range of political strategies by which citizens have sought to influence governmental policy on genetically modified (GM) food. Adam (2000) lists a referendum in Austria, direct action to destroy crops in the UK and various lobbying activities. It is not, of course, inevitable that there will be public participation on particular issues. Adam contrasts Europe with the USA, where there has been relatively little public concern about the use of GM crops in agriculture. What is interesting is that this kind of participation has become, to a limited extent at least, "legitimate", with a UK High Court ruling in 1999 that protesters "could not be banned from interfering with GM crops" (Adam 2000). Furthermore, the FSA's role being to include consultation with the public on a range of issues including food safety, many of their meetings are now held as open sessions theoretically accessible to all. In short, within this contested arena of policy, the portrayal of "the public" as ignorant and in need of nothing more than protection is no longer sustainable.

Choice and Public Constructions of Risk

The construction of food safety in public policy has, then, been predicated on shifting models of what the objects of that policy are supposed to be: the public, consumers or, most recently, active citizens. The role of these different populations in choosing and managing the risks associated with food have similarly shifted. The notion of "choice" is perhaps in itself a rather misleading one, with its implications of "free choice" and "rational choice". In the field of public health nutrition, the most popular models of food choice have been the KAP (Knowledge, Attitude, Practice) models and the various social cognition models, such as the theory of reasoned action (Draper 1991). What these models of food choice have in common is a focus on personal attributes—whether these be knowledge, attitudes or intentions—as the drivers of choice. But, as Wheeler (1992) points out, such a demand-driven approach excludes broader structural influences on the availability and access to food. She argues that to understand the determinants of food choice we need to examine these within what she calls a hierarchy of constraints. This enables us to see that we (or at least most of us) do not have free choice among all the potentially edible substances in the world, but that in fact our choices between different kinds of food are actually increasingly limited or restricted. Wheeler places culture as the primary constraint on food choice, since this divides the edible from the inedible, the desirable from the undesirable, the healthy from the unhealthy, and so forth. Knowledge she places low down the list in determining the utility of different foods, especially what she terms "correct" knowledge, or that which conforms to expert opinion. Reviews of the efficacy of nutrition education show that the provision of information alone has at best a limited impact on shifting consumer choices, in part at least because it neglects the many other influences on what we eat (Reid and Adamson 1998; Tedstone et al. 1998).

So what then does determine our food choice and, specifically, how do the "consumers" or "citizens" of recent policy initiatives decide what are safe foods and what are risky foods? One facet of the emergence of the consumer in public policy from the middle of the twentieth century was the possibility of a "social science" of food choice. If the public were constructed as potential "choosers", rather than passive objects of policy intervention, these choices could be mapped and investigated as objects in their own right. There is now a large sociological and anthropological literature on food and sociocultural influences on eating patterns that dates back to the 1920s, but which did not gain much prominence until the 1980s (Mennell et al. 1992). Individual studies within this literature differ in theoretical slant and also the unit and object of analysis, but most share a focus on the non-nutritional aspects of food and eating (Murcott 1998).

Different approaches range from structural functionalism, ecological and materialist approaches, to conceptual and symbolic approaches (see Messer

1984; Murcott 1988). Each of these conceptualizes the relationship between culture and food in a distinctive way and places a varying emphasis on the material and symbolic aspects of food and the role of food production and consumption in society, but what they share are three broad conclusions. First is the inclusion of the non-nutritional aspects of food and eating in explanations of patterns of consumption. Second, a recognition that the proper unit of analysis is a much broader one than that of the individual and their personal selection of foods for consumption. Third, the empirical evidence demonstrates that the qualities and attributes that we link with particular foods are not related to the material or nutritional qualities of foods, but are largely symbolic. The "classic" account is perhaps Douglas's (1966) interpretation of the Rules of Leviticus, in which she demonstrates that materialist explanations fail to account for the inclusion/exclusion of all the foods covered in the Rules. Her analysis focuses instead on the concept of holiness and its associated symbolic qualities of unity, integrity, perfection of kind. This account arguably provides a more "rational" and certainly a more comprehensive explanation of the classification of certain foods as "unclean"; most explanations focus on the ban on pork consumption and attribute this to the risk of infection with tapeworms, but this does not explain why, for instance, hopping locusts are classified as "clean" and crawling locusts as "unclean".

Taken as a whole the sociological and anthropological literature of food can be read as a form of "lay epidemiology" which illustrates not only that food attributes are often largely symbolic in content, but that food ideologies are not the product of irrational prejudices or ignorance, but are largely socially constructed. In short, rather than being an "ignorant" and passive object of food policy, the "sociological" subject is a rational individual who is a consumer (in that he/she makes individual choices), but whose choices are framed by his/her cultural, social and material circumstances. A social science of food choice is both made possible by the emergence of the consumer in food policy, and contributes to the governance of food policy by providing a source of expertise in the knowledge, attitudes and individual and cultural behaviour of these consumers.

So what empirical evidence is there of how consumers construct risks and dangers in food? Reflecting the rising legitimacy of the "consumer" as the subject of policy has been a proliferation of research into how the public assesses the risks and hazards associated with food from this perspective of lay epidemiology. Alongside this more sociological research is an ongoing production of survey data on food safety commissioned by both government and industry, including the EU-commissioned Eurobarometer, commercial market research and opinion polls (see, for example, Armistead 1998; Northen and Henson 1997).

Choosing safe food

Qualitative studies on how people choose food in terms of managing risk include Caplan (2000) on BSE; the Food Standards Agency (2000), Eldridge *et al.* (1998) and Macintyre *et al.* (1998) on the impact of food scares on food

Alizon Draper and Judith Green

choice; Grove-White *et al.* (1997) on GM foods; and our own study on European perceptions of food safety (Draper *et al.* 2001). Data from the UK participants in this last study illustrate how assessments of risk and safety contribute, although in a relatively minor way, to food choices, but also incorporate a broad range of concerns including the symbolic. The commissioning of this research by the European Union also perhaps illustrates the desire of policy-makers to include public concerns and perceptions about food safety in policy consideration.

The aims of the study were to investigate public perceptions of BSE and vCJD risk in Europe, their interplay with media, policy and surveillance, and their implications for information policy. Only the UK data on risk perceptions are reported here to provide some empirical evidence of the types of risk people attach to food and how these related to food choice. Qualitative research methods and—specifically—focus group discussions were used as the most appropriate methodology to access how people discuss and conceptualize food risk in an everyday context. Natural groups were used to enhance this and were defined as those who shared some social relationship outside the research setting, for instance via work, school or church. Purposive sampling was used to recruit participants from four life-cycle groups: adolescents, young single consumers aged approximately 20–25 years; family food purchasers; and older consumers aged 55+ years. These groups were chosen on the theoretical basis that they might be expected to have different orientations and responsibilities towards choosing foods: with adolescents at the beginning of making food choices for themselves, young singles responsible for themselves but no others, family food purchasers responsible for other household members in addition to themselves, and older people either living alone or with a partner. A total of 11 groups were held in two contrasting locations: London and the south-east; and Coventry and surrounding areas. The groups were conducted over the period December 1999 to February 2001.

In the course of discussions participants used complex "rules of thumb" to assess the relative safety or riskiness of food items. These rules operated to allow them to make practical decisions about food choice in the context of considerable public information about food safety. Many of these rules consisted of either dichotomies of safe versus unsafe foods, or relative scales or degrees of safety.

In these dichotomies of safety the quality of "safety" itself was mostly subsumed under a number of characteristics and articulated as a contrast of opposites. Thus safe food was variously equated with the natural, the organic, the local, the pure, the home-made, the fresh and the traditional. These categories were opposed to unsafe food and this was associated with the chemical and synthetic, the processed and ready-made, and the foreign and imported. In this way food safety was bundled with other food characteristics, including those of nutritional worth and moral value, and choosing food from one side of the opposing categories was a short-cut to a safe choice.

"but I didn't, never have bought and she [daughter] has never liked hamburgers and all the frozen foods which are the things I might have worried more about, you

know, if you were buying ready-made lasagne and hamburgers . . . and maybe at the beginning of that was perhaps the beginning of my disenchantment with supermarkets possibly and wanting to use local shops more . . . I do try to use markets and stuff like that." (Family food purchasers, London)

Scales of safety were also drawn and these were often based on geographical region. Thus foods of local origin were seen as safer than those of more distant origin in a graded scale, with home- or garden-produced safest through to local and regional production to national and, finally, imported food. To some extent this intersected with oppositions of safety, since known versus unknown origins was a salient theme in judging the safety of food, with knowledge of its provenance being an important factor in creating trust in food. It also overlapped with broader issues of trust and faith in local produce, with local retailers, such as butchers, being perceived as more trustworthy than purchasing meat from large supermarkets.

"I think it's a matter of trust. I have a butcher. He is a very good butcher and I trust the meat I buy off of him and all his beef is definitely from BSE free herds and therefore I am very happy to eat his beef, I would not be so happy buying beef at a supermarket even if that was stated and I think again it comes back to trust." (Older citizens, south-east)

"I never worry about eggs personally, I get eggs locally, I just think they are quite fresh, I never worry about eggs." (Family food purchasers, rural south-east)

These scales of safety were not just reflections of practical concerns about food risks (for instance, risk of spoilage during transportation and need for preservatives to counteract this), but also expressions of symbolic identity versus "otherness", in this case of national identity versus somewhat chauvinistic stereotypes of others:

A: *My husband won't allow me to buy anything that isn't organic.* [North American participant]
J: *You'd put that on top?*
A: *It's because he's so freaked out about English meat!*
C: *I take it you're getting American hampers flown over for Christmas!* (Family food purchasers, London)

"Them Spanish things don't do much for me. They could be anything you are eating couldn't they?" (Family food purchasers, rural south-east)

Food safety did not emerge as either a unitary concept or one that was explicit until foregrounded by the research process itself. As participants themselves stated, the quality of safety has many facets:

"Are we going to define safe in terms of genetically safe or bacterially safe or cholesterol safe or are we going to come to any definition?" (Older citizens, rural south-east)

These qualities of safety were mostly framed or characterized in other terms, such as organic, home-made, local and so forth. Safety was also seen as a discrete characteristic, but one that was located in different arenas (for instance, production, transit, sale and storage), timescales (short-term threats of infection versus long-term impacts on health). The rules used to evaluate food safety reflected this complexity and incorporated concerns generally excluded from more formal risk assessments, such as health, morality and ecology.

The data presented above show the complexity of public constructions of food safety/risk and that people use sophisticated strategies to assess the safety/riskiness of food. These strategies and short-cuts allowed for the routinization of food choices and of the management of uncertainty in the context of everyday life. Safety *per se*, however, was *not* a major concern for respondents and provided a limited framework for making decisions about food. Only in discussions of cost did safety emerge as an explicit issue—and here it was seen as clearly counterposed to cost; if food was cheap, a corner must have been cut somewhere.

There were also important definitional issues and conflict with other food discourses. As a multifaceted concept, safety covered a number of different arenas—such as provenance, mode of production—and these competed at times with other food discourses, such as pleasure, socializing, and convenience. Finally, discussions about food largely took place within an assumed framework of trust: that food is safe unless there is a specific breach of trust. Thus these data show that, in relation to the choices participants made about food more broadly, food safety appeared to be only intermittently important. Rather, food choices were made within a framework of trust in both individuals and abstract systems. The starting point would thus appear to be faith in food, not risk and uncertainty, unless ruptured by a sudden invasion of trust, as in April 1996 when the British government announced that BSE was a possible cause of Creutzfeld-Jakob disease.

There is evidence that these broad findings are typical of consumers in other developed countries, in that they reveal a rational approach to decision-making that incorporates risk assessment into other cultural frameworks of food choice. Caplan (2000), for instance, also found that people constructed dichotomies of safety, such as knowledge and confidence versus ignorance and risk, and that social relations were important in creating trust (not only knowing where your beef comes from, but who you buy it from, matters). Also in the UK, Macintyre et al. (1998) found knowledge of provenance and national identity important for people in judging the safety of food. People also balanced and weighed up competing criteria, such as preference versus healthiness, in selecting food. Sellerberg's (1991) study in Sweden argued that people constructed "strategies of confidence" to establish their trust in food against a background of uncertainty and conflicting advice. Like the UK participants in our study, the rural Australians in Lupton's (2000b) study cited frameworks other than safety as being most salient in choosing food, in this case those of "health" and "balance".

However, in the UK-based studies, one significant finding was the evidence of widespread cynicism and lack of faith in policy-makers as a source of advice. In all the focus groups we held in the UK, participants were routinely sceptical about how far one could trust the statements of politicians and policy-makers as sources of information on food safety. This may be a reflection of the post-BSE experience (cf. Eldridge *et al.* 1998), and may be less evident in the accounts of consumers outside the UK. But a corresponding willingness to accept a high degree of personal responsibility for the safety of food (at all stages from choosing produce, storing it and preparing it) is perhaps more generalizable.

Discussion

There have, in short, been interesting shifts in the landscape of food policy over the last 200 years, with different kinds of risk emerging as policy concerns. Embedded within these are changing constructions of the public as the objects of policy, each implying a different proper role for the state. Initial policy concern was with adulteration, with the perceived risks being those of fraud and malfeasance. With the incorporation of infection as a legitimate public health issue, the risks associated with negligence also became a policy concern. Abraham and Lewis (2002) make a similar argument about medicines policy in Europe which was, until the middle of the twentieth century, also largely concerned with adulteration. Only later in the century did legislation address efficacy and safety, with Sweden introducing legislation in 1934 but the UK not until the 1960s (Abraham and Lewis 2002). This reflected a shift in production, from pharmaceuticals being manufactured by small pharmacies to large-scale manufacturers with large research and development functions. Similarly, food production has undergone radical shifts over the twentieth century, with a dominance of retailing by the supermarket multiples and a rise in the vertical integration within the food sector and an increasing "technologization" of food production, perhaps especially evident in the merged chemical and food production industries (Tansey and Worsley 1995; Sorj and Wilkinson 1985). The role of the state consequently shifts from that of merely protecting consumers through legislation on fraud, to regulatory control on behalf of consumers, using technical expertise to assess such qualities as nutritional content and microbial contamination.

Most recently, there has been an emphasis on the public as citizens who not only passively consume, but may to some extent be active as participants within policy formation, consulted through formal mechanisms and heard as informal activists. Although most food policy is still orientated towards the conception of informed choice, the public is increasingly seen as consisting of potentially active "citizens", with a role in shaping the food policy agenda, the content of policy and the ways in which it is communicated. The rise of a social science of food choice has gone hand in hand with this policy shift. It is in part a key source of expertise on lay accounts of choice, but has been made possible (in terms of available funding) by a rising concern with including "users' views" in policy development. The function of the state thus becomes more overtly partisan. From being a neutral regulator of food quality on behalf of the public, the state's role is contested, with the BSE inquiry in the UK and the protests around GM crops evidence of an "active" citizenry with a critique of state policy.

One reading of the emergent interest in including public views in policy is a liberal one of a democratizing of food policy, and a growing responsiveness to users' views on the part of policy-makers. Such a view presupposes "mature consumers", able to assess expert advice on food safety and quality and lobby policy-makers on the values of food policy. However, there are two arguments that limit this interpretation. First, in terms of the kinds of formal consultation exercises considered by government departments, there are, of course, limits to the topics consulted on and the range of views invited. More significantly, the moral obligation for consumers now to contribute as well as respond to policy interventions can be read as a facet of a neoliberal citizenship which is as much about increasing control of the population as it is about democratization.

Petersen defines neoliberalism as "a form of rule which involves creating a sphere of freedom for subjects so that they are able to exercise a regulated autonomy" (Petersen 1997: 194). The key feature of neoliberal governance is the way in which individuals are brought into the business of managing their own lives as an enterprise through rational decision-making. Petersen discusses the implications of self-governance in neoliberal welfare states with respect to health promotion policies, which increasingly posit the individual as "at risk" and in need of constant self-examination, reflection and action to maintain the "healthy self". This argument has considerable resonance for the field of food policy. The increasing focus on the provision of information to a public encouraged to assess (for instance) ever more detailed product labelling and process increasingly complex nutritional messages, and then become involved in the production of policy, brings with it a set of obligations as well as rights. This is a new model of citizenship, in which being a "responsible" citizen involves not only making the "right" nutritional choices for oneself and one's family, but also engaging actively with food policy issues, whether they be the development of GM food or the regulation of infection. Higgs (1998) makes a similar argument with respect to social policy for the elderly, suggesting that the concept of citizenship now emphasizes individual agency and choice, with an individuation in the governance of risk. The model citizen of the new order "learns to engage with risks constructively" (Higgs 1998: 193), and the role of the state is to shape this self-governance, rather than to manage risks on behalf of the population.

There is, then, a moral dimension to the new citizenship, in which citizens are obliged to actively "self-govern" as rational risk assessors. There is a wide literature on governance of the self in a range of health and welfare provisions, including health promotion (Petersen 1997), HIV (Rhodes 1997), and personal safety and injury risk (Green 1997). Here, we argue that the incorporation of the "consumer's voice", and the evidence on how consumers are willing to accept responsibility as active citizens, suggest that this analysis could be extended to food policy.

Note

1. Accum's *Treatise on the Adulteration of Food and Culinary Poisons* was published in 1820. It sold out in a month and was reissued four times in two years.

References

Abraham, J. and Lewis, G. (2002), Citizenship, medical expertise and the capitalist regulatory state in Europe, *Sociology*, 36: 67–88.

Adam, B. (2000), The temporal gaze: the challenge for social theory in the context of GM food, *British Journal of Sociology*, 51: 125–42.

Armistead, A. (1998), The National Health Survey—consumer attitudes to health and food, *British Food Journal*, 2: 95–8.

Atkins, P. J. (2000), The pasteurisation of England: the science, culture and health implications of milk processing, 1900–1950. In *Food, Science, Policy and Regulation in the Twentieth Century: International and Comparative Perspectives*, London and New York: Routledge, ch. 3, pp. 37–51.

Bufton, M. and Berridge, V. (2000), Post-war nutrition, science and policy making in Britain *c.* 1945–1994: the case of diet and heart disease. In *Food, Science, Policy and Regulation in the Twentieth Century: International and Comparative Perspectives*, London and New York: Routledge, ch. 13, pp. 207–21.

Cabinet Office (1998), An introductory guide: how to consult your users. Online at http://www.cabinet-office.gov.uk/servicefirst/1998/guidance/users/.

Caplan, P. (2000), "Eating British beef with confidence": a consideration of consumers' responses to BSE in Britain. In P. Caplan (ed.), *Risk Revisited*, London: Pluto Press, pp. 184–203.

Collins, E. J. T. (1993), Food adulteration and food safety in Britain in the 19th and early 20th centuries, *Food Policy*, 18: 95–109.

Craig, F. W. (1970), *British General Election Manifestos 1918–1966*, London: Political References Publications.

Douglas, M. (1966), *Purity and Danger: An Analysis of the Concepts of Pollution and Taboo*, London: Routledge and Kegan Paul.

Draper, A. K. (1991), Vegetarianism in the UK. Doctoral thesis, University of London.

Draper, A. K., Green, J. and Dowler, E. (2001), Public perceptions of BSE and CJD risk in Europe, their interplay with media, policy initiatives and surveillance issues: drawing the lessons for information policy. Task 1, Qualitative study of public perceptions of risk of BSE, trust in information sources and their determinants. European TSE Project PL 987028.

Drummond, J. C. and Wilbraham, A. (1958), *The Englishman's Food: A History of Five Centuries of English Diet*, rev. edn, London: Jonathan Cape.

Duff, J. (1999), Setting the menu: dietary guidelines, corporate interests and nutrition policy. In J. Germov and L. Williams (eds), *A Sociology of Food and Nutrition*, Oxford: Oxford University Press, pp. 77–97.

Eldridge, J., Kitzinger, J., Philo, G. and Reilly, J. (1998), The re-emergence of BSE: the impact on public beliefs and behaviour, *Risk and Human Behaviour Newsletter*, 3: 6–10.

Figlio, K. (1985), What is an accident? In P. Weindling (ed.), *The Social History of Occupational Health*, London: Croom Helm.

Flynn, A., Harrison, M. and Marsden, T. (1998), Regulation, rights and the structuring of food choice. In A. Murcot (ed.), *The Nation's Diet*, Harlow: Addison Wesley Longman, pp. 152–67.

French, M. and Phillips, J. (1999), Protecting consumers' health and pockets: approaches to food safety laws in Britain 1860–1938. Paper presented at the Society for the Social History of Medicine Spring Conference 1999: Science, Medicine and Food Policy in the Twentieth Century, Aberdeen University.

FSA (2000), *Qualitative Research to Explore Public Attitudes to Food Safety*, prepared by Cragg Ross Dawson Ltd, London.

FSA (2002), http://www.foodstandards.gov.uk/foodindustry/regulation/foodstandardsact.

Gabriel, Y. and Lang, T. (1995), *The Unmanageable Consumer: Contemporary Consumption and its Fragmentations*, London: Sage.

Green, J. (1997), *Risk and Misfortune: The Social Construction of Accidents*, London: UCL Press.

Grove-White, R., Macnaghten, P., Mayer, S. and Wynne, B. I. (1997), *Uncertain Worlds: Genetically Modified Organisms, Food and Public Attitudes in Britain*, Lancaster: Centre for the Study of Environmental Change, University of Lancaster.

Hardy, A. (1999a), Food, hygiene, and the laboratory: a short history of food poisoning in Britain, *circa* 1850–1950, *Social History of Medicine*, 12: 293–311.

Hardy, A. (1999b), Food poisoning: surveillance, research and regulation in central government circa 1880–1950. Paper presented at the Society for the Social History of Medicine Spring Conference 1999: Science, Medicine and Food Policy in the Twentieth Century, Aberdeen University.

Higgs, P. (1998), Risk, governmentality and the reconceptualization of citizenship. In G. Scambler and P. Higgs (eds), *Modernity, Medicine and Health*, London and New York: Routledge, pp. 176–97.

Klein, R. (2000), The politics of risk: the case of BSE, *British Medical Journal*, 321: 1091–2.

Lang, T. (1997), Going public: food campaigns during the 1980s and early 1990s. In D. Smith (ed.), *Nutrition in Britain: Science, Scientists and Politics in the Twentieth Century*, London and New York: Routledge, pp. 238–60.

Lang, T. (1999), Food as a public health issue. In S. Griffiths and D. J. Hunter (eds), *Perspectives in Public Health*, Oxford: Radcliffe Medical Press, pp. 47–55.

Lupton, D. (2000a), Food, risk and subjectivity. In S. Williams, J. Gabe and M. Calnan (eds), *Health, Medicine and Society*, London: Routledge, pp. 205–18.

Lupton, D. (2000b), The heart of the meal: food preferences and habits among rural Australian couples, *Sociology of Health and Illness*, 22: 94–109.

Macintyre, S., Reilly, J., Miller, D. and Eldridge, J. (1998), Food choice, food scare, and health: the role of the media. In A. Murcott (ed.), *The Nation's Diet: The Social Science of Food Choice*, London and New York: Longman, pp. 228–49.

Mennell, S., Murcott, A. and van Otterloo, A. (1992), *The Sociology of Food: Eating, Diet and Culture*, London: Sage.

Messer, E. (1984), Anthropological perspectives on diet, *Annual Review of Anthropology*, 13: 205–49.

Miller, D. and Reilly, J. (1995), Making an issue of food safety: the media, pressure groups, and the public sphere. In D. Mauer and J. Sobal (eds), *Eating Agendas: Food and Nutrition as Social Problems*, New York: Aldine de Gruyter, pp. 305–36.

Murcott, A. (1988), Sociological and anthropological approaches to food and eating, *World Review of Nutrition and Dietetics*, 55: 1–40.

Murcott, A. (1998), Food choice, the social sciences and the "Nation's Diet" research programme. In A. Murcott (ed.), *The Nation's Diet: The Social Science of Food Choice*, London and New York: Longman, pp. 1–22.

Northen, J. and Henson, S. (1997), *National Consumer Behaviour Report: the United Kingdom. Volume 2: National Report on Consumers of Meat in the UK*. Quality Policy and Consumer Behaviour Project FAIR-CT 95–0046. Http://www.uni-hohenheim.de/~apo420b/eu-research/euwelcome.htm

Petersen, A. (1997), Risk, governance and the new public health. In A. Petersen and R. Bunton (eds), *Foucault, Health and Medicine*, London: Routledge.

Reid, M. and Adamson, H. (1998), *Opportunities for and Barriers to Good Nutritional Health in Women of Childbearing Age, Pregnant Women, Infants Under 1 and Children Aged 1 to 5*, London: Health Education Authority.

Rhodes, T. (1997), Risk theory in epidemic times: sex, drugs and the social organization of "risk behaviour", *Sociology of Health and Illness*, 19: 208–27.

Sellerberg, A.-M. (1991), In food we trust? Vitally necessary confidence—and unfamiliar ways of attaining it. In *Palatable Worlds*, Oslo: Solum Forlag, pp. 193–201.

Shaw, A. (1999), "What are 'they' doing to our food?": public concerns about food in the UK, *Sociological Research Online*, 4: 258–71.

Smith, M. J. (1991), From policy community to issue network: *salmonella* in eggs and the new politics of food, *Public Administration*, 69: 235–55.

Sorj, N. and Wilkinson, J. (1985), Modern food technology: industrialising nature, *International Social Science Journal*, 37: 310–14.

Tansey, G. and Worsley, T. (1995), *The Food System: A Guide*, London: Earthscan.

Tedstone, A., Aviles, M., Shetty, P. and Daniels, L. (1998), *Effectiveness of Interventions to Promote Healthy Eating in Preschool Children Aged 1 to 5 Years: A Review*, London: Health Education Authority.

Wheeler, E. F. (1992), What determines food choice and what does food choice determine? *BNF Bulletin*, 17: 65–73.

5

Food Security: Rights, Livelihoods and the World Food Summit–Five Years Later

Karim Hussein

Introduction

Food insecurity and hunger remain central issues in development and aid policy in the current international consensus to prioritize poverty elimination. This is not surprising: food insecurity has a devastating impact on poor people, their capacities and the development opportunities of individuals, households, communities and states. The scale of the problem is daunting: despite reductions in the numbers of food-insecure over recent decades, the latest estimate of numbers of undernourished people in the world is at 815 million (FAO 2001).

This paper aims to analyse recent policy debates on food security in the context of the World Food Summit—five years later (WFS–fyl) hosted by the UN Food and Agriculture Organization (FAO) in June 2002 (see box 1). Essentially, the paper attempts to do two things: (1) it outlines some of the issues that the WFS–fyl aimed to address and why they matter; (2) it explains some key technical debates surrounding rights, food security measurement and action since 1996, and areas that need to be explored and deepened from 2002. The paper begins with a brief overview of the concepts of food security, hunger and poverty used. It then analyses contemporary debates regarding the three substantive issues that need to be addressed to reduce hunger.

- *Reaffirmation of the right to food* and, related to this, *underlining the importance of participation* of the food-insecure and their empowerment in addressing WFS goals.
- *Improving the analysis of food insecurity* so as to ensure that appropriate actions are developed. It is suggested that emerging livelihoods approaches provide a link between the right to food and freedom from hunger, improved measurement and action.
- *Recognition of the roles of diverse actors* in measurement and defining policies and actions to reduce hunger. Indeed, implementing the right to food entails a shift of power in all initiatives, from measurement and monitoring of food insecurity through to the development, implementation and

---

Box 1

FAO, the World Food Summit and food security measurement

The United Nations Food and Agriculture Organization (FAO) is financed by some 180 member nations and its member organization (the European Union). The FAO, based in Rome, is the largest specialized agency within the UN system, with a leading role in agriculture, forestry, fisheries and rural development. It has a mandate to raise levels of nutrition and standards of living, to improve agricultural productivity and to better the condition of rural populations. Since its inception in 1945, FAO has worked to alleviate poverty and hunger by promoting agricultural development, improved nutrition and the pursuit of food security.

In 1996, FAO hosted the World Food Summit (WFS) which drew together the leaders of 185 countries and the European Community. The Summit aimed to address the persistent scourge of food insecurity in the world and develop actions to eliminate hunger. Delegates at the WFS pledged in the Rome Declaration on World Food Security to work towards the achievement of food security for all, to undertake an ongoing effort to eradicate hunger in all countries and, specifically, to reduce the number of undernourished people in the world to half by the year 2015 (estimated at 841 million in 1996—FAO 1996b).

The Summit placed particular emphasis on monitoring progress towards the WFS hunger target, and established the Food Insecurity and Vulnerability Information and Mapping Systems (FIVIMS) to monitor global and national efforts to reach WFS goals. The WFS also developed a Plan of Action to move towards these goals. FIVIMS states in its most recent annual report that current trends in reduction of food insecurity indicate that this target will not be met by 2015 (FAO 2001).

In this context, the WFS–fyl reassembled government representatives in Rome from 10 June to 13 June 2002 to review progress towards ending hunger since the 1996 World Food Summit, and to consider ways to accelerate the process. Preparations for the WFS–fyl focused on two issues: enhancing political will among developing countries and partners to reach the WFS goal; and mobilizing sufficient additional financial resources to identify the food-insecure more accurately and identifying concrete actions (to reduce hunger in the short term and underlying poverty in the longer term). The event was articulated around a number of plenaries and roundtables. While it was primarily an intergovernmental event, over 600 representatives from NGOs and civil society took part in various open events at the Summit. Unfortunately, developed and industrialized countries preferred to have lower-level representation than the developing countries, which sent their heads of state to represent them. Initial reports indicate that while key issues such as measurement and the role of agriculture were debated, there was little commitment to increased resources for food security or a major shift in approach by powerful stakeholders.

---

evaluation of programmes. This suggests a radical departure for the national governments of the international donor community.

The WFS–fyl appears to have been unable to make dramatic headway in addressing these issues, hampered by the lack of high-level representation from donor countries. However, there remain other means and fora through which to take them forward.

Karim Hussein

Core Concepts and Definitions

Narratives on the nature of food insecurity and hunger and how they relate to poverty differ widely between development actors. Others have effectively reviewed the evolution in thinking on food security in recent years (e.g. Devereux and Maxwell 2001) and this exercise will not be repeated here. Nonetheless, four interrelated concepts are central to food security and merit some explanation.

Food security

The World Bank has referred to food security as access by all people at all times to sufficient food, in terms of quality, quantity, and diversity for an active and healthy life without risk of loss of that access (World Bank 2000). In 1996, the WFS described the state in the following terms.

> Food security at the household, national, regional and global levels [is achieved] when all people, at all times, have physical and economic access to sufficient, safe and nutritious food to meet their dietary needs and food preferences for an active and healthy life.

Others include the importance of *stability* in food supplies (FAO) or, more radically, the removal of the fear that there will not be enough to eat (Maxwell 1991). At least four main dimensions emerge from most contemporary definitions of food security:

- availability
- access for all
- consumption, over-consumption and quality
- appropriate utilization.

Food security is considered in this paper to refer to secure and regular access by all people at all times to enough food for a healthy and active life. This food has to be safe, nutritious and meet food preferences. Food security can be achieved by ensuring sufficient supply (e.g. through agricultural production or food aid) and improving access (e.g. through more secure and sustainable livelihoods; entitlements[1] to food or the amount of food someone can command through a combination of production, sale or exchange of assets, sale of labour or via transfers through social networks).[2] *Food insecurity* is the opposite state of a lack of access to food or an adequate diet—either temporarily (transitory food insecurity) or continuously over time (chronic food insecurity).

Hunger

Hunger is central to poor people's experience and definitions of poverty and ill-being (DFID 2002a) and is widely perceived to be the most severe and direct manifestation of poverty. Subjective definitions of hunger by the poor vary. However, hunger generally refers to a strong desire for food or a specific nutrient or a state of lack of access to food. This state is often characterized by pain and leads to weakness, debilitation, malnutrition and, in extreme cases, death. Like food insecurity, hunger can be chronic or seasonal.

Poverty

Poverty is now broadly perceived to be a multidimensional state beyond deficiency in income. Poverty may be relative or absolute and, like food insecurity, may be chronic or transitory. *Absolute poverty* is a condition where survival needs are not met or where consumption falls below an established set of needs. This is often measured by low level of calorie consumption converted into a level of monetary income (Greeley 1994). *Relative poverty* refers to "a lack of resources to obtain the types of diets, participate in the activities and have the living conditions . . . which are customary . . . in the society to which they belong" (Townsend 1974).

Vulnerability

Vulnerability cuts across the food security and poverty literature. It encapsulates the dimensions of risk, stress, shocks and lack of ability to cope with these. FIVIMS incorporates vulnerability as it refers to the range of factors that place people at risk of becoming food-insecure, including factors that affect their ability to cope. Vulnerability captures the dynamic and uncertain nature of food insecurity for the marginally better-off or transitory food-insecure: while one day a family may have enough to eat, a poor agricultural season, unavailability of wage labour, conflict or other factors outside their control may tip the family into a state of food insecurity. However, vulnerability is difficult to measure quantitatively.

Linking food security, hunger and poverty

Food insecurity is multidimensional and can affect both the absolute poor and relatively poor—for example, through nutritional deficiencies. Lack of adequate nutrition and access to food have long been recognized as one of the most severe manifestations of poverty reflected in use of calorie consumption estimates to set income-based poverty lines and identify the poorest (see Lipton 1984). However, there is some confusion over the attribution of cause and effect, with implications for the identification of priority actions. For example, while FAO acknowledges that hunger is both the cause and effect of poverty, it argues that "the eradication of hunger is instrumental to the eradication of other dimensions of poverty" (CFS 2001). Meanwhile, the United Kingdom's Department for International Development (DFID) asserts that "Poverty reduction is essential to eliminating hunger" (DFID 2002a). Food insecurity, hunger and poverty are clearly closely related; however, different actors disagree on cause and effect. This is not simply a platitudinous debate. If poverty causes hunger, it indicates that actions are necessary both to address the structural causes of poverty and inequality, as well as to address the symptoms of hunger in the short and medium term.

Despite these differences, there is growing convergence on the implications for action. While FAO states that "hunger needs specific targeting within broader poverty reduction initiatives" (CFS 2001), DFID acknowledges that "a focus on food security within poverty reduction initiatives is critical, in order to ensure that such initiatives meet the needs of the hungry and that they address both the chronic and transitory aspects of food security" (DFID 2002a).

However, while there is a consensus that hunger needs to be addressed in its own right and that food policy has a role in poverty reduction, there is less certainty concerning priorities for action to address hunger. Emerging livelihoods approaches may provide a practical tool to tie together these concepts, providing the link between a multidimensional and people-centred view of poverty, an analytical framework based on people's strategies, assets and capacities and the identification of actions appropriate to diverse contexts and population groups. In short, livelihoods approaches present a useful analytical tool to address issues in food security measurement, particularly at the subnational level. They provide a framework for identifying problems related to disempowerment and developing appropriate actions to address these.

A significant literature has built up around livelihoods approaches (see e.g. Carney 1999; Carney *et al.* 1999; Hussein forthcoming) and the strong complementarities between rights-based and livelihoods approaches (Moser *et al.* 2001; Farrington 2001). Elements of these approaches that are particularly relevant to the analysis of food insecurity include:

- a focus on the diverse strategies (farming and/or livestock rearing, non-farm employment, migration, etc.) and assets (e.g. human, economic, financial, social, natural and political assets) used by people to survive and gain a living;
- analysis of the constraints faced by people in pursuing these strategies or accessing these assets;
- the impact of policies, politics and formal and informal institutions;
- analysis of the effects of factors outside the control of vulnerable groups (e.g. shocks such as war and HIV/AIDS, floods, etc.; constraints related to seasonality and so on);
- a focus on the outcomes people aim to achieve through the pursuit of livelihood strategies (e.g. increased income, security or well-being).

Rights, Participation and Empowerment

Rights-based approaches emerge from an inclusive human rights framework based on the perception that all people everywhere should have the capacity to claim a number of fundamental civil, political, economic, social and cultural rights irrespective of race, culture, religion, or gender. These rights are guaranteed in international law by the 1948 Universal Declaration of Human Rights and other subsequent UN instruments. The right to food and the right to be free from hunger are inseparable from other economic and social rights such as the right to a means of living.

Socio-economic rights have generally received less attention than civil and political rights. However, in theory, the two sets of rights have always been considered to have equal importance in international law. In this context, there has been growing interest generally among campaigners and international NGOs and some donors, in anchoring efforts to address food insecurity in a rights framework.

The Rome Declaration on World Food Security of 1996 reaffirmed the

> right of everyone to have access to safe and nutritious food, consistent with the right to adequate food and the fundamental right of everyone to be free from hunger. (FAO 1996a)

The Resolution for the WFS–fyl affirmed this commitment. However, as with all social and economic rights, it continues to face the problem of implementation.

Key intergovernmental agencies responsible for food and agriculture have highlighted the right to food, to push food security and agriculture up the donor agenda (see Van de Sand 2001). For these agencies, commitment to the right to food should lead not only to increased investment in agriculture, but to initiatives to strengthen the broader livelihood opportunities, economic bargaining power and political influence of the poor and their organizations (e.g. the International Fund for Agricultural Development—IFAD)—and to the development of participatory, livelihoods-centred programmes to promote sustainable development (e.g. FAO's Special Programme for Food Security).

International non-governmental organizations (NGOs) have also championed the right to food in their campaign for action against hunger,[3] highlighting the importance of:

- strong civil society participation in initiatives to combat hunger;
- food sovereignty, or the right of the peoples of each country to:
  - counter destructive effects of international trade liberalization
  - determine their own policies concerning sustainable food production, distribution and consumption
  - develop their own strategies to ensure the realization of the right to adequate food for all;
- shifting the emphasis away from bolstering the influence of food-centred international institutions (e.g. FAO) in relation to the World Bank and the International Monetary Fund, to promoting reform in the international economy and political processes at the national level, specifically in fostering a greater role for civil society and local initiatives.

Some observers have argued that General Comment 12 of the UN Committee of Economic and Social Rights provides a legal and authoritative interpretation of the right to food. However, for others, the implementation of a rights-based approach to food security has been hampered by the lack of a detailed definition of these rights and of the instruments to enforce them.

Further, guaranteeing the right to food may be seen as a support to achieving other rights. Hence, the WFS Plan of Action stated the need for the UN system and governments to "better define the rights related to food in article 11 of the Covenant [on Economic, Social and Cultural Rights] and to propose ways to implement and realize these rights as a means of achieving the commitments and objectives of the World Food Summit, taking into account the possibility of formulating voluntary guidelines for food security for all" (Commitment 7, objective 7.4 of the Plan of Action).

Consequently, a draft International Code of Conduct on the Human Right for Adequate Food was proposed, in September 1997, by a group of civil society organizations with some support from donors such as Germany.[4] This draft Code of Conduct was founded on the premise that adequate financial and material resources are available in the world to eliminate hunger and that the right to adequate food is key to resolving hunger, since it implies the right to feed oneself or, where this is impossible, to access social safety nets. Promoters argue that such a Code would provide a mechanism to empower the hungry and make governments and international actors accountable for reducing hunger. However, others, including the UK and USA, are not convinced of the added value provided by such a Code over existing mechanisms to promote rights-based approaches. Concerns include that such a Code may undermine existing legal mechanisms to promote rights and take the right to food out of the wider human rights context—hence weakening arguments in favour of such rights. It is also argued by some donors that this emphasis reinforces a stilted view of food security as an issue primarily related to food production and agriculture, rather than linked to the promotion of poverty reduction, sustainable development and multisectoral approaches to development.

Hence, while there is, as FAO argues, a need to mobilize additional resources and confirm the political will to address hunger at all levels, rights, empowerment at the local level and accountability are also vital. The Director-General of FAO reaffirmed the importance of the WFS–fyl addressing the right to food in a speech in Berlin in May 2002: hunger being a manifestation of persistent disparities in power in the world. Similarly, the Assistant President of IFAD has recently argued:

> food security is an issue of *empowering* people to influence or shape institutions, policies, and service organizations. It is about enabling poor men and women to guide and direct changes in "the rules of the game".

This generates a key message for the international community:

> Empowerment *with* more resources will reduce hunger. Resources *without* empowerment are not the answer. (Van de Sand 2001)

Windfuhr (2001) and Swaminathan (2001) explore the implications for practice if the right to food is to be translated into reality. They highlight the need to shift power and decision-making over priorities and resource allocation regarding food security initiatives from the donor community to national governments and within countries empowering food-insecure people and their organizations. This leads to three observations:

- *Decision-makers* need to deepen their understanding of the complex interplay between formal rights-conferring bodies and institutions that affect the capacity of people to attain a state of food security.
- *National governments* must acknowledge their role as central actors in defending and guaranteeing attainment of the right to food—implying a need to strengthen the ability of developing country states to protect and fulfil the citizens' right to food, through measures that both stimulate supply and access to food.
- *The food-insecure and their organizations* must develop appropriate strategies and tactics to claim rights, demand legal instruments and practical actions that will address food insecurity at national and subnational levels. The second point here is important: rights might be agreed and accorded at summits and enshrined in international law, but they will only take shape and be constituted in a specific context by and through struggle: "They [rights] articulate a vision of entitlements, of how things might be, which in turn has the capacity to advance political aspiration and action" (Hunt 1991: 247). This struggle is likely to be of a political nature and there is a need to develop specific measures and interventions. International leaders have an important role in confirming rights and establishing a framework by which the right to adequate food can be claimed by the hungry and their representatives over time. However, they may be reluctant to do so: they may generate a struggle that could have momentous political implications for *all* concerned.

The shift of power entailed in implementing the right to food should influence all initiatives, from measurement and monitoring of food insecurity through to the development, implementation and evaluation of programmes. This suggests a radical departure that is as difficult for the international donor community as for national governments to accept.

Indeed, despite many references to stakeholder and civil society participation in achieving WFS goals at the 1996 Summit, little interest was subsequently observed in mobilizing stakeholders to get involved in drawing up and implementing national action plans to reduce hunger (SID 2001). This effectively disenfranchised non-state actors—a factor that can only contribute to difficulties in achieving WFS goals.

In sum, rights-based approaches provide a framework for demanding action to eliminate hunger and empowering the food-insecure to have a real stake in the process. A human rights approach to food security is useful as it refocuses attention on:

- the responsibility of international institutions and states to champion and guarantee fundamental human rights;
- the agency of the food-insecure: highlighting the importance of heeding their "voice", empowering them to take action to eliminate hunger and claim their rights;

- the need to identify performance standards to which governments can be held accountable, in the absence of the capacity to enforce these rights (see e.g. Maxwell 1998); and
- ways of incorporating rights-based indicators and monitoring into food insecurity measurement (see Jonsson and Patel 2001).

However, as pointed out elsewhere, a rights-based approach to food has been difficult to implement. Doubtless this is due to the change in power relations and distribution of resources thus implied.

A people-centred approach also has implications for the analysis of food insecurity, as actions need to be based on an analysis that is sensitive to subnational variations and livelihood diversity. The following section examines the current international system for measuring progress towards WFS targets coordinated by FIVIMS, and draws on recent ODI research to propose key improvements. This is followed by a section that suggests livelihoods approaches could be a useful link between rights-based approaches, measurement and analysis, and action.

Improving the Analysis of Food Insecurity

Background

The WFS emphasized that countries and the international community require reliable, accurate and consistent information on the extent and magnitude of food insecurity at subnational, national, regional and global levels. Reliable information is clearly necessary in order to develop appropriate policies and interventions and to underpin advocacy for action to address food insecurity if it is to be effective. One of the key decisions of the WFS was, therefore, to establish the inter-agency Food Insecurity and Vulnerability Information and Mapping Systems (FIVIMS) to contribute to the reduction of food insecurity and vulnerability through better information on food security at global and national levels (see box 2).

Using FIVIMS data, FAO argues that progress towards the reduction of food insecurity is not currently sufficient to reach WFS targets by 2015. For example, FIVIMS *State of Food Insecurity in the World* reports paint the gloomy picture of a world in which the number of hungry people is actually increasing in most of the developing world and particularly in areas vulnerable to conflict and disaster. SOFI 1999 (FAO's annual report on the "State of Food Insecurity in the World") states that "if the pace in reducing [food insecurity] is not stepped up, more than 600 million people will still go to sleep hungry in the developing countries in 2015" (FAO 1999). Hence, it is argued that, to achieve the Summit goal, a much faster rate of progress is required. The SOFI 2001 report continues to assert that while progress has been made in reducing the absolute number of hungry people in the world, it is not happening fast enough: the average rate of decline in numbers of undernourished needs to speed up from 6 million people a year to 22 million a year to reach the target (FAO 2001). However, these figures contrast with the more positive story told by data on poverty reduction.[5]

Box 2

FIVIMS—an international instrument for food security measurement and analysis

FIVIMS is a network of systems that assembles, analyses and disseminates information about people who are food-insecure or at risk (i.e. vulnerable to food insecurity).

FIVIMS has three core objectives:

(a) international comparative monitoring of undernutrition and global food insecurity indicators to evaluate progress towards achieving global food insecurity targets (including, principally, halving the *number* of undernourished by 2015) and further targets included in the Millennium Development Goals, including halving the *proportion* of hungry people in the world by 2015;
(b) promotion of best practice across agencies in food insecurity and vulnerability information and mapping at the country level;
(c) facilitating the coordination of food insecurity measurement and response at the national level and improving performance of national food security information systems.

Although FIVIMS has a small secretariat based at FAO and most data collection and analysis activities are undertaken by FAO technical divisions, it is an inter-agency initiative with over 25 members including multilateral, bilateral and non-governmental organizations. At the global level, FIVIMS provides estimates of undernutrition and monitors a range of global food security indicators. At the national level, it undertakes activities to improve national food security information systems.

FIVIMS capacity to influence policies and actions to reduce hunger has been undermined by debate on the validity of its measure of food insecurity—the number of "undernourished" or those suffering from undernutriton defined by lack of access to calories or micro-nutrients. This indicator is based on per capita food supply estimates drawn from national food balance sheet data. These are then adjusted for distribution using a controversial methodology based on broad assumptions of national and individual calorie intake needs and national income distribution. Further, the Millennium Goals preferred to refer to halving the *proportion* of under-nourished in the world by 2015. Recent work has studied the strengths and weaknesses of the undernourishment headcount measure and the potential contribution of nutritional indicators with a view to improving reliability and policy relevance over time.

Improving the international measure of undernutrition

Haddad *et al.* (2001) recall that according to the FAO's measure, some 841 million people were undernourished in 1996, translating into a goal of reducing this figure by over 400 million by 2015. While this is not a measure of access or consumption but of per capita food availability, based on fixed assumptions about distribution, the FAO methodology at least generates headcount estimates of undernutrition that are comparable across countries over time. They therefore provide a way to compare country progress against food insecurity targets that is not sensitive to subnational variation.

There has been a growing debate on the adequacy of this methodology and the usefulness of the information generated, for defining specific interventions. The measure generates data and conclusions which differ from country-level poverty assessments. Specialists such as Svedberg have severely criticized the methodology for being based on imperfect data and ambiguous assumptions (e.g. about population distribution and consumption patterns), arguing that an alternative approach based on anthropometric surveys is more appropriate as these would provide more relevant indicators of nutritional status (Devereux 2001).

Haddad *et al.* (2001) arrive at five major conclusions:

1. Qualitative data on Bangladesh, Ethiopia and Tanzania reveal significant differences between aggregate global figures generated by FIVIMS and country-level data. These subnational data generally point to a more negative trend in reducing food insecurity. They highlight the importance of innovations in agricultural technology (Bangladesh), the devastating impact of shocks such as HIV/AIDS (Tanzania), the need to harmonize and analyse data collected (Ethiopia and Tanzania) and the need to monitor the capacity and institutional aspects of food security-related development aid (Tanzania). A general conclusion is the importance of analysing qualitative data on the distribution of food insecurity across regions within a country.

2. There was a mismatch between the FAO's numbers of "undernourished" and actual levels of food insecurity. The number of "undernourished" indicator only really reflected physical access to food/calories at national level. It did not reflect the multidimensionality of food insecurity and livelihood diversity at the subnational level. Nor could the indicator capture issues related to economic, social or physiological access, or vulnerability and safety. However, many of these aspects of food insecurity measurement could be integrated into FIVIMS as they all revolve around using existing household surveys and integrating such data with the food balance sheets.

3. At the same time, new methods need to be developed to analyse the relationships between shocks (HIV/AIDS, war, etc.), subnational variation, diverse livelihood strategies and food security trends.

4. National government capacity for data collection and analysis needs to be strengthened.

5. An improved indicator for global inter-country food security measurement is required but this will take time and investment. Methodologies need to be developed to integrate existing subnational data on food availability, access and nutritional status of regions and livelihood groups into national statistical systems that feed into global food security monitoring. Such initiatives would have to address the varying quality and coverage of food security information systems in developing countries. Indeed, no clear substitute for "the number of undernourished" indicator exists where national-level data are not readily available. However, immediate improvements might include: updating the underlying assumptions behind data analysis (e.g. population distribution and spread

of agricultural production/consumption in a country; stability and peace . . .); the collection of new data that are better able to predict shocks to food insecurity (e.g. HIV/AIDS, weather extremes, conflict . . .); improved capacities for in-country monitoring of food insecurity, focusing on trends among specific population groups vulnerable to food security. This would require inter-agency cooperation, drawing together analysis from a variety of agencies (e.g. World Food Programme Vulnerability Assessment and Mapping (VAM) units or NGO household food economy surveys). This information could be reconciled to existing quantitative data, providing a bridge between assessment and action.

Nutritional indicators

Shoham *et al.* (2001) provide an analysis of the use of nutrition indicators in surveillance systems that can feed into decision-making at the national level and global food insecurity measurement. Nutrition indicators include anthropometric measures such as weight deficiency, stunting or wasting in children and micro-nutrient deficiency indicators to identify conditions such as anaemia or vitamin A deficiency.

The study observed that while nutritional indicators are not exact measures of food insecurity or poverty, they are an important component of national-level nutritional surveillance systems that feed information into food security monitoring. Investments have tended to focus on anthropometry. However, more investment in monitoring micro-nutrient deficiencies is needed to avoid public health crises, especially in disasters.

Nevertheless, case studies show that the existence of "good" nutritional surveillance information has not always produced an appropriate or timely decision or intervention to bolster food security. This confirms conclusions from extensive research at Cornell University in the 1980s and 1990s: that nutritional surveillance systems with no practical link to decision-making are of limited use in addressing hunger (see e.g. Tucker *et al.* 1989). This deficiency is often due to the lack of an institutional framework setting out organizational linkages and how information should be used and acted upon at the country level. To address this, decision-makers at country level need to be involved from the design stage of nutritional surveillance systems. However, such cooperation is not always present and actors frequently act as if they are competitors rather than collaborators working towards the same end goals.

Finally, livelihoods approaches promote best practice that should make nutritional surveillance systems more relevant to decision-making by emphasizing:

- evolution of surveillance systems away from measuring and monitoring the impact of nutritional status towards monitoring people's responses to food insecurity;
- identification of the nutritional condition of specific livelihood groups;
- the need to draw micro–macro linkages: analysing the underlying causes of food insecurity for specific vulnerable groups and macro-level factors

determining their access to food, health and care and feeding this information back to decision-makers;

- adoption of a consultative and participatory approach to information gathering and analysis, involving the food-insecure in the analysis of data and identification of interventions.

Food security measurement, rights and empowerment

The quality and reliability of national and global food insecurity information matters. Decision-makers need information on food security trends that is believed to be reliable and accurate in order to be persuaded to take action. Indeed, data on the world food security situation frequently underpins calls by developing countries and international agencies for funding for new programme interventions and investments. FIVIMS has an important role in collating reliable information that can inform decision-makers at national and global levels and has the potential to generate more appropriate interventions. However, this is somewhat undermined by limitations in the methodology used and in the reliability of data.

ODI-coordinated research has highlighted that the data collected through monitoring the FIVIMS undernourishment indicator can provide orders of magnitude and rough trends on food insecurity, thus providing some leverage to argue for action to mitigate hunger (see Haddad *et al.* 2001). However, the calculation of the number of undernourished is based on disputable assumptions, giving rise to questions over accuracy. Some actors have rightly questioned the relevance of this measure. For example, DFID has recently stated:

> We need to refine our indicators of hunger. "Undernourishment" is a limited concept in that it measures only food production, modified by distribution ... Conceptually, it is a long way from the notion of "food security", which also covers availability, access and the ability to utilize available food. Further work is needed to improve this indicator and to use it in conjunction with the "underweight" indicator and other relevant information that better demonstrates people's access to food. (DFID 2002a: 11)

Ways in which to improve the indicator have been discussed at a FIVIMS International Scientific Symposium on the measurement and Assessment of Food Deprivation and Under-nutrition held in Rome in June 2002. This examined undernourishment indicators and complementary quantitative and qualitative approaches to assessing hunger. It also attempted to directly address decision-makers' information needs.

However, it is important to recognize that if the rights perspective is taken, issues of participation, empowerment and livelihood diversity also need to be addressed. While food security and hunger are global phenomena, the reasons, dimensions, severity and actions to address it will vary across contexts. This requires a radical shift of power in which local ownership of food security analysis and local initiatives to address hunger are prioritized. How can this be reflected in food insecurity measurement and analysis of progress towards WFS targets?

Standard technical methods of measuring food insecurity and targeting interventions used by agencies and national governments are not always consistent with rights-based and empowering approaches. In the literature on poverty, it has been argued that such an approach fails to identify the poorest. Furthermore, approaches in which outsiders decide who is the most vulnerable and how they are to be assisted are essentially non-participatory and related to "top-down" blueprint approaches to development (see Chambers 1983; Harrell-Bond and Leopold 1992). Indeed, if the food-insecure themselves are not in control of the process, measurement and targeting simply become a manifestation of the way in which power is retained by the agent giving resources (Harrell-Bond and Leopold 1992). This retention of exclusive power by the giver may work against effectiveness—leading to misdirected investments in actions against hunger and thus, ironically, preventing attainment of the very targets set by donors.

Hence, at the subnational level at least, it is vitally important to fully engage the food-insecure in defining targets, undertaking monitoring and measurement and planning actions against hunger. There are a range of recognized participatory methodologies that can facilitate this: e.g. participatory rural appraisal, the household economy approach (see Save the Children 2000), and strengthening local organizations.

One central problem remains, however: generating information that is considered to be objective, accurate and relevant to decision-makers so that they feel confident that they can identify and target appropriate interventions. This reality has to be addressed in the short term to ensure the continued flow of donor resources. However, as we move towards a rights-based approach, information systems at the national level should be designed so that the food-insecure are in the driving seat, defining the information necessary for them to measure progress and allocate resources.

What might livelihoods approaches have to offer to food security measurement?

Livelihoods-oriented approaches are used by many NGOs in collecting data on and analysing food security. The Household Economy Approach, developed by Save the Children, has been applied across a number of countries in east and southern Africa to assess the vulnerability of households with considerable success (Save the Children 2000). As a result, the utility of incorporating a livelihoods approach into food insecurity analysis and measurement is being examined by FIVIMS. Initial livelihoods work with FIVIMS might usefully focus on:

- capturing a consensus, if one exists or can be created, on best practices at a district/regional level;
- examining how to scale up innovative district-, regional- and national-level data collection initiatives that have yielded cost-effective results that have effectively fed into decision-making.

However, it is not clear how livelihoods approaches might be incorporated into national government data collection and decision-making processes which lie at the heart of global food insecurity measurement initiatives. These still tend to be dominated by sectorally defined departments and budget lines, which have a disincentive to take on board multisectoral approaches.

Livelihoods are nevertheless a useful complement to a rights-based approach. Specifically, rights analysis provides insights into the distribution of power and a tool for focusing state actions on the livelihoods of the poor; whereas livelihoods analysis offers a way to prioritize efforts and actions to obtain rights for poor groups (Moser *et al.* 2001). Here, it is argued that livelihoods approaches can be a practical vehicle for linking rights-based approaches, measurement and action to reduce food insecurity by providing tools for:

- addressing the realities of subnational variation and diversified livelihoods;
- improving indicators on food insecurity by drawing on contextual realities;
- analysing food insecurity in a given context and incorporating vulnerability and policy into the analysis;
- linking poverty and food insecurity with issues related to social capital, empowerment and participation;
- identifying appropriate policy measures to realize rights in a participatory way.

The challenge remains to identify mechanisms for effectively combining the two perspectives in order qualitatively to improve the food security measurement processes.

This should also help move food security analysis and action away from a narrow focus on agriculture towards addressing diversified (and non-agricultural) livelihood strategies. It could highlight the need for food security analysis to begin by understanding people's experiences of hunger and the relationship between food insecurity and the constraints and opportunities to their existing livelihoods, prior to deciding on interventions. Livelihoods analysis is also likely to be key to interpreting the relationship between short- and long-term phenomena that affect food security, particularly at the national level. In sum, livelihoods approaches provide an analytical framework on which to build appropriate operational interventions to eliminate hunger in diverse contexts. Building on core principles of participation and empowerment, they complement an approach centred on enabling the food-insecure to demand their rights, entitlements and access to food. Livelihoods analysis is also likely to be key to interpreting the relationship between short- and long-term phenomena that affect food security, particularly at the national level.

Nonetheless, there are a number of challenges to incorporating livelihoods approaches into food insecurity analysis. These include:

- integrating local livelihoods data gathered by a range of agencies into central statistical systems at the national level that can provide national averages for making global comparisons;
- financing the costs of scaling up resource-intensive methods used principally at the district level and developing satisfactory methods to aggregate information while retaining a relevant degree of livelihood information.

Conclusions

This paper has highlighted the importance of a human rights and empowerment perspective in relation to reaching targets for hunger reduction and
has demonstrated the relevance of technical debates over food insecurity
measurement to actions to reduce hunger. However, unless there is a strong
political commitment to realize the right to food—particularly on the part of
donors and national governments of countries in which the food-insecure
live—the debates over food security measurement and numbers affected will
remain little more than an end in themselves.

Improving the analysis of food insecurity and developing appropriate
responses is beyond the capacity of one agency or institution. It is a process
involving increased investments, the development of improved methodologies
and enhanced analytical capacities at the level of communities, national governments and agencies. It is important not only to measure achievement of
targets to reduce food insecurity, but also to address the root causes of hunger. Thus, prior to developing meaningful actions, a practical rights-based
approach to hunger and food security needs to be reaffirmed. This is
required to underpin an enhanced role for a range of actors at all levels in
measurement, policy formulation and decision-making. A strategic shift is
required at all levels and by all actors: balancing the stress on the important
role of donors and international agencies in providing resources, increasing
investment in agriculture but also in increasing broader entitlements to food,
and debating ways forward while increasing emphasis on local livelihoods,
empowerment and a strengthened role for civil society in developing actions
to address *their* priority food security concerns.

The evidence presented leads to at least three priority issues that need to
be addressed by the international community.

1. *Reaffirmation of the right to food and freedom from hunger*, and development of a
   strategy to implement it through actions by a range of actors and community empowerment. While a "Code of Conduct" could provide a firm
   moral basis and practical impetus for implementing policies and actions
   to reduce food insecurity, it might also simply provide cover for inaction
   among national and international decision-makers unless accompanied
   by financial commitments, concrete action plans and follow-up.
2. *Improvement of the measurement of food insecurity at national and international levels.*
   This involves refining and complementing the undernourishment measure
   used by FAO; drawing in livelihoods approaches sensitive to subnational
   variation; and developing frameworks for subnational data systems to
   feed into national FIVIMS and decision-making processes.[6] It also implies
   an injection of additional funding for international measurement initiatives
   and for national government departments in poor countries responsible
   for collecting relevant statistics. Support for initiatives to strengthen
   mechanisms for local information to feed into national and international
   systems is also needed.
3. *Recognizing the need to address micro- and macro-level factors determining food
   security at the local level and the roles of diverse actors in actions to reduce hunger at*

multiple levels. Excessive emphasis on a few international agencies or donors is a mistake. Responsibility and accountability for addressing the diverse supply and access, macro- and micro-economic, social and physiological dimensions of food security are spread across a range of actors. Donors, international agencies, national governments and the public sector, the private sector and civil society (e.g. community-based and producer organizations, international and national NGOs) all have roles to play and must work in partnership if WFS targets are to be achieved. Important lessons on this are emerging from work on achieving food security through community-based food systems.[7] This is accepted in principle (e.g. in the Draft Resolution for the WFS–fyl), but still needs to be worked out in practice. For example, in relation to defending the right to food, *international agencies and donors* have a special responsibility for promoting the right to food at an international level, mobilizing resources to monitor progress and supporting interventions; *national governments* have the primary responsibility to put in place legal instruments to defend the right to food for all; and *civil society, the food insecure and their representatives* are responsible for the political struggle needed to achieve action to uphold the rights of the hungry. It is important to underline here the link between acknowledging local experiences of hunger, empowering the food-insecure at community level and shifting decision-making power closer to them (see Mancusi-Materi 2000). A strategy for civil society and representatives of the food-insecure to be engaged in the analysis of food insecurity, development of concrete actions to eliminate hunger at all levels and monitoring achievements needs to be established.

What might this mean for international action to fight hunger?

The WFS–fyl provided an opportunity for the international community to renew commitments to halving the number and proportion of food-insecure in the world. In the context of recent donor pledges to substantially increase the financial resources available for poverty reduction and development at the Monterrey Financing for Development conference in Spring 2002,[8] the Summit had the potential to give impetus to prioritizing actions against food insecurity and hunger within the broader context of international and national efforts to eliminate poverty.

The agenda of the WFS–fyl also included a wide range of policy issues beyond those considered in this paper, all of which are relevant to reducing hunger in the world: from the role of economic growth,[9] trade reform, increased investment in agriculture and rural development, and good governance to dealing with HIV/AIDS and conflict.

However, it is unclear how much the Summit actually achieved in terms of prioritizing the fight against hunger. The heads of state present solemnly renewed their commitments to eradicating hunger and to achieving WFS targets, with increased emphasis on multi-stakeholder partnerships between actors. However, it is unclear what tangible value added was provided by this exercise. While developing countries sent their heads of state, demonstrating the priority they place on food security, representation of rich, industrialized countries tended to be limited and lower-level (i.e. below head of state or even minister in many cases). There were no major new commitments to provide resources to fight hunger.

Furthermore, despite the right to food and related Code of Conduct being one of the most debated themes in the run-up to and at the Summit, it was not a centrepin of the Declaration. While Paragraph 10 of the Summit Declaration reaffirms in the preamble "the right of everyone to have access to safe and nutritious food", a number of powerful states (headed by the USA, but including the EU, Australia, New Zealand and Canada) declined to subscribe to the Code of Conduct and blocked reference to this in the Summit Declaration. Thus, the Summit Declaration referred only to the establishment of "voluntary guidelines to achieve the progressive realisation of the right to adequate food" over the next two years.[10] Voluntary guidelines might, if used effectively, provide civil rights organizations and other actors with a useful tool for monitoring the realization of the right to food in specific situations and for specific groups and contexts.[11] However, it is argued here that a commitment to a Code of Conduct would have been an important step towards action and would have demonstrated political will to meet WFS targets. Further, voluntary guidelines do not guarantee *action* from states. If the FAO is right that the key to achieving WFS–fyl targets is political will, these examples indicated that this "will" is still lacking.

The final Summit Declaration was at best opaque, and emphasized some well-trodden issue-areas: e.g. the importance of linking urban and rural development; the continued importance of effective measurement; and the significance of agricultural development.

The final Declaration also watered down mention of rights and stepped back from the idea of a Code of Conduct: rather, it agreed to set up intergovernmental mechanisms to draw up a set of voluntary guidelines on the right to food over a two-year period. This process is to be led by FAO in conjunction with international treaty bodies (e.g. the UN High Commission for Refugees). However, voluntary agreements make it difficult to hold states or other actors to commitments. Further, heads of state and senior ministers from key developed countries were absent from the Summit, there was a lack of commitment to increasing resources available for new food insecurity initiatives, and still limited engagement of civil society. In this context it seems unlikely that the Summit will generate rapid changes in policy and practice.

So—what can make a difference in combating hunger? The WFS–fyl may not have achieved much more than discussing issues and problems in addressing hunger. It is now essential for all actors to move beyond vague commitments towards the implementation of actions to guarantee rights and eliminate hunger at national and subnational levels.

While it is good that the Summit highlighted the importance of rights to freedom from hunger, key donors' refusal to support the implementation of a Code of Conduct to achieve these rights generated a weak Summit Resolution. Nor did the Summit do enough to highlight the importance of adopting new approaches to improve the analysis of food insecurity, the necessity of empowering the food-insecure, and defining a path forward for the implementation of actions to reduce hunger that are based on partnership between actors. The next step, therefore, needs to be the elaboration of concrete plans for the involvement of the food-insecure in decisions on priority actions at national and global levels and monitoring progress on implementation so as to achieve WFS goals.

Notes

In developing the thinking behind this paper, the author is indebted to discussions and helpful materials provided by a number of specialists taking part in the DFID-funded ODI Food Security Technical Support Facility in 2001–2002 (see papers at www.odi.org.uk/RPEG/foodsec/frontpage.html). These include: David Wilcock, Stephen Devereux, Simon Maxwell, Lawrence Haddad and Jeremy Shoham. Comments from Rachel Lambert of DFID, and the editors of this volume were also useful. Responsibility for the arguments in this paper remains with the author alone.

1. See Devereux and Singer (1999) for an overview of entitlements concepts in relation to food security.
2. See World Bank (1986) and DFID (2002a).
3. Amalric (2001).
4. *International Code of Conduct on the Human Right to Adequate Food*, September 1997. Endorsed by FoodFirst Information and Action Network, International Human Rights Organization for the Right to Feed Oneself; World Alliance for Nutrition and Human Rights, and Institut Jacques Maritain International. Mimeo.
5. Results cited in the following two sections rely heavily on two papers commissioned by the ODI Food Security Technical Support Facility: Haddad et al. 2001 and Shoham et al. 2001. These are available from the food security pages of the ODI website: www.odi.org.uk/RPEG/foodsec/homepage.html
6. These issues were explored through a major international scientific symposium coordinated by FAO in June 2002 on "Measurement and Assessment of Food Deprivation and Under-Nutrition" and in new research on "food insecurity measurement, livelihoods approaches and policy: applications in FIVIMS".
7. A useful seminar was held on community-based food systems and local initiatives to address food security in Salzburg in May 2002. It underlined the importance of grassroots collective programmes against hunger, the need to address macro-level factors that shape food insecurity (e.g. globalization of trade, agricultural policies, etc.) and efforts to scale up successful local-level initiatives to the macro-level.
8. At the International Conference on Financing for Development in Monterrey, Mexico, 18–22 March 2002, the European Union made commitments to inject some US$20 billion additional resources into overseas development assistance between 2000 and 2006 and the US president called for an increase in US overseas development assistance of $5 billion (see www.un.org/esa/ffd).
9. See Arcand (2001), which argues that there is a significant relationship between better nutrition and economic growth.
10. The WFS–fyl Declaration can be found at the FAO Home Page (http://www.fao.org/DOCREP/MEETING/004/Y6948E.HTM). An intergovernmental working group will start to work on guidelines for policy on food as a human right shortly. This is to be appointed at the FAO Council meeting in November 2002. It is intended that FAO along with other UN agencies, including the Office of the High Commissioner for Human Rights, lead the development of the guidelines.

11. This point was recently made by an FAO technician during an electronic forum on food security.

References

Amalric, A. (2001), *Preparing Strategically for World Food Summit–five years later*, SID Policy Papers. May, Rome: Society for International Development.

Arcand, J.-L. (2001), Undernourishment and economic growth: the efficiency cost of hunger, *FAO Economic and Social Development Paper* 147, Rome: FAO.

Carney, D. (1999), Approaches to sustainable livelihoods for the rural poor, *ODI Poverty Briefing*, 2, January.

Carney, D. *et al.* (1999), *Livelihood Approaches Compared*, London: DFID.

CFS (2001), The World food summit Goal and the Millennium Development Goals. Committee on World Food security, 27th session, Rome, 28 May–1 June.

Chambers, R. (1983), *Rural Development: Putting the Last First*, Harlow: Longman.

Devereux, S. (2002), Book review of P. Svedberg, 2000, *Poverty and Undernutrition: Theory, Measurement and Policy, Journal of Development Studies*, 38, 2: 189–91.

Devereux, S. and Maxwell, S. (eds) (2001), *Food Security in Sub-Saharan Africa*, London: ITDG.

Devereux, S. and Singer, H. (1999), A tribute to Professor Amartya Sen on the occasion of his receiving the 1998 Nobel Prize for economics, *Food Policy*, 24, 1.

DFID (2002a), *Eliminating Hunger: Strategy for Achieving the Millennium Development Goal on Hunger*, May, London and Glasgow: DFID.

DFID (2002b), *Better Livelihood for Poor People: the Role of Agriculture: Consultation document*, May, London and Glasgow: DFID.

FAO (1996a), *Rome Declaration on World Food Security*, Rome: FAO.

FAO (1996b), *The Sixth World Food Survey*, Rome: FAO.

FAO (1999), *The State of Food Insecurity in the World 1999*, Rome: FAO.

FAO (2001), *The State of Food Insecurity in the World 2001. Food Insecurity: When People Live with Hunger and Fear Starvation*, Rome: FAO.

Farrington, J. (2001), Sustainable livelihoods, rights and the new architecture of aid, *Natural Resources Perspectives*, 69, London: ODI.

Greeley, M. (1994), Measurement of poverty and poverty of measurement, *IDS Bulletin*, 25, 2.

Haddad, L. with Gill, G. Kassa, A. and Tierney, A. (2001), Theme 1: Deepening the analysis of the factors behind progress towards WFS targets, IFPRI, OPM, ODI. ODI Food Security Technical Support Facility, Facility Manager: Karim Hussein. The full papers are available at *www.odi.org.uk/RPEG*.

Haddad, L. and Gillespie, S. (2001), Effective food and nutrition policy responses to HIV/AIDS: what we know and what we need to know. Draft FCN Discussion Paper, International Food Policy Research Institute, March.

Harrell-Bond, B. and Leopold, M. (1992), Counting the refugees: the myth of accountability, *Journal of Refugee Studies*, 5.

Hawkins, K. and Hussein, K. (2001), *Impact of HIV/AIDS on Food Security*, ODI Policy Briefing Note to DFID Food Security Advisor for Committee on World Food Security, Overseas Development Institute, May. (Available at www.odi.org.uk/RPEG/foodsec/frontpage.html)

Hunt, A. (1991), *Explorations in Law and Society: Towards a Constitutive Theory of Law*, New York and London: Routledge.

Hussein, K. (forthcoming), Livelihoods approaches compared: a review of current agency practice, London: ODI and DFID.

Jonsson, U. and Patel, M. (2001), Benchmark and indicators for the rights to food, health and care for nutritional well-being. Paper presented at the IUNS Workshop on "A New Paradigm in Human Nutrition? Assessing and addressing adequate food and health as basic human rights in nutrition", 17th International Congress on Nutrition, Vienna, August.

Lipton, M. (1984), The poor and the poorest: some interim findings, *World Bank Discussion Paper*, no. 25, Washington DC: World Bank.

Mancusi-Materi, E. (2000), Working for sustainable livelihoods and food security: voices from the grassroots, *Development*, 43, 4, December: 85–92. See also Special Issue of *Development* devoted to the politics of food security (44, 4).

Maxwell, S. (1991), Introduction. In Maxwell (ed.), *To Cure All Hunger: Food Policy and Food Security in Sudan*, London: IT Publications.

Maxwell, S. (1998), Saucy with the gods: nutrition and food security speak to poverty. Paper presented as a keynote address to the World Bank Human Development Week, 2–6 March.

Moser, C. and Norton, A. with Conway, T., Ferguson, C. and Izard, P. (2001), *To Claim our Rights: Livelihood Security, Human Rights and Sustainable Development*, London: ODI.

ODI (2002), Food Security, *Key Sheets for Sustainable Livelihoods*, no. 8, Policy Planning and Implementation. Supported by DFID and Netherlands Ministry of Foreign Affairs.

Save the Children (2000), *The Household Economy Approach: A Resource Manual for Practitioners*, London: Save the Children.

Shoham, J., Watson, F. and Dolan, C. (2001), Theme 2: The use of nutritional indicators in surveillance systems, Nutrition Works/ODI. ODI Food Security Technical Support Facility, Facility Manager: Karim Hussein (available at www.odi.org.uk/RPEG/foodsec/frontpage.html).

SID (2001), From aid to community empowerment: food security as a political project. Rome: SID (available at *www.sidint.org*).

Swaminathan, M. S. (2001), The right to food: from analysis to action. UNESCO Chair in Ecotechnology, MSSRF, Chennai, India (mimeo).

Townsend, P. (1974), Poverty as relative deprivation: resources and styles of living. In D. Wedderburn (ed.), *Poverty, Inequality and Class Structure*, Cambridge: Cambridge University Press.

Tucker, K., Pelletier, D., Rasmussen, K., Habicht, J.-P., Pinstrup-Andersen, P. and Roche, F. (1989), *Advances in Nutritional Surveillance: The Cornell Nutritional Surveillance Program 1981–1987*, Cornell Food and Nutrition Policy Program Monograph 89–2, CFNPP, Cornell University, Ithaca, New York.

Van de Sand, (2001), IFAD and the right to food: addressing the challenge of ending rural poverty, Rome, September (mimeo).

Windfuhr, M. (2001), The role of the Code of Conduct to implement the right to food. Presented at the occasion of the International Seminar The Right to Food: a Challenge for Peace and Development in the 21st Century. Organized by International Jacques Maritain Institut, Rome, 17–19 September.

World Bank (1986), *Poverty and Hunger: Issues and Options for Food Security in Developing Countries*, World Bank Policy Study, Washington, DC.

World Bank (2000), Food security. Nuts and Bolts Brief from the World Bank Poverty Group, Washington, DC.

6

Food Banks and Food Security: Welfare Reform, Human Rights and Social Policy. Lessons from Canada?

Graham Riches

Introduction

Two juxtaposed headlines in the *Guardian Weekly* (*Washington Post* section, 7–13 March 2002) highlight the current crisis of food insecurity in North America, and indeed in many first-world societies. One article, headlined "Putting a human face on the scandal of hunger", is the story of relief agencies, engulfed by a largely unseen crisis, calling for more money to assist them in feeding America's poor. The other headline reads "Reports suggest economy is growing". In other words, in the midst of a strengthening and increasingly healthy US economy, food banks and emergency soup kitchens are failing to cope with the enormity of food poverty in their society. This is not a new phenomenon but it does invite critical policy questions about the capacity and effectiveness of voluntary and faith-based organizations—of which food banks are key players—adequately to respond to the continuing crisis of food poverty, let alone ensure food security.

In the past 20 years charitable food banks in North America, in Europe, Australia and New Zealand (Riches 1986, 1997; Poppendieck 1998; Hawkes and Webster 2000; Dowler *et al.* 2001) have emerged as significant community responses to the needs of hungry or food-insecure people. In March 2001, 2.4 per cent of the Canadian population received emergency assistance from food banks (Wilson and Tsoa 2001; CAFB 2002). This suggests food banks play a primary role in meeting the food needs of vulnerable populations and that their role in the redistribution of surplus food lies at a critical interface between food security and social policy, particularly in the relationship between health and nutrition, income security and welfare reform and the human right to food. The international rise of food banks in first-world societies raises important questions not only for food security and how best to achieve it, but also for debates about the current direction of welfare reform and social policy.

Graham Riches

Food Security, Food Poverty and Food Banks

Food security, as defined by the World Food Summit in 1996, "exists when all people at all times, have physical and economic access to sufficient, safe and nutritious food to meet their dietary needs and food preferences for an active and healthy life" (Canada 1998: 5). This definition is limited in that it omits any reference to the important question of who controls the food supply and its distribution. Yet, as recognized in *Canada's Action Plan for Food Security* (1998), it does identify three critical elements of food security: an available and reliable food supply, the importance of access to food and to sufficient, safe and nutritious food which must also be culturally acceptable (1998: 5).

From this perspective, the food bank question can be understood within the "food security box" as a debate about the merits of this particular form of surplus food distribution as a means of extending access to food in order to achieve food security. The relevant policy question is whether food banks are more effective than other community-based food programmes such as food stamps, good food boxes, collective kitchens or community gardens at meeting the food and nutritional needs of hungry people. While this is an important question it begs a more critical and inclusive policy analysis and debate about eradicating food poverty. It fails to address people's "inability to acquire or consume an adequate or sufficient quantity of food in socially acceptable ways, or the uncertainty that one will be able to do so" (Radimer *et al.* 1992). Dowler has asked the key question: "Why should such citizens not be able to shop for food like everyone else?" (Dowler *et al.* 2001). This, of course, means that people require sufficient income in terms of wages or benefits if household food security is to be assured. Moreover, the stigma associated with charitable food banking suggests it is not a normal channel of food distribution and is a socially unacceptable way to obtain food.

The rapid emergence and institutionalization of food banks as a critical player in the field of charitable and emergency food relief is at the same time a significant indicator of the prevalence of food poverty and the failure of the welfare state and the public safety net or income support programmes in first-world societies. Indeed, the growth and expansion in food banks since the early 1980s suggests on the one hand that food poverty and inequality are increasing (Robertson *et al.* 1999; Pulkingham and Ternowetsky 1996) and on the other that food banks are an inadequate response to the complex issue of social exclusion and the state's failure to "respect, protect and fulfill" the right to food. From the perspective of social policy analysis it is imperative to ask who is benefiting and why from food banking. This is particularly so in relation to current debates about welfare reform and the human right to food and all that it implies for the full realization of social justice.

This paper seeks to address these questions, reflecting on the experience of 20 years of food banking in Canada. Bearing in mind the limits of comparative social policy (Jones 1985: 5) and of the transferability of policy ideas and practices between different welfare regimes, there are perhaps lessons to be drawn from a re-evaluation of the role of food banks in Canada and a consideration of the extent to which they have become part of the problem of food poverty or one contributing to its solution. Given Canada's highly decentralized federal system, and the difficulties of generalizing about social policy and programmes which for the most part fall constitutionally within provincial domains, the food bank phenomenon is nevertheless worth examining.

In countries such as the United Kingdom where food banks are in their infancy (Hawkes and Webster 2000; Dowler *et al.* 2001), the question of whether to support their development should be a question for an urgent and informed public debate and not a question to be left to community food policy organizations and charitable foundations. In countries where they are now institutionalized, as in Europe, the United States and Canada, their potential role in public education and policy advocacy should be considered as more significant in the struggle to achieve food security than the food they provide.

Re-assessing the Role of Food Banks in Canada

Food banks can reasonably be defined "as centralized warehouses or clearing houses registered as non-profit organizations for the purpose of collecting, storing and distributing surplus food (donated/shared), free of charge either directly to hungry people or to front line social agencies which provide supplementary food and meals" (Riches 1986). However, it would be unwise to consider this description as definitive in that organizations in Canada, and indeed in other countries, which describe themselves as food banks vary in their aims and objectives, their size and scope and in their roles and functions.

Some food banks such as Toronto's Daily Bread Food Bank, the Greater Vancouver Food Bank or the system of Moissons in Quebec are large coordinating food collection and distribution clearing houses which provide food to emergency feeding programmes, soup kitchens or community kitchens. Others are small, local church-run social agencies which both collect donated foods and hand out groceries or provide meals to hungry people. Even the large food banks may deal directly with people needing food. Some food banks purchase foods when running low while others rely entirely on donated products. Some engage in advocacy and public education while most prefer simply to provide a charitable service of feeding the hungry. However, the fact of the matter is that food banks, however they are defined, are now big business in Canada. Indeed, it has recently been observed that while they were first established to provide emergency relief for those in need of food, "20 years later they have become an integral part of contemporary Canadian society" (Theriault and Yadlowski 2000: 206).

Origins and purposes

The origins of Canadian food banks can be traced back to the establishment of the first one in Edmonton, Alberta, in 1981. The immediate cause was the onset of a deep recession generated by a bust in the oil industry and the inadequate response of federal unemployment insurance and the provincial social assistance programme to meet the income needs of swelling numbers of unemployed people (Riches 1986).

93

Graham Riches

However, the seeds of food banking had been planted in US soil as early as 1967 with the setting up of the first food bank in North America in Phoenix, Arizona. Its philosophy was "simply to marry the interests of the food industry to cope effectively with surplus, unsaleable food with those of grass roots poverty organizations" (DBFB 1999: 10). In essence, "the idea was that a modern, wasteful society could act as one that provides a resource to others" (ibid.).

While this philosophy was certainly one supported by the Edmonton Food Bank and others in Canada which quickly followed its lead, Gerard Kennedy, the first director of the Edmonton Food Bank (and now member of the Liberal opposition in the Ontario Legislature) has observed that Canadian food banking has been about more than the alleviation of food poverty or redistributing surplus food (DBFB 1999). Some food banks, and especially the Daily Bread Food Bank in Toronto and the Canadian Association of Food Banks, have been powerful advocates, provincially and nationally, for the eradication of hunger. There has also been a rejection of the institutionalization associated with US food banks which employ large numbers of people and operate "in the manner of large industries, as warehouses only with complex systems of inspection and regulation" (ibid.: 11).

Institutionalization

However, there is evidence that food banks in Canada have themselves become institutionalized. There would appear to be three processes at work: the creation and development of a strong national food bank organization and movement; the corporatization of food banks through their partnerships with national food companies and the media support they receive; and the increasingly significant roles they have come to play as charitable partners with governments in Canada's public safety net (social assistance), thereby contributing to the introduction and implementation of neo-conservative welfare reform.

The dramatic increase in food banks and their national organizational development suggests the creation of a new form of charitable social institution with a long-term life expectancy. In 2001, according to the Hunger-Count Survey conducted annually by the Canadian Association of Food Banks/Association de Banques Alimentaires du Canada, 632 food banks and 2,123 affiliated agencies provided emergency groceries to 718,334 people in the month of March (Wilson and Tsoa 2001: 3; CAFB 2002). While the numbers using food banks declined by 1.2 per cent from the previous year, they represent a 90 per cent increase in food bank use since March 1989. It is important to note that this survey is conducted in March each year as "it is an unexceptional month, without predictable high or low food bank use patterns" (2001: 4). The report itself comments that "food banks have become an institution rather than a temporary response to the effects of the recession as they were intended in the 1980s" (2001: 3).

The formal institutionalization of food banks in Canada could be said to date from 1988 when the Canadian Association of Food Banks (CAFB) was established. As a national coalition of food banks it coordinates donations of food and transportation (using the donated services of transportation companies) across the country to ensure food is distributed quickly and efficiently to member food banks; provides liaison between food banks, industry and government and acts as the voice of food banks (CAFB 2002). The CAFB represents food banks serving 80 per cent of food bank recipients in Canada and receives no financial assistance from any level of government. In more recent years it has played an active role in national anti-poverty advocacy and support for a food security movement in Canada.

Perhaps, however, the critical turning point in the institutionalization of food banks was the setting up in 1995 of the National Food Sharing System when the CAFB became the sole distributor across the country of food donations from major food companies and some national and provincial marketing boards. This Fair Share System, as it is called, was supported in 1997 by 63 corporate food sponsors including companies such as Campbell Soups, Kraft, Kelloggs, H. J. Heinz and Quaker Oats. This food is then transported by rail and road across Canada to local food banks courtesy of the two national rail companies (CP Rail and Canadian National) in 40 ft shipping containers supplied by NYK Line (Canada) and Montreal Shipping and with the support of numerous truckers. In 1997 over 6 million pounds of food was distributed in this way (CAFB website 2002).

The corporatization of food banks is best exemplified by the role played by corporate partners in the activities of the Greater Vancouver Food Bank (GVFB), an organization which provides food to 25,000 people on a weekly basis. Approximately 60 per cent of the food distributed by the GVFB comes in bulk from the food industry (GVFB website). This includes food donations from large national companies through the National Food Sharing System, from national and provincially based supermarket chains and grocery stores. Support for operational services is also provided by major companies in the transportation and communication industry as well as by the print media and commercial and public radio and television. In fact, the role played by the Canadian Broadcasting Corporation (CBC) in sponsoring annual food bank fundraising drives, which in 2001 raised over $140,000 for the GVFB, highlights the role played by the media in socially constructing the issue of food poverty (or hunger as it is referred to in Canada) as a matter of charity and not politics. The CBC has been sponsoring such drives for 15 years and along with the commercial media has helped shape the public perception of food banks as acceptable and necessary social agencies. Whether this is a legitimate role for the country's public broadcasting agency is a matter of some concern in light of the fact that the problem of food poverty continues to increase at the same time as Canada's system of social security is being eroded and is failing to meet minimum international standards.

It is also increasingly evident that food banks have become "institutionalized at the level of individual household economies and community based projects" (Tarasuk and MacLean 1990). As Tarasuk points out, those seeking assistance do so repeatedly and are becoming dependent on food aid (*ibid.*). Food banks have also become an institutionalized part of Canada's system of income security programmes or public safety net. These include provincial and municipal social assistance programmes and the federally administered

Employment Insurance (formerly Unemployment Insurance). Indeed, it was argued over a decade ago that food banks have become an integrated and institutionalized second tier of Canada's social welfare system (Gandy and Greschner 1989; Tarasuk and Davis 1996). Government financial aid staff and social workers frequently refer their clients to food banks as the programmes of last resort. Social assistance benefits fall thousands of dollars below Canada's low income cut-offs (the unofficial but conventionally accepted poverty lines) and fail to meet the budgetary requirements for adequate and nutritious food, to say nothing of meeting rental and other household costs (NCW 1999, 2000). There is little doubt that the view expressed in 1986 that food banks "act as the voluntary back-up to a public safety net that has fallen apart" has been confirmed (Riches 1986).

Indeed, there is government support for this view. The governments of Alberta and Quebec, in responding to the UN Committee monitoring Canada's compliance with the provisions of the International Covenant on Economic, Social and Cultural Rights (UN 1998), stated that food banks made valuable contributions and provided an important means of resource distribution. The question to which they were responding asked if the government considered the need for food banks in so affluent a country as Canada to be consistent with article 11 of the Covenant. This article "recognises the right of everyone to an adequate standard of living for himself and his family including food, clothing and shelter" and "the fundamental right of everyone to be free from hunger" (UN 1998). Interestingly, more than half of Canada's provincial and territorial governments, including the federal government, chose not to respond to this question, suggesting ambivalence, if not embarrassment, at the nature of the question (*ibid.*).

There can be little doubt that food banks in Canada today enjoy broad government, business and media support and a high degree of public legitimacy. They have become key institutions in the newly resurrected residual welfare state with governments relying on them as charitable partners providing feeding programmes of last resort. They permit the state to neglect their obligation to protect vulnerable and powerless people. They encourage the view that food poverty is not a critical public policy issue. They allow the corporate food industry to be viewed as responsible community partners. However, the question then arises: what relationship is there, if any, between the role of food banks as agents of surplus food redistribution in the amelioration of food poverty, the promotion of adequate nutrition and the achievement of food security? These questions will be addressed from three perspectives: food bank usage, effectiveness and consumer perspectives.

Usage

Food banks in Canada provided assistance to 1.25 million people in 1989 and more than twice that number in 1997 (Theriault and Yadlowski 2000: 208). However, these figures may well include double counting, and more reliable data were not available until the CAFB commenced its annual hunger count survey in March 1997. The most recent survey reports that in 2001, 718,334 people living in Canada (2.4 per cent of the population) used a food bank in March of that year. Some 294,516 (41 per cent) of these food bank users were children and young people under the age of 18 years despite the fact that this age group includes 25 per cent of the Canadian population (Wilson and Tsoa 2001). The CAFB estimates that almost 60 per cent of households accessing food banks were families with children. As the report itself notes, it is important to realize that in 1989 an all-party resolution in the House of Commons committed itself to the eradication of child poverty in Canada by the year 2000. What these figures suggest is that women as mothers, and particularly single mothers, are significant users of food banks and that food poverty is as much a problem for families as it is for unemployed individuals.

The majority of people (65 per cent) using food banks received social assistance (income support/provincial "welfare"), though it is notable that 7 per cent were in receipt of some form of disability benefit, 6.7 per cent were seniors and 12 per cent were employed but members of the working poor (Wilson and Tsoa 2001). A socio-demographic study of food bank users in Montreal found that 41.6 per cent lived alone and that 83.5 per cent were receiving social assistance benefits. Interestingly, over a third were well-educated and had either completed technical school or had a college or university education (Starkey *et al.* 1998). This finding is reflected in the CAFB study that "an estimated 9.6 per cent of households accessing food banks were adult students" (Wilson and Tsoa 2001: 15). Indeed, a previous study had estimated that between 1 and 3 per cent of the total enrolled student university population used food banks (Theriault and Yadlowski 2000; see Westaway 1993: 29). Other recent studies have documented hunger among women and families (Tarasuk *et al.* 1998), schoolchildren (Campaign 2000 1999) and the elderly (Azad *et al.* 1999).

At the same time, given that Canada's poverty rate in 1998 was 16.8 per cent (NCW 2000) and that the National Population Health Survey reported 2.4 million Canadians experienced "compromised diets" (i.e. food insecurity) in 1998/9 (Che and Chen 2001) it is reasonable to assume that food banks are in fact underutilized.

People access food from food banks in a number of ways: either directly from the banks or their outlets (pantries, depots, churches) which involves standing in queues and receiving on average a 3–4 days' supply of groceries every month, or through meals provided in a variety of agencies such as soup kitchens, shelters and hostels, school meal programmes and community kitchens. Nor is access always assured. The CAFB March 2001 survey reported that nearly 40 per cent of food banks restrict food bank use employing a variety of rationing devices: closing early, turning people away and giving less. They also resort to additional fund raisers and community appeals and buying food (Che and Chen: 9). The bottom line is that food banks are supply-dependent and must frequently ration scarce supplies of donated foods.

Volume of food distributed

The volume of food distributed is one measure of the work of food banks, and provides one picture of their scale of operation and their potential effectiveness.

In 1999 Second Harvest, the largest food bank umbrella organization in the United States distributed 458 thousand tonnes (1,009 million pounds) of non-perishable processed food through 50,000+ agencies, to 26 million people (Hawkes and Webster 2000). Total food distributed including perishable and prepared food, perishable produce and agricultural surplus supplied by other agencies amounted to approximately 660 thousand tonnes. In the same year the European Federation of Food Banks (EFFB) distributed 116,000 tonnes of food products through 13,200 associations to 2.2 million beneficiaries (EFFB website, 2002). In the UK 3,195 tonnes of food (8 million meals on an annual basis) were redistributed by a variety of agencies including one food bank which contributed 20–27 tonnes of food (*ibid.*).

The amount of food collected and distributed by food banks in Canada has not been systematically recorded. However, it is clear from CAFB reports and that of the Greater Vancouver Food Bank that the amounts are far from insignificant. In terms of volume the CAFB and its members expected to distribute over 45,248 tonnes of food (100 million pounds) in the twelve months from April 2002 (CAFB website, 24 April 2002). In 1997, it reported that the National Food Sharing System, endorsed by the Food and Consumer Products Manufacturers of Canada and representing more than 170 companies with national brand products, distributed 6 million pounds (2,715 tonnes) of non-perishable food across the country. To place this in a local perspective the Greater Vancouver Food Bank distributes 5 million pounds (2,262 tonnes) of food annually. It reports providing 45 tonnes (100,000 pounds) of food to 25,000 individuals each week. On an individual basis, this translates into 4 pounds of food per person or a little over half a pound of food per day, though this says little about the nutritional benefits of such foods. Some 9,000 people, of whom a third are children, receive the food in the form of hampers and 16,000 individuals (a 45 per cent increase compared to 2001) access this food through meals provided by a variety of social agencies (GVFB website).

In March 2001, 91 food banks reported serving a total of 1.9 million meals across Canada. However, this was considered an underestimate as research assistance to track the meal usage was not available and in the previous March 2.7 million meals were reported served. As the CAFB points out, "these figures reflect a fraction of the meal programmes in Canada" (Wilson and Tsoa 2001). In 2000 the GVFB reported serving 250,000 meals on a monthly basis or 970,000 pounds (438 tonnes) of food to thousands of people living in Downtown Eastside, Vancouver's and indeed Canada's most impoverished community (GVFB website).

Effectiveness

Despite the significant, some might argue overwhelming, numbers of people receiving emergency foods, and the massive volume being distributed, what evidence is there that food banks are effective? Many food banks would rightly claim that their purpose is not to solve the problem of food poverty in Canada, but rather to provide emergency relief. Their function is ameliorative and should be judged in that light. At the same time it has been argued that food banks can fulfil important health prevention functions, a role which it is suggested has been "completely unrecognised by public health authorities" (Theriault and Yadlowski 2000). "Food banks", it is asserted, "can play an important role in feeding the poor. In the case of indigent children, the food bank intervention can be crucial in promoting healthy development; indeed, it may well contribute to reducing occurrences of costly, chronic health problems" (*ibid.*). Yet it is difficult to make the case that food banks are an appropriate response to food poverty or that their ameliorative functions or contributions to nutritional well-being are meeting with success.

As noted earlier, findings from the National Population Health Survey (1998/9) revealed that 2.4 million Canadians (8.4 per cent) of the population had to compromise their diets because of lack of money. In other words they were unable to obtain the variety or quantity of food they wanted and/or they did not have enough food to eat (Che and Chen 2001: 13). The study reported that "about 20% of economically disadvantaged people use food banks" (Campbell and Desjardins 1989; Badun *et al.* 1995, cited in Che and Chen 2001). The NPH survey also "found that 22% of respondents in food insecure households had sought help from food banks, soup kitchens or other charitable agencies in the past year (19% reported occasional use; 3% used food assistance often)." The majority using food banks reported receiving food mainly towards the end of the month (Che and Chen 2001: 19).

Furthermore, a recent study assessing the food insecurity and nutritional vulnerability of a sample of 153 women of families using food banks in Toronto in 1998 found that "seventy percent of the women reported some level of absolute deprivation, despite using food banks" (Tarasuk and Beaton 1999). The authors draw the inescapable conclusion that "while charitable food assistance may have alleviated *some* of the absolute food deprivation in the households studied, it clearly did not *prevent* members from going hungry" (*ibid.*: 112). In light of the accumulated evidence that food banks have become the institutionalized and poor cousin of an increasingly enfeebled welfare system which itself is unable to address people's basic food needs (Vozoris *et al.* 2002; DC/CNC-BC 2001), it is highly unlikely that charity alone can adequately feed the hundreds of thousands of hungry Canadians, let alone address their nutritional well-being in other than *ad hoc* and socially unacceptable ways.

In assessing the effectiveness of food banks it is important also to consider consumer perspectives. Based on the little that has been recorded on this subject in Canada it is fair to say there are divergent views. Swanson has rightly pointed out that "the Code of Ethics of the Canadian Association of Food Banks states that everyone has 'the right to their daily sustenance' and pledges that members will organize activities to 'bring about the greatest degree of personal dignity possible.' The Code also states that members should ensure that they do not 'reduce the impetus of improvements to government social assistance programs' and that they will bring the 'greatest attention possible to the problems of hunger and of food surplus'" (Swanson 2001: 144). Some food banks, as Swanson herself writes, live up to these commitments, treating people with respect and campaigning on social justice issues.

The Daily Bread Food Bank in Toronto is a good example of this. It is the largest food bank in Ontario and is continually to the fore working to build a strong food security movement and campaigning, in the face of federal and provincial cutbacks, for adequate social assistance benefits, affordable rents, social (public) housing and national child care programs. A review of as yet unpublished data from a recent survey of Daily Bread Food Bank users (2001) suggests that many food bank recipients are highly appreciative of the service provided and of the attitudes of the staff. Some do, however, have criticisms of the food they receive—it is not sufficient, lacks variety, is not the most nutritious food and so on. Indeed, the key criticisms are directed at the government in terms of inadequate social assistance housing and the public lack of support.

Yet, an earlier 1991 study of food bank users' attitudes towards being on the receiving end of charity suggests that not all food banks are as highly regarded as Daily Bread. The study, conducted by End Legislated Poverty, a Vancouver-based anti-poverty organization, interviewed food bank recipients about their attitudes to a US-organized charity event in the city which raised $70,000 "to take the left-overs from the tables of the rich to feed the poor" (Hobbs et al. 1993: 94). Questions were also asked about how people got treated at food banks, about food quality and quantity and what it was like to wait for handouts. Typical responses were statements such as: "You know there's a lot of hostility here. They demean you, they yell at you, they treat you like children, and they have this attitude, you know, that they are better than you because they're volunteering", or "There should be a variety of foods because this is a multicultural centre", or "The food here is nothing special . . . well, damn awful actually", and "It's degrading to make people stand in line-ups to beg for food" (1993: 98–100). Swanson's conclusion about such attitudes and behaviours seems incontestable: they amount to poor-bashing (Swanson 2001: 140).

At the same time there is also evidence to suggest that food bank users have come to accept charitable food assistance as a necessary part of their food coping and provisioning strategies (Tarasuk and Beaton 1999) and as an accepted community resource (Starkey et al. 1998). This is despite the fact that, as Tarasuk notes in her survey, "the vast majority (84%) of women described feeling shame, embarrassment, degradation and humiliation at this first visit" to a food bank (Tarasuk and Beaton 1999).

Perhaps there are two conclusions to be drawn from these studies about the effectiveness of Canadian food banks. Whatever the degree to which some food banks are appreciated by those who use them, there is little evidence on the basis of the foods already received that they ameliorate food poverty, prevent hunger or contribute to nutritional well-being. The structural causes of food poverty are not addressed by surplus food redistribution. At the same time, however much food banks enable governments to offload their welfare responsibilities, it is critical that food banks themselves should not be held responsible for statutory neglect. The documented evidence of 20 years of food poverty and food banking in Canada points rather to the massive failure of welfare reform policies and the abandonment by the federal and provincial governments of their international obligations to respect, protect and fulfil the human right to food (Riches 1997; see also Dowler *et al.* 2001).

Welfare Reform and the Commodification of Social Assistance

The rise of food banks in Canada during a period of increasing economic growth, labour market restructuring and widening income inequality (Kitchen 1995: 266; Pulkingham and Ternowetsky 1996: 4) prompts policy questions which move the debate about their effectiveness beyond questions of surplus food redistribution and the role of charity. The fact is that Canada along with many OECD countries has in the two decades since 1981 engineered a profound shift in federal and provincial social policy towards market-driven, neo-liberal concepts of social welfare. There has been a retreat from the welfare state and the modest social rights established in the period 1966–73 towards a welfare environment marked by the re-commodification of social benefits and the collapse of entitlements (Lightman and Riches 2000). The influence of US-style welfare reform has become marked in terms of a return to residualism, privatization and charitable or faith-based responses to the meeting of basic human needs.

The growth of food banks in the early 1980s was the warning sign of what was in store. They provided concrete evidence of the breakdown of Canada's social safety net, particularly the federal unemployment insurance programme and provincial social assistance (Riches 1986). In the 1990s the newly elected Liberal federal government, committed to the elimination of a significant fiscal deficit and a private sector-led recovery based on a free trade agenda with the United States, embarked on a programme of social security reform. This entailed reducing unemployment benefits, introducing stringent eligibility criteria and renaming the programme Employment Insurance. This reflected the new market mantra that social security was no longer a "passive" programme of entitlements and benefits but an "active" set of policies placing responsibility on beneficiaries to move back, or be moved, into the labour force.

The federal government also sought to limit its financial support to provincial social assistance programmes and in 1996 scrapped the 30-year-old Canada Assistance Plan (CAP). Since its introduction in 1966 CAP had provided federal cost-shared dollars to the provinces and territories on the condition that they provide assistance to all people judged to be in need (in other words they could not be required to work in order to obtain assistance); that they establish appeal tribunals; and that claimants from out of province were not debarred from receiving social assistance (NCW 1995). Under the new block funding formula of the Canada Health and Social Transfer, introduced in 1996, the provinces are no longer required to provide assistance on the basis of need and the right of appeal no longer stands. While the provinces still receive transfer payments for social assistance they are now free to allocate such funding as they see fit between health care, post-secondary education and social welfare. As a consequence, a welfare reform agenda of work-fare and learn-fare has been introduced, most noticeably by neo-conservative administrations in Alberta, Ontario and British Columbia.

Welfare reform has successfully undermined the idea of universality and collective social rights. Key features of the new reforms include the privatization of welfare administration, increasingly stringent eligibility criteria, the reduction of already inadequate benefits, requirements regarding work, job searches and training programmes and, most recently, in British Columbia, the lifetime denial of benefits to anyone convicted of welfare fraud and the restriction that claimants are only permitted to receive benefits for two years out of five. So much for the human right to food.

Welfare reform has resulted in the re-commodification of social assistance based on the Poor Law principle of less eligibility and the idea that the only legitimate claim to such benefits is when the claimant has an established commitment or relationship to the labour market. In other words, people's entitlements to income support, and thereby to food security, are directly related to their capacity to sell their labour power as a commodity in the market place. As Esping-Andersen has pointed out, this means that "people's rights to survive outside the market are at stake" (Esping-Andersen 1990: 35). The commodification of welfare rejects the notion that the state has a legitimate role in addressing basic human needs including the right to food and to be free from hunger. In Canada, the scrapping of CAP has set the social policy clock back a generation to residual times. It also represents state endorsement of the public legitimacy of charitable food banks as the programmes of last resort in the fight against food poverty. However, if, as the evidence suggests, the issues presented by food poverty are beyond the resources and good will of the food banks it is important to consider an alternative agenda. While food banks themselves may not have solved the problem of either food poverty or food security in Canada they may have a role to play in advancing a political response.

Food Security and the Human Right to Food

Food and food poverty are political questions (Robertson et al. 1999) and as Dowler et al. (2001) have argued "solutions to food poverty go beyond welfare transfers or health services to include issues of basic human rights, sustainable development, health inequalities and social inclusion". As a question for social policy food security is about the courses of action and social arrangements whereby society provides for the individual and/or collective welfare of its peoples (Titmuss 1974; Jones 1985). Food as a human right is clearly an important way of reframing the debate about food poverty and suggests an agenda for action which goes beyond the welfare/human capital responses which Dowler has discussed in relation to the United Kingdom (Dowler et al. 2001).

From a human rights perspective there is in Canada a certain irony to the question of what to do about food poverty and food security. While the human right to food lacks constitutional entrenchment in Canada in that neither the Canadian Bill of Rights (1960) nor the Canadian Charter of Rights and Freedoms (1982) contains explicit language setting out the human right to food (Robertson 1990: 195), Canada, along with the majority of the

world's nations but excluding the United States, has historically acknowledged this right. As long ago as 1976 the federal government, supported
by the provinces, ratified the International Covenant on Economic, Social
and Cultural Rights thereby committing itself in international law to
respect, protect and fulfil the human right to food. It has also since that
time ratified the International Convention of the Rights of the Child (1992)
and signed the World Declaration on Nutrition (Rome, 1992), the recent
World Declaration on Social Development (Copenhagen, 1995) and the
Declaration on World Food Security (Rome, 1996). It has also, in conjunction with community partners, introduced Canada's Action Plan for Food
Security (1998) setting out agendas for both domestic and international
action. It also committed itself to full participation at the World Food
Summit held in Rome in June 2002. The problem has been that "the treaties
to which Canada is a party are not self-executing. Their incorporation into
domestic law is dependent on implementing legislation" (Robertson 1990:
205).

Despite this lack of implementation, the human right to food would
appear to have legs both in terms of public education and political advocacy.
Human rights have become a well-articulated discourse and a significant
challenge to transnational corporate power in and between countries of the
North and South. Food security itself is central to global debates about
poverty, environmental sustainability, social justice and democracy itself.
Who is controlling the world's food production and supply is a critical question now receiving significant international attention. Within Canada the
human right to food and its application to issues of food poverty is now on
the agenda of an emerging Canadian food security movement and is being
addressed in academic courses, food policy councils, community nutrition
organizations, municipal community-based food security networks as well as
by the Canadian Association of Food Banks. There is as well a growing
public awareness that food issues are political questions providing an opportunity to explore the interconnectedness of issues of poverty, health and
nutrition, the environment (agriculture and fisheries) and social justice. The
proclamation of the Toronto Food Charter in June 2001 is one example of
how the public debate about food security is being reframed and advanced
at the municipal level.

In conclusion, it is clear that the evidence of two decades of food banking in Canada confirms it as an inadequate response to food poverty
while allowing governments to look the other way and neglect hunger
and nutritional health. Food banks are confirmation of the re-emergence
of the residual welfare state and sit at the interface between critical questions of public health, welfare reform and social policy. While they have
in some measure played a role in raising community awareness of food
insecurity, it remains to be seen whether they will become a part of the
solution to food poverty. This will only occur if they use their public legitimacy to critique the new welfare residualism and advocate a rights-based
approach to the achievement of food security for all. Given their institutionalization as part of Canada's system of social welfare, this is an unlikely
prospect.

Graham Riches

References

Azad, N., Murphy, J., Amos, S. and Toppan, J. (1999), Nutrition survey in an elderly population following admission to a tertiary care hospital, *Canadian Medical Association Journal*, 116, 5, 7 September: 511–15.

Badun, C., Evers, S. and Hooper, M. (1995), Food security and nutritional concerns of parents in an economically disadvantgaed community, *Journal of the Canadian Dietetic Association*, 56, 2: 75–80.

CAFB (2002), website http://www.icomm.ca/cafb/about.html

Campaign 2000 (1999), *Ontario Report Card 2000*, Toronto: Family Service Association.

Campbell, C. C. and Desjardins, E. (1989), A model and research approach for studying the management of limited food resources by low income families, *Journal of Nutrition Education*, 21: 162–71.

Canada (1998), *Canada's Action Plan for Food Security: A Response to the World Food Summit*, Agriculture and Agri-Food, Ottawa, Canada.

Che, J. and Chen, J. (2001), Food insecurity in Canadian households, *Health Reports*, Statistics Canada vol. 12, no. 4, 11–22 (Catalogue 82-003-XPE).

DBFB (1999), *Still Hungry for Change: Fifteen Years of Daily Bread*, Report of the Daily Bread Food Bank, Toronto, Ontario, 18 February: 53.

DC/CNC-BC (2001), *The Cost of Eating in BC—The Challenge of Healthy Eating on a Low Income*, Report by the Dieticians of Canada and the Community Nutritionists Council of BC, October.

Dowler, E., Turner, S. and Dobson, S. (2001), *Poverty Bites: Food, Health and Poor Families*, London: Child Poverty Action Group (CPAG).

EFFB (2002), website: www.eurofoodbank.org/eng/lcl.htm

Esping-Andersen, G. (1990), *The Three Worlds of Welfare Capitalism*, Cambridge: Polity Press.

Gandy, J. and Greschner, S. (1989), *Food Distribution Organizations in Metropolitan Toronto: A Secondary Welfare System?* Working Papers in Social Welfare in Canada, University of Toronto, Faculty of Social Work.

GVFB website: http:www.foodbank.bc.ca/

Hawkes, C. and Webster, J. (2000), *Too Much and Too Little? Debates of Surplus Food Redistribution*, London: SUSTAIN, The Alliance for Better Food and Farming.

Hobbs, K., MacEachern, W., McIvor, A. and Turner, S. (1993), Waste of a nation: poor people speak out about charity, *Canadian Review of Social Policy/Revue canadienne de politique sociale*, Spring, 31: 94–104.

Jones, C. (1985), *Patterns of Social Policy*, London: Tavistock.

Kitchen, B. (1995), Declining living standards in a changing economy. In J. C. Turner and F. J. Turner, *Canadian Social Welfare*, Scarborough: Allyn and Bacon, ch. 15.

Lightman, E. and Riches, G. (2000), From modest rights to commodification in Canada's welfare state, *European Journal of Social Work*, 3, 2: 179–90.

Lightman, E. and Riches, G. (2001), Canada: one step forward, two steps back? In P. Alcock and G. Craig (eds), *International Social Policy*, London: Palgrave, ch. 3.

NCW (1999), *Poverty Profile 1997*, National Council of Welfare Reports, Ottawa: Minister of Public Works and Government Services.

NCW (2000), *Poverty Profile 1998*, National Council of Welfare Reports, Ottawa: Minister of Public Works and Government Services.

Poppendieck, J. (1998), *Sweet Charity? Emergency Food and the End of Entitlement*, New York: Viking.

Pulkingham, J. and Ternowetsky, G. (1996), The changing landscape of social policy and the Canadian welfare state. In J. Pulkingham and G. Ternowetsky (eds), *Remaking Canadian Social Policy*, Halifax: Fernwood, ch. 1.

Radimer, K. L., Olson, C. M., Greene, J. C., Campbell, C. C. and Habicht, J. P. (1992), Understanding hunger and developing indicators to assess it in women and children, *Journal of Nutrition Education*, 24: 363–455.

Riches, G. (1986), *Food Banks and the Welfare Crisis*, Ottawa: Canadian Council on Social Development.

Riches, G. (1997), *First World Hunger: Food Security and Welfare Politics*, London: Macmillan/New York: St Martins.

Riches, G. (1999), Advancing the human right to food in Canada: social policy and the politics of hunger, welfare and food security, *Agriculture and Human Values*, 16: 203–11.

Robertson, A., Brunner, E. and Sheiham, A. (1999), Food is a political issue. In M. Marmot and R. G. Wilkinson (eds), *Social Determinants of Health*, Oxford: Oxford University Press.

Robertson, R. E. (1990), The right to food—Canada's broken covenant, *Canadian Human Rights Year Book* 1989–90: 6.

Starkey, L. J., Kuhnlein, H. V. and Gray-Donald, K. (1998), Food bank users: sociodemographic and nutritional characteristics, *Canadian Medical Association Journal*, 158, 9: 1143–9.

Swanson, J. (2001), *Poor-bashing: The Politics of Exclusion*, Toronto: Between the Lines Press.

Tarasuk, V. S. and Beaton, G. H. (1999), Household food insecurity and hunger among families using food banks, *Canadian Journal of Public Health*, 90, 2: 109–13.

Tarasuk, V. S. and Davis, B. (1996), Responses to food insecurity in the changing Canadian welfare state, *Journal of Nutrition Education*, 28, 2: 71–5.

Tarasuk, V. S. and MacLean, H. (1990), The institutionalization of food banks in Canada: a public health concern, *Canadian Journal of Public Health*, 81, July/August: 331–2.

Tarasuk, V. S., Beaton, G., Geduld, J. and Hilditch, S. (1998), *Nutritional Vulnerability and Food Security among Women in Families using Food Banks*, Toronto: Department of Nutritional Sciences, Faculty of Medicine, University of Toronto.

Theriault, L. and Yadlowski, L. (2000), Revisiting the food bank issues in Canada, *Canadian Social Work Review*, 17, 2: 205–23.

Titmuss, R. M. (1974), *Social Policy: An Introduction*, London: Allen and Unwin.

UN (1998), Responses to the written questions from the Committee on Economic, Social and Cultural Rights Review of Canada's Third Report on the International Covenant on Economic, Social and Cultural Rights, Chapter Committee on Poverty Issues, United Nations E/C. 12/Q/CAN1.

Westaway, N. (1993), Food for thought: starving student no longer a cliché, *Campus Canada*, November/December: 29–31.

Wilson, B., with Tsoa, E. (2001), *HungerCount 2001: Food Bank Lines in Insecure Times*, Canada's Annual Survey of Emergency Food Programs, Canadian Association of Food Banks, Toronto.

Vozoris, N., Davis, B. and Tarasuk, V. (2002), The affordability of a nutritious diet for households on welfare in Toronto, *Canadian Journal of Public Health*, 93, 1: 36–40.

7

Food Aid in Complex Emergencies: Lessons from Sudan

Elizabeth Ojaba, Anne Itto Leonardo and Margaret Itto Leonardo

Introduction

This paper reviews the nature of "complex emergencies", and briefly examines the motives for humanitarian aid responses in such conditions. It is written out of the authors' experiences of living and working in Sudan and for aid agencies working in Sudan and in other countries experiencing complex emergencies. In particular, it draws on the current programme known as "Operation Lifeline Sudan" (OLS) as a case study to examine:

- how food aid is used in "complex emergencies" as part of a general aid package;
- how such usage contributes to development as "emergencies" turn into "chronic situations".

The overall objective is to share experiences and lessons learned.

Sudan has been in a state of war for nearly 40 years, with devastating effects on the civilian population, particularly in South Sudan. Since 1983, over 2 million people have died from the effects of the war; 5 million have been displaced internally; about 500,000 have sought refuge in neighbouring countries, and thousands more have fled to almost every country on the globe (Burr and Collins 1995). Years of drought, flood, famine and underdevelopment have led to economic and social crises of enormous proportions across southern Sudan, aggravating people's vulnerability to disease, malnutrition and psychosocial traumas. Women have been especially and specifically vulnerable because of the traumas of rape and physical violence, excessive workload and increased responsibilities with men away fighting, guilt and the loss of self-esteem which comes from their actual or perceived inability to care for their families. This human suffering has attracted the attention of the United Nations (UN), together with international and national non-governmental organizations (NGOs), to provide humanitarian assistance to the people affected in South Sudan. The current ongoing assistance programme, dubbed Operation Lifeline Sudan, has been running since 1989, following a UN-negotiated agreement between the government of

Sudan (GOS) and the Sudan People's Liberation Army-Movement (SPLA-M) to allow humanitarian aid to reach civilians on either side.

Overview of Food Aid in the Context of International Emergencies

Complex emergencies

"Complex emergencies" or "complex political emergencies" are phenomena characterized by a multiplicity of causes, such as civil wars and ethnic conflicts, famine, population displacement, disputed sovereignty, and the breakdown of national government (Commack 1998; Commins 1996). The term was coined by the UN to describe the major crises which have proliferated since 1989 and which have required a "system-wide" response, i.e. a combination of military, peacekeeping, and relief interventions, together with high-level diplomacy. The complexity refers both to the multi-causal nature of the emergency and the "multi-mandate" nature of the response. It also involves recognition of the fact that major crises are necessarily political and economic in their causes and consequences, not just humanitarian.

Complex emergencies destroy political, economic, social and environmental systems to an extent more devastating than in the case of other "mere" emergencies. Complex emergencies are also more horrific because they involve:

- use of civilians as targets—bombing civilians, raping women, displacing whole populations;
- destruction of social networks—burning homes and displacing people, fragmenting communities, massacring people through organized militias;
- creation of economic chaos—starvation and famine, disruption of markets and trade, massive accumulation of wealth by the powerful at the expense of the poor;
- total failure of the state—weakened government structure, collapse of public/social services, absence of law and order;
- manipulation of relief goods—control of relief aid by protagonists for their own benefit;
- political upheavals—ideological brainwashing or political incitements, the arming or empowering of some segments of society to "rise up" against existing structures;
- psychosocial traumas—conflict-related death and disabilities, a sense of powerlessness;
- environmental destruction—burning of villages, forests or wildlife.

(Lautze 1997)

Given the nature of such assaults, self-sufficiency becomes a critical survival strategy for most people caught up in complex emergencies. Innovative approaches to providing relief and recovery assistance are essential in such situations, and need to address both life-saving, medium- and long-term development needs. Lautze (1997) outlined options for response, ranging from no intervention because conditions for operations would be unattainable, through rapid distribution of free relief supplies for urgent life-saving, to strategic forms of intervention for livelihood regeneration in the medium or long term. The distribution of free seeds to ensure a crop within a few months would be a common example of the former; restocking livestock and appropriate market support would be examples of the latter. Responses should ideally support people's own capacity and desires for self-sufficiency.

Humanitarian aid

Humanitarian intervention originally implied military intervention to prevent widespread suffering or death among a country's inhabitants (Folleras 1998). The term is now used of humanitarian efforts to intervene in emergency situations, not necessarily involving the use of armed forces or with the support of the governments concerned (Roberts 1996). Such efforts are guided by the Geneva Conventions, codes of conduct from NGOs and multi-agency guidelines, which humanitarian workers try to follow. The Geneva Conventions of 1949 and additional Protocols of 1977, state that "governments are obliged to allow the free passage of medical supplies, religious items and other essentials to children, pregnant women, and nursing mothers and must avoid the use of starvation of civilians as a method of combat" (Minear and Weiss 1993). In 1994, the International Red Cross and Crescent Movement, together with other NGOs, outlined a Code of Conduct for Disaster Relief, based on 10 principles, geared to the alleviation of human suffering, the protection of life and health, and the assurance of respect for all human beings. This has been sanctioned by the International Court of Justice, which warned that such principles "must be limited to the purpose indicated in the code of practice for the International Red Cross" and "must be given without discrimination to all in need". In short, humanitarian assistance, as currently understood, is to be implemented in ways which emphasize "provision of basic requirements, that meet people's needs for water, sanitation, nutrition, food, shelter, and health care, including the rights to expect minimum gender-sensitive standards in humanitarian aid" (Sphere Project 1998: 131–2).

However, humanitarian organizations have different conceptual approaches to complex emergencies. Some emphasize traditional, humanitarian values, focusing on provision to meet immediate needs. Others stress developmental objectives and, in addition to addressing the conflict itself as the cause of the crisis, work to enable people to resume production, to learn new skills, to "develop" and move out of the passive receipt of relief goods, even in the midst of conflict-induced upheaval. Finally, increased awareness of the politicization of aid, and the contested distinctions between "relief" and "development", has led some agencies to bypass national governments and operate largely outside the public domain or formal sectors, and instead channel aid through NGOs. Whether or not funding NGOs is an appropriate means of ensuring the delivery of relief in ways which meet the objectives of donor governments has itself been questioned, in terms of its potential detrimental impact on local capacity-building or more structural developments (Goodhand and Chamberlain 1996). Delivering development aid by supporting a national institution, particularly a civil institution, makes practical sense, although the choice of which institutions to support is rarely straightforward, given the complex economic and political context and sensitivities of most situations.

Motives for giving aid

Official motives. Food aid is one of the mechanisms designed for responding to both natural disasters and complex emergencies in order to save lives, as well as to reactivate production and marketing systems to optimize food security and self-sufficiency. Indeed, one key rationale for giving food aid is that it allows the beneficiaries to keep their livestock, production tools and seed, rather than selling these assets to buy food. This prevents further impoverishment of the affected people, and facilitates their recovery to resume their normal activities after the crisis has abated (Thirion and Grunewald 1999).

Actual motives. Motives for giving aid are not always altruistic in practice. They arguably date back to the cold war era and were directly related to the need to form solidarity and have "friends" in the so-called developing world, since social tensions in these countries could result in their movement towards one or the other of the superpowers. It was believed that, through the injection of capital into traditional societies, economic growth would automatically result, as well as changes in popular perception and social inequality, thus creating a modern society. Unfortunately, despite the injection of large amounts of capital into the economies of specific countries over the last 20 to 30 years, most remain at the level of traditional societies. By and large, international humanitarian responses to complex emergencies continue to be dogged by claims of false neutrality, and claims that agencies deny the reality of aid being increasingly politicized. Too often, it is asserted, the warring parties have manipulated humanitarian aid for their own strategic and propaganda purposes (Folleras 1998) rather than for the good causes they were supposed to help.

So why, then, do rich, industrialized countries still continue to give humanitarian aid at all to those in the developing world? Plausible answers from the literature and observation are as follows:

- *A fear of bad media publicity*: a predominant motive for giving aid in humanitarian crisis (Folleras 1998).
- *Northern governments' accommodation with violence*: characterized by a continued trickle of humanitarian assistance in lieu of development aid (Duffield 1994).
- *Moral hesitation*: preventing donors from cutting aid altogether, even when they are trying to attach conditions to development aid (Folleras 1998).
- *Post-cold war developments in humanitarian considerations*: making it more difficult to cut aid on the grounds of political necessity; in particular the need for "transparency" has increasingly become the everyday jargon of

Elizabeth Ojaba, Anne Itto Leonardo and Margaret Itto Leonardo

relief, and failure to be "aid-transparent" would attract wide publicity which most governments would rather avoid (Folleras 1998).

- *The humanitarian imperative*: has progressively become so strong that the threat to withdraw is not always realistic, and therefore not useful (Folleras 1998).
- *Solidarity approach*: the policy which supports siding with those in a conflict who are deemed to be fighting a just struggle against oppression, or who constitute an authentic liberation movement for freedom and the realization of human dignity. This, for instance, was the basis of support for the SPLA-M by Kenya, the only African country to play a major role in relief assistance to South Sudan (Kenya viewed the SPLA-M as allies needing assistance from black African states against Arab and Muslim adversaries —Minear 1991).
- *Strategic monitoring*: based on the belief that the mere presence of international aid workers allows for a continuous watch to be kept over civilian needs and well-being, as well as over military activities (Folleras 1998).

Motives for receiving aid

Just as there are many reasons for giving aid in a civil war, there are many for receiving it. The most obvious is the resulting reduction in a government's need to cater for the humanitarian needs of its own people. When NGOs and other aid agencies take responsibility for an area, warring parties are essentially free to direct their resources towards the costs of fighting. For example, in Mozambique, over 60 per cent of the government's budget came from foreign aid, 40 per cent of which was used for military purposes (Folleras 1998). In Sudan, where the war was costing the state US$1 m per day in 1990, relief operations paid a civil war surcharge for virtually all expenditures. Relief food replaced home-grown sorghum, which the government was instead able to export, to obtain the foreign currency desperately needed to fund the war (Afif 1994; Minear 1991).

The Role of Food Aid in a Complex Emergency: The Case of Sudan

Political, economic and socio-cultural context

Sudan, covering some 2.5×10^6 km^2 in area, is the largest country in Africa and potentially one of the richest. The country gained independence from Great Britain in 1956, since when it has been in political turmoil, conflict and civil war. A combination of factors relating to the country's religious, racial, cultural, political and economic make-up, contribute to this situation. Tensions along ethnic, tribal and religious lines have been exacerbated by claims of differential shares of government and international aid, and benefits from the development of natural resources.

For instance, the population of North Sudan is largely Muslim, with many identifying themselves as Arabs, and the population of South Sudan is largely black and practises Christianity and traditional African religions. However, in some parts of the country, Arabs and Africans are neighbours and have intermarried, and in towns throughout the country, Arabs and Africans live as close neighbours and may be friends. Nevertheless, within North and South Sudan alike, there are widely diverse ethnic and tribal groupings with different lifestyles and political allegiances. In recent years, religious and racial differences have become more sharply drawn, not least because of increasingly assertive Muslim fundamentalism which has made the imposition of Islamic laws a "national" crusade (Minear 1991). Conflict and civil wars have heightened tribal tension in the south—a weakness exploited by the GOS to foster political differences along tribal lines.

The conflicts have an important economic dimension in that, despite having more arable land and natural resources than northern regions, the south has received less of the government's annual budget allocations, international aid and commercial investments. Externally financed projects to develop Southern oil and water resources have triggered conflicts and memories of exploitation, leading to violence and civil war.

The first civil war (1955–72) ended with peace accords signed in Addis Ababa, Ethiopia, which promised the south more economic and political autonomy within a loosely federated Sudan. But barely 10 years on, in 1983, the second and currently ongoing civil war erupted when various provisions of the 1972 Addis Ababa agreement were abrogated. (A major grievance at the time was the decision by the GOS to impose sharia laws on the non-Muslim south.) As part of its strategy of containing the rebellion in the south, the GOS armed tribal militias, who turned against civilians suspected of loyalty to the SPLA-M. The SPLA-M in turn, heightened its attacks on the government-held garrison towns, to apply pressure on the central authority in Khartoum. Such policies disrupted normal agricultural and economic life, forcing people to migrate away from villages and roads into towns—or out of the south altogether.

The Operation Lifeline Sudan (OLS): an example of humanitarian aid

The early attempts. In early 1986, the Sudan Council of Churches (SCC), an ecumenical grouping of the country's Protestant and Catholic churches, and Sudanaid, the relief and development arm of the Sudan Bishops' Conference, alerted international aid agencies to the existence of food shortages in the south and to the war's interference in the regional recovery from the drought of 1984–6. They estimated that 30 per cent of the population had already been displaced. Their advocacy, together with support from Oxfam-UK, UNICEF and donor governments, led the GOS to set up a committee to monitor the situation (Minear 1991). In 1986, SCC and Sudanaid, supported by local church leaders, negotiated a safe passage agreement with local government authorities and SPLA-M commanders for the transport of relief supplies, including food, into a region that had had no access to food for two years. In the same year, a similar effort, to provide food relief to the Equatoria region from neighbouring Kenya, failed because SPLA-M would not agree to let food pass through their territories to the government-controlled town of Juba, so long as the GOS would give no assurances that its troops,

Elizabeth Ojaba, Anne Itto Leonardo and Margaret Itto Leonardo

Map 1

The Republic of Sudan

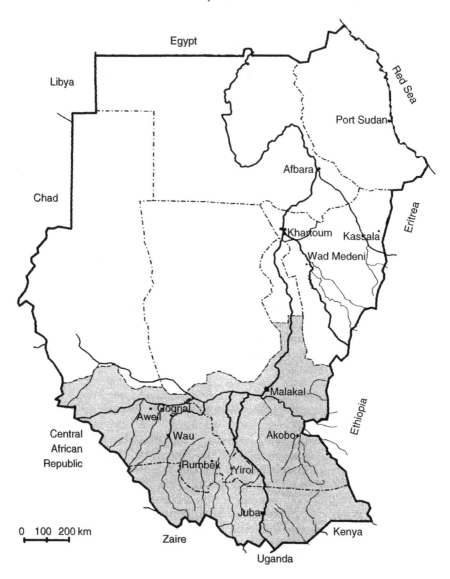

Note: The shaded area represents South Sudan.

in turn, would not attack convoys of food bound for SPLA-M areas. In 1986 again, SCC and Sudanaid, in collaboration with World Vision International, managed to negotiate a delivery of 2,000 metric tonnes of food and non-food items for the beleaguered civilians of Wau in the Bahar el Ghazal region (see map 1). The success of the latter operation encouraged NGOs to establish a system in western Equatoria that would allow them to supply Wau with food flown in from neighbouring Zaire. The following year, 1987, saw another successful negotiation with GOS and SPLA-M, this time for a vaccination programme for over 50,000 head of cattle.

The first major UN initiative for humanitarian assistance in the south came with "Operation Rainbow" in 1986. Supported by 11 donor governments, the effort to supply civilians on both sides was spearheaded by the Sudan Representative of the UN Secretary-General, and managed by the World Food Programme (WFP). The operation encountered problems from both parties to the conflict—neither of which acknowledged the scale of the need nor was willing for relief to go to the other side. For instance, the SPLA-M threatened to shoot down any relief planes bound for the government-held towns of Juba, Wau and Malakal which it had not previously cleared for flight passage. The government offered no guarantees of safety either (Minear 1991). Thus the international effort failed where local effort had succeeded.

The second UN attempt came in 1989, following an agreement negotiated by the UN with the GOS and the SPLA-M to allow humanitarian assistance to pass through specifed "corridors of tranquillity" (as they were labelled), to reach civilians on either side of the conflict. OLS was launched to address the needs of people living with conflict, and was the first UN relief effort ever to operate cross-border in a war zone with the full agreement of both the sovereign government and the other parties to the conflict. In fact, it was also set up shortly after a devastating famine in 1988, during which some 250,000–300,000 people in southern Sudan had died (UNICEF-OLS 1994). OLS functions on the basis of two sectors: a northern sector, operating from Khartoum, and a southern sector, operating from Lokichoggio in Kenya. By 2001, the southern sector comprised a consortium of over 30 organizations (as compared with fewer than 10 in 1989), working closely with the humanitarian wings of the two main southern insurgent armies.

OLS aims and objectives. OLS's primary aim is to help the people of southern Sudan during the current conflict, through measures to support their survival, protection and development. Much of the programme focus is of necessity on emergency food, medicine and shelter. However, although the general objective is to bring relief and rehabilitation to civilians caught up in the war and famines, OLS agencies have also sought to provide assistance in a way which would enhance people's food security and self-reliance, and would protect the rights of war-affected civilians, particularly children and women (UNICEF-OLS 1994; Commack 1998).

In short, OLS aims to save lives, promote self-reliance, protect people's safety and dignity, and enable people to invest in their future. The agencies within OLS operate under codes of conduct based on international guidelines (Commack 1998):

- The humanitarian imperative has priority.
- Aid is given regardless of race, creed or nationality and without adverse distinction of any kind, and priorities are based on need alone.
- Aid is not used to further a particular political or religious standpoint.

- OLS will endeavour not to act as an instrument of government foreign policy.
- OLS will respect culture and customs.
- OLS will attempt to build disaster response on local capabilities.
- Ways will be found to involve beneficiaries in the management of relief aid.
- Relief aid will be used to reduce future vulnerabilities to disaster and to meet basic needs.
- OLS is accountable both to those it seeks to assist and to those from whom it accepts resources.
- OLS information campaigns will recognize disaster victims as dignified human beings and not as objects of pity.

Programme components. OLS was set up to respond to a complex emergency where the population had been affected for a long period of time by a combination of drought, flood, civil war, clan raiding and banditry, economic collapse, displacement and (hence) chronic underdevelopment. A substantial part of the southern sector remained inaccessible due to insecurity, lack of infrastructure and transportation, and GOS bans on movement. In some areas the emergency nature of the programme was very evident, with massive hunger and new population movements generated by political insecurity and a succession of natural disasters. In other areas, local indigenous people had returned from refugee camps and other "safe havens" to their homes, where they were trying to rear livestock, clear fields and plant crops, rebuild their houses and the local infrastructure, re-establish the civil administration, and thus re-establish their lives. Such varied conditions have increasingly required different response strategies from OLS agencies, ranging from food drops and emergency distributions to the extension of NGO-implemented development projects, such as construction of water and environmental sanitation, and household food security support (Commack 1998). Sometimes these two combine: the World Food Programme, for instance, was recently required to structure developmental activities into its emergency operations, through the provision of food-for-work and micro-projects. By these means, OLS intended to address the need for both emergency and rehabilitation phases in its southern sector operations (WFP 1997).

Who needs food aid? Targeting "vulnerability". In 1998, OLS was ranked the world's largest ever relief operation, channelling aid to 2.6 million people, feared to be dying at the rate of 120 per day (Sudan Catholic Information Office 1998). However, there is never enough food aid to provide for all, and agencies target aid to the most vulnerable groups. Yet notions of "vulnerability" differ by culture and professional understanding (Appleton 2000). Certainly in Sudan, differences between the aid community's and local Sudanese definitions of "vulnerability" have led to confusions over the targeting of relief food (Commack 1998). For instance, the OLS agencies define "vulnerability" by means of objective or scientifically defined measures (e.g. individuals or families who have no food stocks or who show physical signs of having no food, such as children whose growth or body size is markedly reduced) and in terms of physiological vulnerability. Thus the eligible "vulnerable groups" were young children aged under 5, pregnant and lactating women, the sick, and the elderly. However, to the southern Sudanese, who define "vulnerability" on the basis of livelihood needs or social assets, the eligible "vulnerable groups" were: men without cattle, farmers and fishermen with no livestock/fish, male returnees with nothing to share, and families without daughters. The only groups these two lists have in common are widows, the destitute, the disabled and the poor. By Sudanese standards, a child whose family or clan has sufficient cattle should not receive special attention, even if they happen to be very thin occasionally (Appleton 2000).

Discussions with women about "who were the most vulnerable people in the society and why?" yielded the following responses (Commack 1998; Wittenveen *et al.* 2001):

Widows: because they are weak and cannot hunt—they do everything for the family, they are the mother and father in one.

Widowers: because even though they can hunt/fish, they have a bigger problem of raising children on their own and are constrained by lack of cattle to remarry and get stepmothers for their kids.

Women whose husbands are away: because their situation is just as bad as widows'—men who are away from their wives do not, necessarily, send remittance to their families.

Orphans, disabled and elderly: because they are incapacitated by their social and physical circumstances—orphans are not cared for separately but shuffled between families and many elderly are without families and dependent on charity.

Almost all newly displaced persons, returnees and the poor: because they have not or cannot acquire assets (grains, livestock, goods) and must trade away their relief food to gain other essential items, e.g. salt, sugar, soap.

Women in general: because they can be attacked while collecting food, water, firewood or trading. Women do not hunt and, in some areas, only men can fish.

These different perspectives have somehow to be reconciled by workers and by recipients themselves, on the ground. These issues require response because OLS has been operating for so long and so publicly, and because it has espoused the Codes of Conduct outlined above, in particular to involve beneficiaries in the management of relief aid, and to be accountable to those it seeks to assist, as well as to those from whom it accepts resources. International NGOs and UN agencies both have to justify the allocation and targeting strategies for aid to an increasingly sceptical and informed public in rich donor nations. Recognizing the perspectives and wisdom of those with

Elizabeth Ojaba, Anne Itto Leonardo and Margaret Itto Leonardo

Figure 1

Food aid delivered to OLS southern sector over time

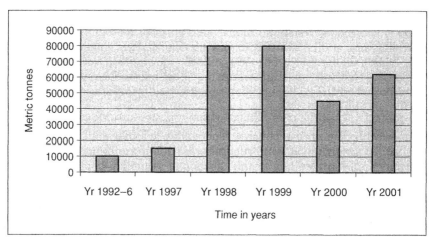

Source: Wittenveen *et al.* (2001).

long experience of living with conflict, as well as respecting local views and customs, is a particular contemporary challenge.

Who needs food aid in the south? Quantities and areas. Needs in the south have fluctuated from an estimated annual requirement as low as 10,000 metric tonnes in 1992, up to 80,000 in 1998–9 (see figure 1). These food gaps were consistent with trends in nutrition and mortality data over the same period (see table 1). Latest estimates, derived from the most recent Annual Needs Assessment (ANA) (Wittenveen *et al.* 2001), indicated the overall food gap in southern Sudan for 2001 to be 62,000 metric tonnes.

Food needs tend to peak in the "hungry" months of May–June, when most households are cultivating and have run out of grain reserves. However, the areas of highest need were primarily those that were the most insecure. These include: Northern Bahr el Ghazal and Lakes provinces (because of bandit attacks); Eastern Equatoria province (because of drought); Upper Nile Province (because of GOS/SPLA-M fighting around the oil fields); and Jonglei province (because of inter-clan fighting). Indeed, the characteristics of food-insecure areas listed by the ANA team were as follows (Wittenveen *et al.* 2001):

- they are close to oil fields and therefore near the front line of the war;
- they have experienced sustained conflict, displacement and cattle raiding;
- their crops have been affected by erratic rains;
- they are prone to drought;
- they have poor access to health services and suffer from a high prevalence of guinea worm, malaria and other infectious diseases;

Table 1

Trends in nutrition status

Location	Global malnutrition < −2 Zscore (%)	Severe malnutrition < −3 Zscore (%)	CMR/ 10,000/day	< 5 yrs MR/ 10,000/day	NGOs
Ajiep, Gogrial County					
July 1998	80	48	26	46	MSF-B
Sept. 1998	48	13	13	25	
Jan. 1999	14.6	1.5	5.3	9.8	
June 1999	4.9	1.1	1.03	2.2	
July 2000	5.9	0.4	1.5	2.4	
Malualkon, Aweil E.					
Sept. 1998	36.2	29.1	no data	no data	Tear Fund
May 1999	29.1	6.1			
Oct. 1999	34.3	5.2			
Aug. 2000	12.2	1.3			
Akobo (Bien State)					
Oct. 1998	24.8	1.9	4.7	6.5	MSF-B
April 1999	33.4	4.8	2.0	2.5	
Sept. 1999	17.0	2.0	2.6	2.8	
June 2000	33.8	7.7	3.2	3.7	
Oct. 2000	25.2	3.3	no data	no data	
Yirol (Lakes)					
Sept. 1998	17.7	2.2	2.9	3.8	LWF
Feb. 1999	11.7	1.6	no data	no data	
June 1999	6.8	2.1	0.3	0.2	
Dec. 1999	22.7	3.0	no data	3.06	
June 2000	11.3	1.6	0.4	0.3	
Rumbek (Lakes)					
Feb. 1999	11.9	1.3	no data	no data	LWF
June 1999	6.8	1.4	0.8	0.5	
June 2000	8.5	1.1	0.9	0.7	

Source: Wittenveen *et al.* (2001).

- a high percentage of households are incapacitated by weakness, a lack of inputs and non-seasonal migration;
- a high percentage of households have small tangible and exploitable assets base;
- implemented relief interventions are below the level planned;
- they have little, if any, access to markets and cash flows.

In 2001, for instance, the delivery of the 62,000 metric tonnes of food needed was never met, because of air bombardment of the areas most accessible to humanitarian assistance, leading to under-deliveries which caused alarming

Elizabeth Ojaba, Anne Itto Leonardo and Margaret Itto Leonardo

levels of malnutrition in young children. The ANA report (Wittenveen *et al.* 2001) detailed this and the problems faced by people in these areas in trying to maintain their livelihoods and thus their own self-sufficiency. These included: late and erratic rains, which had a detrimental effect on crops, so that many households had to replant, but often ran out of seeds due to their own previous poor harvest or lack of access to seed markets. Livestock production was poor where drought had dried up grazing land, prompting tribal competition and fights. Distress livestock sales, by people displaced into towns and anxious to avoid losses, further aggravated matters. Military insecurity and landmines hampered the collection of wild foods by women and young girls. River fish catches were low because of the lack of flooding due to drought. Food markets functioned badly because few traders were willing to walk long distances or take risks associated with entering government-controlled areas.

Southern Sudanese welfare systems were traditionally built on the unity of the clan, lineage or village, whereby the chief took responsibility for ensuring that the weak or vulnerable members of his area were provided for. Inevitably, the hardships of war and natural disaster have weakened this system to near collapse. Widows and their children can no longer expect obligatory support from brothers-in-law; chiefs have no food to offer to the poor; widowers can no longer afford the bride price to remarry and to secure a stepmother to care for their children.

Food aid in the south: who stands to benefit? Despite OLS agencies' espousal of international codes of conduct for aid, maintaining impartiality and transparency during implementation of aid programmes has never been easy. The claim that food aid will benefit only civilians is increasingly hard to substantiate (Roberts 1996). Indeed, Omaar and Waal (1994) argue that any involvement by international NGOs in a complex emergency must also benefit the parties to any conflicts. Various analysts have addressed this issue in relation to the operation of OLS (Minear 1991; Omaar and Waal 1994; Folleras 1998) and their conclusions, broadly summarized, are:

- *GOS and SPLA-M* both used OLS as a "breathing space" to consolidate their military power. Each agreed to participate in it only when their respective political interests seemed to be clearly served by doing so. Each welcomed the temporary suspension of military activities, the chance to re-establish international goodwill, and to use food to win the allegiance of civilians or at least to dampen unrest. Relief food also freed resources to spend on preparing and fighting the war. GOS and SPLA-M soldiers benefited from OLS food aid. Eyewitnesses reported finding relief foods whenever military posts were overrun: "the men with the guns always eat first—or at least they always eat"; "they are not going to starve whether they are GOS soldiers in garrison towns or SPLA" (Roger Winters of the US Committee for Refugees).
- International aid agencies and donor governments expanded their role and influence through such activities as OLS, particularly as the cold war drew to an end. The USA was lead donor in the international response

118

to the Sudan famine in 1984–5 and subsequently: arguably to protect its interests in rights to military bases for rapid deployment and access to the Red Sea, together with its interests in strategic proximity to Marxist Ethiopia, oil investment opportunities, and support for Sudan's ally, Egypt and for the Sudan itself—which, alone among Arab states, backed the Camp David Agreement on the Middle East. US criticism of Khartoum policies on humanitarian/human rights grounds was thus subdued.

Local communities in Sudan benefited from an international aid personnel presence, which helped moderate the worst excesses of the warring parties in the south, and contributed to breaking merchants' monopoly on food market prices. The agreement creating "corridors of tranquillity" removed hostility and allowed relief vehicles, supplies and personnel to accomplish their work, and also enabled civilians to pursue their own farm or livestock production activities. OLS succeeded in helping avoid widespread starvation and displacement, and some agencies working specifically with SPLA-M got food aid to areas no other agency could reach, which avoided starvation deaths in recipient populations.

The Contribution of Humanitarian Aid to Long-term Development in Sudan

The concept of developmental relief

International NGOs and other humanitarian agencies have traditionally assumed a dichotomy between "relief" and "development" work. This assumption informs the allocation of funds by bilateral donors, and, occasionally, donors refuse to support long-term projects in programmes deemed as essentially emergency (Commins 1996). In the past, emergency situations resulting from war or acute famine were seen as temporary interruptions to the development process (Duffield 1999). Given the concept of a linear continuum of "relief-to-rehabilitation-to-development", it was assumed that—after short spells of crises—"normal" conditions would resume (Roche 1996). Duffield (1999) argues that such approaches can lead to long-term dependence on relief, thus weakening the capacity of local populations to adapt to ongoing changes. Assumptions about "the continuum of development" are increasingly seen as no longer valid because—unlike a natural disaster—complex emergencies are not resolved in a matter of months.

This challenges us to ask: "what does development actually mean in such circumstances? How do we balance the distribution of relief and provision of services to achieve sustainable self-reliance, and implementation of operational activities with concerns about human rights and political freedom?" (Roche 1996). Over the past decade, progress has been made towards establishing clear links, both conceptually and operationally, between initial relief operations and longer-term development goals. As a result, NGOs working in complex emergency situations are moving to a wider understanding of development, which is not simply tied to economic indicators. Issues of social relations of production, including gender analysis, and the ways in which human and natural resources are managed beyond the simplicities of relief,

Elizabeth Ojaba, Anne Itto Leonardo and Margaret Itto Leonardo

are critical (Commins 1996). Operating in a conflict-related emergency requires different skills and a different time-frame, plus the recognition that—unlike in a natural disaster which deprives people of all possessions—local communities can and do pursue their own strategies in conditions of emergency, to maximize the trade-off between lives and livelihoods in order to achieve not just present but future survival (Lautze 1997). NGOs' experience provides a valuable base for other agencies to identify development potential within conflict situations, to review their priorities and adjust their capacity for work in different settings, and to present policy challenges to government and donors (Commins 1996).

OLS: positive contributions to development

OLS's main focus was on emergency provision of relief food and this in itself played an important part in preventing collapse of the rural economy (Fielding *et al.* 2000). However, the programme's non-food components have, in the long run, brought more durable benefits with substantial impact, in turn contributing to food security (Minear 1991). Major elements have included distribution of agricultural tools and seeds, with livestock vaccination and provision of fishing equipment, to improve household food production capacity; accelerated immunization campaigns, primary health care and essential drugs programmes; and improved access to potable water, greatly disrupted by the war, through installation of water and sanitation equipment, training of local staff to repair hand pumps and rehabilitate bore holes, and establishment of mobile teams to repair and construct water sources.

In addition to the positive outcomes from the presence of international aid personnel mentioned above, they have monitored human needs and military activities, enabling rapid resumption of emergency assistance where necessary, and contributed to a sense of well-being among the people throughout the southern Sudan (Folleras 1998). OLS has also created opportunities for many southern Sudanese to participate or be involved in relief and development-oriented activities themselves, thereby acquiring new knowledge, skills and practical experience through on-the-job training. Some agencies explicitly adopted local "capacity-building" schemes, which led to the creation of a cadre of experienced, trained Sudanese professionals, highly sought after by other organizations (COWI 1997; Minear 1991).

It has often been said that, despite its limitations, emergency relief can nudge open the door for peace, though it cannot hold it open for ever. This has proved true in the case of OLS. Although earlier ceasefires provided a breathing space for the warring parties, after which conflict was resumed with renewed strength and vigour, the truth remains that the later ceasefires and truces declared by the warring parties—especially the one mediated by the US President Jimmy Carter to ensure safe passage for relief supplies and needs assessment—have had broader results. Closed to military vehicles but open to relief convoys, the "corridors of tranquillity" have ensured reduced military activities over wider areas, encouraging the resumption of normal commerce and other economic activities. This has greatly benefited the surrounding countryside, giving people the courage and energy to plant their crops and grow their own food (Folleras 1998). "The narrow corridors of tranquillity became broader zones of peace", observed Deng and Minear (1992), a view shared by the UN, which regards the corridors of tranquillity and the associated relief efforts as instrumental in paving the way for peace negotiations. Both the GOS and SPLA-M have acknowledged that the OLS experience contributed to the peace process (Hay 1990).

Of all its achievements, OLS deserves most praise for having established and preserved humanitarian principles in extremely difficult circumstances (Minear 1991). It has mobilized a large-scale international response and helped ensure that relief supplies reached those in need, notwithstanding problems of coordination, and considerable expense.

OLS: negative contributions to development

Donor governments arguably find themselves in a "catch-22" position over assistance. For instance, in 1989, the same donor governments that provided substantial emergency aid virtually cut off all development and economic assistance in order to put pressure on the GOS to change its military, economic and human rights policies (Minear 1991; Folleras 1998). Was this ultimately constructive towards development? Deng and Minear (1992) expressed concern that the lack of donor investment in increased food production would have the effect of increasing people's vulnerability to famine. Indeed, General Beshir (Sudan's prime minister) had logic on his side when he commented that "the donor countries are not forthcoming in helping us to increase our local food productivity. With a little assistance, we could produce enough food for displaced people, refugees from other countries, and even send food to our neighbours" (Minear 1991). Deng and Minear (1992) further warned that dwindling trends in long-term aid donation could actually reduce donor leverage against objectionable policies. Indeed, as it turned out, the policy in 1989 of exclusively providing emergency aid simply infuriated the GOS and failed to produce any change in its political approaches and activities.

The achievement of the OLS food assistance programme has also been disputed. Although it has been hailed as life-saving, it has also been charged with hindering peace efforts, in that the availability of relief food enabled the warring parties to consolidate their hold over their respective populations (Deng and Minear 1992). It eased their responsibilities to provide such food or to foster conditions in which food could be produced locally. There is also evidence that the negotiated "corridors of tranquillity" were used to prepare for renewed offensives (Minear 1991). There were difficulties with the focus of some OLS agencies towards particular areas or ethnic groups, which, it has been claimed, contributed to some extent to inter-ethnic animosity on both sides (COWI 1997).

OLS has also contributed to the marginalization of many southern Sudanese women, who had already been faced with problems from the war environment that neither they nor their society had previously dealt with. It is common to find women left to deal alone with problems of food, health care, displacement and general security, for their children, the sick, the disabled, and the elderly (Young *et al.* 2001). They face problems of assault and lack of protection while collecting food, water and firewood, and this affects food security and capacity to plan or settle in a community (Commack 1998). Excessive workloads prevent women from participating in community activities, or gaining access to information on humanitarian assistance. The international humanitarian system further marginalizes them: for example, the OLS seeds and farm tools protocols demand these production inputs be distributed through heads of household, who in most cases are men. The same applies to skills training programmes organized by NGOs, which are intended to improve production and thus household food security; these too are mainly targeted at men. Yet women account for 80 per cent of food production, and in most cases they are also responsible for tending crops, and selecting and storing seeds for the future.

Finally, projects and programmes for the large numbers living for long periods in refugee or displaced persons camps sometimes do not have quite the impact donors intend. For instance, the provision of seeds and of farm tools have been "fashionable" donor projects designed to enable displaced people to grow their own food. It has been found, however, that beneficiaries were not generally using the seed types and varieties distributed by OLS NGOs for planting—rather, these were being washed and eaten. This was partly because the beneficiaries, being unfamiliar with the relief seeds being distributed, preferred their local seeds; partly because the relief seeds performed poorly; and partly because they tended to arrive either too early or too late. A new approach is currently being tested by the Catholic Relief Service: local resident farmers are encouraged to bring their varieties of seeds to a "seed fair" where displaced people living in camps can buy them using vouchers or cash provided by the relief agencies (Oketayot 2001). The problem with this approach, unfortunately, is that it is more appropriate as an emergency response—rather than as a revitalization project, where the emphasis has to be on sustainability and agribusiness.

Conclusions and Lessons Learnt

This paper has reviewed some of the general principles of humanitarian food aid, as applied to complex emergencies, and explored the lessons learned from Operation Lifeline Sudan. One key lesson is that humanitarian concerns, creatively managed, can be a forceful influence in their own right, even where political and military agendas dominate (Minear 1991). OLS has been described as one of history's largest humanitarian interventions in an active civil war, which also facilitated the peace process. The "corridors of tranquillity" eventually became peace zones (Folleras 1998), and OLS-negotiated agreements on several occasions helped keep alive the hopes for a peace process, through the reaffirmation of commitments from both parties to the war on the grounds of humanitarian and patriotic considerations that the people suffering were "no strangers but Sudanese children".

Nevertheless, there were negative practical outcomes, in that quantities of food allocated for certain areas were never transported, despite protracted negotiations, and certain areas were never reached at all, which, given its enormous operational budget, reflects poorly on OLS. Indeed, while the OLS experience has highlighted the many positive reasons for giving humanitarian aid (obligatory humanitarian imperative, media phobia, moral hesitation, solidarity), it has also demonstrated the more unscrupulous motives for receiving aid. Both the GOS and the SPLA-M, in their pursuit of political and military objectives, have involved strategies which violated the humanitarian and human rights of Sudanese civilians. Nevertheless both parties to the conflict came to realize that they could not continue antagonizing civilians and using food as a weapon indefinitely—SPLA-M, because it depended for material and moral support on the local population and GOS because it could not afford a widespread civilian uprising that could make governance more difficult (Minear 1991).

OLS has had its share of critics as well as admirers, and regularly comes under scrutiny for its lessons for the international donor and aid communities. While no one questions the significance of OLS's intervention in preventing mass starvation and death (Smock 1996), some nevertheless believe that the programme has exacerbated conflict rather than contributing to peace. Omaar and Waal (1994) argue that because war strategies have come to revolve around relief—and because relief has been diverted to the military on both sides—the provision of aid prevents either side from being forced to be accountable to their constituents. The implementation of relief and development activities also comes under challenge. For instance, in decisions over resource allocation, tensions between groups can be reinforced, although NGOs may argue this can equally help prevent further conflict by helping to counterbalance disequilibria in power and resources. Nevertheless, when NGOs have more funds than local government, it can create an imbalance between external and domestic resources, making it difficult for local institutions to build for peace. Also, NGOs can hire much of the best talent, at the expense of domestic agencies. The experiences demonstrate there is no clearcut solution: no matter how great the need for prompt action, weighing the pros and cons of interventions in complex emergencies is always a challenge.

The international codes of conduct on impartiality and "neutrality" proved difficult for OLS agencies to maintain because of the responses by the GOS and SPLA-M, each of which laid down (different) conditions on agencies operating in the opposing side's areas. For instance, an attempt by a few NGOs to fly relief supplies to the south without GOS permission fuelled that authority's suspicions about relief flights, leading to a temporary withdrawal of cooperation (Deng and Minear 1992). As a result, in practice most relief agencies chose to work on one side or the other, dealing as best they could with the pressure which this inevitably induced (Minear 1991). In some instances, it worked particularly well, enabling agencies to move within occupied areas and achieve remarkable results in delivering goods and services to targeted beneficiaries in otherwise inaccessible areas (COWI 1997).

In complex emergencies, the survival of food market systems is often threatened, and the rapid deployment of support systems is needed, to monitor prices, supply and production. This is necessary both for local populations and for the relief agencies themselves, who are faced with problems of availability, quality, reliability of operators and transport (Thirion and Grunewald 1999). Under OLS operations, regional purchasing proved a very viable means of maintaining and boosting local production and markets; a simple system to monitor market and production trends made it possible to assess when and where local purchases could best be made. It also made it possible to supply foods adapted to local dietary habits and to supply these more rapidly (as in the case where fish preserved traditionally by sun-drying were purchased from surplus areas and distributed, or sold at fair prices, in deficit areas). This by itself is a good demonstration of OLS's achieving its long-term objective to promote livelihoods through increased production.

There was no evidence that OLS recipient populations became totally reliant on food aid, nor of a disincentive effect on local food production (Holt and Lawrence 1993). The following quotation from a speech by Prime Minister Gazouli Dafalla affirms the Sudanese attitude to receipt of food aid:

> it is painful for us to accept these gifts you bear us ... It is painful to listen to your admonitions as to the manner in which we are using what you are giving us. The Sudanese way is to bestow gifts upon the people who come to this country, not the other way around. While you are doing a noble thing, it is hurting us. Every grain [of food] in effect is hurting the Sudanese. It is painful to receive it for nothing. (Folleras 1998)

An aid worker's impression of the people from southern Sudan adds a further perspective:

> Working in Southern Sudan is one of the most demanding but reward-ing tasks one can imagine. Even if the work is difficult ... time spent in southern Sudan amongst these proud people is among the most unforgettable memories. The Nilotic people live a lonely, difficult, and often dangerous life. To survive in a generally hostile environment where nothing is given freely, they have had to develop independence, courage, patience, prudence, and physical as well as mental strength ... If one remembers that really nothing good ever came to the Nilotes from outside ... (Minear 1991)

Nonetheless, the desire to provide a quick, technical response, without com-mitting to continuous provision of humanitarian assistance or longer-term development, is still dominant among OLS donors. Their preference is still largely for funding short-term humanitarian assistance dealing with food, shelter and health services—as well as funding of seeds and tools pro-grammes, with marginal impact on food security—rather than long-term rehabilitation interventions addressing the root causes of problems. These include widespread illiteracy, lack of primary education and skills, problems of trauma, rapes and other hardships prevalent in the war-affected areas. Equally important would be assisting local civil societies and authorities to establish democratic and accountable forms of government. The latter has the potential to enable elders and local authorities again to take responsibil-ity for the well-being of the people. The potential for capacity-building among recipient populations is considerable, by working with them to create cadres of well-trained people with management experience. This has manifestly been one of the success stories of the OLS.

References

Afif, B. Y. (1994), *New African Yearbook*, London: IC Publications.

Appleton, J. (2000), *Food Aid: Who Needs It?* Briefing Paper OXFAM-GB Food and Nutrition Office. *www.oxfam.org.uk/policy/gender/00jul/0700faid.htm*

Burr, J. and Collins, R. (1995), *Requiem for the Sudan: War, Drought and Disaster Relief on the Nile*, Boulder, CO: West View Press.

Commack, D. (1996), *Promoting Gender Sensitive Operations*, World Food Programme/ Operation Lifeline Sudan, Southern Sector.

Commins, S. (ed.) (1996), *Development in States of War*, Development in Practice Readers, Oxford: Oxfam Publishing.

COWI (Centre for Operation Water Initiatives) (1997), *Evaluation of Norwegian Humanitarian Assistance to the Sudan*, Oslo: Royal Ministry of Foreign Affairs.

Deng, F. M. and Minear, L. (1992), *The Challenges of Famine Relief: Emergency Operation in Sudan*, Washington, DC: Brookings Institution.

Duffield, M. (1994), Complex emergencies and the crisis of developmentalism, *IDS Bulletin: Linking Relief and Development*, 25, 4: 37–45.

Duffield, M. (1999), The Crisis of International Aid. In C. Priotte, B. Husson and F. Grunewald (eds), *Responding to Emergencies and Fostering Development: The Dilemmas of Humanitarian Aid*, London: Zed Books, pp. 19–21.

Fielding, W., Gullick, C., Coutts, P. and Sharp, B. (2000), *An Introduction to the Food Economy Research in Southern Sudan*, London: World Food Programme/Save the Children Fund UK.

Folleras, A. (1998) *Humanitarian Aid as a Tool for Peace: a Case Study on Humanitarian Organizations in Sudan*. MA thesis, European University Centre for Peace Studies, Stadtschlaining, Austria.

Goodhand, J. and Chamberlain, P. (1996), "Dancing with the prince": NGOs' survival strategies in the Afghanistan conflict. In S. Commins (ed.), *Development in States of War*, Development in Practice Readers, Oxford: Oxfam Publishing, pp. 39–50.

Hay, R. (1990), *Humanitarian Cease-fire: an Examination of their Potential Contribution to the Resolution of Conflict*, Ottawa: Canadian Institute for International Peace and Security.

Holt, J. and Lawrence, M. (1993), *Making Ends Meet: a Survey of the Food Economy of the Ethiopian North-East Highlands*, London: Save the Children Fund UK.

Lautze, S. (1997), *Saving Lives and Livelihoods: The Fundamentals of a Livelihoods Strategy*, Feinstein International Famine Centre, School of Nutrition Science and Policy, Tufts University.

Minear, L. (1991), *Humanitarianism under Siege: a Critical Review of Operation Lifeline Sudan*, Trenton, NJ: Red Sea Press.

Minear, L. and Weiss, T. G. (1993), *Humanitarian Action in Times of War: a Handbook for Practitioners*, London: Lynne Reinner.

Oketayot, C. (2001), *Comments on the CRS/Sudan Seed System and Seed Fair Training*. Unpublished report, Catholic Relief Service Sudan Programme.

Omaar, R. and Waal, A. (1994), *Humanitarianism Unbound? Current Dilemmas facing Multi-mandate Relief Operations in Political Emergencies*, London: Africa Rights.

Roberts, A. (1996), *Humanitarian Action in War: Aid, Protection and Impartiality in a Policy Vacuum*, London: IISS/Adelphi papers.

Roche, C. (1996), Operationality in turbulence: the need for change. In S. Commins (ed.), *Development in States of War*, Development in Practice Readers, Oxford: Oxfam Publications, pp. 15–25.

Elizabeth Ojaba, Anne Itto Leonardo and Margaret Itto Leonardo

Smock, D. R. (1996), *Humanitarian Assistance and Conflict in Africa*, Washington, DC: United States Institute of Peace.

Sphere Project (1998), *The Sphere Handbook: Humanitarian Charter and Minimum Standards in Disaster Response*, Sphere Project, available from Oxford: Oxfam Publishing.

Sudan Catholic Information Office (1998), *Sudan Monthly Report*. 15 August.

Thirion, M. C. and Grunewald, F. (1999), Emergency food aid. In C. Priotte, B. Husson and F. Grunewald (eds), *Responding to Emergencies and Fostering Development: the Dilemmas of Humanitarian Aid*, London: Zed Books, pp. 173–4.

UNICEF-OLS (1994), *Review of 1994 Activities*, UNICEF–Operation Lifeline Sudan Southern Sector.

Wittenveen, A., Muchomba, E. and Nanok, J. (2001), *The Food Security Situation in Southern Sudan—A Summary Report Based on Data Collected during 2000–01 Annual Needs Assessment (ANA)*, London: World Food Programme/Save the Children Fund UK.

WFP (World Food Programme Strategy and Policy Division and Technical Support Service, Sudan) (1997), *An Emergency in Transition: Case Study Linking Relief and Development*, October. Unpublished report, WPP-OLS Southern Sector.

Young, H., Jaspars, S., Brown, R., Frize, J. and Khogali, H. (2001), *Food Security Assessments in Emergencies: a Livelihoods Approach*, HPN paper, Overseas Development Institute, London.

8

School Meals Policy: The Problem with Governing Children

Ulla Gustafsson

Introduction

School meals policy has been intrinsic to many Western welfare states. In the UK such policies have sparked intense discussion in recent decades. This has partly been a result of dietary concerns resulting from the deregulation of national nutritional guidelines in 1980. The immediate focus of such discussions has been on the nutritional impact of school meals on the present health of children (White *et al.* 1992), but the attention has also demonstrated a concern with the future health of the next generation (Baggott 2000). Children are regularly surveyed, the adequacy of their nutritional intake is assessed, and the results are noted in policy discussions (see, e.g. Gregory *et al.* 2000).

This longitudinal case study of school meals policy in the UK may at first glance seem uncomplicated and uncontroversial, in that it is focused on the issue of ensuring a well-nourished and healthy future generation. However, the examination of school meals policy over time reveals this to be emblematic of far broader central government preoccupations. Indeed, school meals policies point to issues of fundamental importance with regard to the governance of the nation. In particular, they may inform our understanding of the relationship between the state, the family and children—and of the ways in which such institutions are conceptualized. In a society where the current involvement of its citizens in the policy process has become increasingly important for the legitimacy of democracy, school meals policies highlight some central dilemmas.

This paper outlines the history of school meals policy in England and Wales[1] firstly in terms of its nutritional focus. Here we are able to note a shift from concerns over the sheer lack of food to concerns over excesses in children's diets, indicating that issues of nutrition have continued to be of primary interest. The paper will next seek to locate school meals policies within a broader social policy context. The trends here will reflect a change in emphasis from the overt control of a population to forms of governance run on more participative lines. Finally, the paper seeks to elucidate the role and function of children in the policy process, through a re-examination of relationships between the state, the family and children. It will become apparent that children, the intended and actual recipients of school meals policies, have not been the policy-makers' central focus or direct concern.

School Meals and Nutrition

The link between nutrition and health is well recognized in school meals policies. It could even be argued that this has been the main motivating factor behind the institution of such policies. Even so, we have seen a shift in focus over time, from merely providing children with enough food, to trying to ensure the best appropriate composition of the food they actually consume. Let us consider the emphasis given to the link between diet and health in the policies enacted on school meals in Britain, over the twentieth century.

The first legislation making public provision of school meals available was the 1906 Education (Provision of Meals) Act. Local education authorities (LEAs) were given power to provide free or reduced-charge meals for those children who would otherwise be unable to profit from the education provided (DHSS 1973). Considerable concern had been raised regarding the health of the population as revealed by the experience of recruitment to the Boer War, and this had alerted the government to the need for intervention with regard to the children of the poor (Webster 1993).

Nevertheless, free school meals were only made available to children deemed, by medical experts, to be suffering from malnutrition. *Feeding* (as it was called) was more like a form of medical treatment, aimed at the very poorest (Ivatts 1991). Such a medical definition permitted the separation of school meals provision from the provisions of the Poor Law.[2] In other words, a child could receive school food regardless of whether his/her parents were receiving assistance through the Poor Law. Local authorities were also enabled to provide school meals to children other than the needy, provided they charged at least the cost price (Sharp 1992). Even so, this last was not a popular option, since the meals provided were based on the soup-kitchen model, with consequent stigmatizing connotations. Hence, only a small proportion of school children, the most needy, were touched by this particular reform.

Next came the Education Act of 1944. Now LEAs had a *duty* to provide school meals. A universalist national system was set up, financed largely from central government funds. There was therefore a shift from a system providing the most basic nutrients to the poor, to a regime offering a meal to all school children. There were clear nutritional guidelines drawn up by experts, specifying the precise proportions of various nutrients necessary for the growing child (such as: 29 g protein, 880 kcal energy, 32 g fat—DHSS 1973). This was partly a consequence of the successful rationing that took place during the Second World War (Murcott 1994), but it also had to do with the popularity of the scientific approach adopted by nutritionists at the time (Lupton 1996). Nevertheless, although the guidelines were in place they were not standardized for the whole country until 1965. So it was the policy rather than the implementation which was in place. But there was also a set price stipulated, fixed at the same level for the whole country; and these school meals were intended to provide about one-third of the daily allowance of nutrients and energy for every child.

The provisions of the 1944 Act in this respect did not arise out of a vacuum. Indeed, there had been a number of developments during the inter-war years which had helped to shape it. It had become apparent that "school feeding" was seriously inadequate. A parallel school meals system, the "school canteen", had emerged in the grammar schools, providing middle-class children with a wholesome meal, paid for by their parents. In 1937 a cost comparison between the "school canteen" and "school feeding" indicated that the free school meal was nutritionally inadequate (Ivatts 1991). The cost of the free meal was 9d (old pence) while in a typical grammar school the cost could be over 2s (old shillings). Evidence also came to light that the provision of free food to poor children was in any case patchy. By 1914 only 160,000 children were being provided for (Sharp 1992). Flaws in the old system were thus identified and a positive model developed. It was recognized that, in order for school meals to achieve their intended purpose of providing nourishing lunches for pupils throughout the country, the prevalent system for organizing the feeding of the poor was not enough. Hence the emphasis placed upon a national system, in the context of postwar reconstruction.

Yet by the 1970s, again all was not well with school meals. The report of a DES Working Party (1975) noted that children's tastes had changed and they were no longer appreciating the standard school meal. A note of caution was therefore struck. "A nutritious meal will benefit pupils only if they eat it" (cited in Rose and Falconer 1992: 353). Nevertheless, a mere sufficiency of food intake was no longer deemed to be the object. Instead, concerns were being raised over the excesses in children's diets. In a context of increased wealth for many and the rise of consumerism, children had begun to reject the "nutritious" lunches being provided at school, in favour of options more attractive.

A radical change of policy on school meals came finally with the 1980 Education Act.[3] Here the duty of LEAs to provide school meals was removed (except for pupils entitled to free meals). At the same time nutritional standards and fixed pricing systems were also removed. This was followed by the 1986 Local Government Act's introduction of competitive tendering, whereby contracts had to be given to the caterer offering the cheapest price. "Specifications could include 'quality' standards, but no clauses which might be considered 'un-competitive' were allowed" (Cole-Hamilton et al. 1991).

Most LEAs now changed the type of school meal provision available in secondary schools. Cash cafeterias were created, where the pupils were allowed to pick and choose whatever foods they wanted, and pay for their selection. This was very much in line with government thinking on efficiency, consumer choice and reduction in waste. The same year (1986) the Social Security Act was passed (to take effect in 1988).[4] The entitlement to free school meals was limited to children whose families were receiving Income Support, and was removed from children whose families were receiving

Family Credit. The net result was some 400,000 children no longer being entitled to free meals (White *et al.* 1992).

Deregulation coupled with reduction in the entitlement to school meals gave rise to concern across a range of pressure groups—for example, the Child Poverty Action Group, the National Children's Bureau, the then Health Education Authority (now known as the Health Development Agency). Indeed, some 50 different organizations joined together and, in 1992, formed the School Meals Campaign to put the nutritional case for school meals. Many groups pointed to the reduction in the uptake of school meals as proof of the detrimental effects of deregulation and the reduction in entitlement. For example, in October 1979, 4.9 million schoolchildren (64 per cent) ate school meals, whereas by October 1988 this had gone down to 2.8 million (47 per cent) (White *et al.* 1992). Furthermore, studies of children's diets indicated that their eating habits had deteriorated. For example, a government study showed that children consumed too much fat and sugar and too little fruit and vegetables (DHSS 1989). The prevalence of children consciously involved in dieting and slimming was a further cause for concern. The *Guardian* reported that girls as young as six claimed to be unhappy about their bodies and were conscious of monitoring their food intake (*Guardian*, 28 November 1997). In addition, low intakes of iron and calcium, particularly among girls, were noted (White *et al.* 1992).

The reason why children's diets are of importance is partly to do with the fact that eating habits are formed in childhood (MacDonald 1998). Given the body of evidence setting out the links between disease and diets high in fat/sugar but low in fruit/vegetables (Baggott 2000), the concern about the health of the future generation seems well founded. In the case of children, there is a link established not merely between poor diet and growth and development in general, but between diet and more particular health problems—such as dental disease, anaemia, mental performance, obesity and even non-insulin-dependent diabetes (Sharp 1992). Furthermore, the health problems which emerge in adulthood as a result of poor nutrition in childhood include obesity, diabetes, coronary heart disease, stroke, hypertension and a number of cancers, in particular colon cancer (Sharp 1992).

Once in power, the New Labour government published a White Paper, *Excellence in Schools* (DfEE 1997), which included a commitment to the reintroduction of nutritional standards for school lunches. This was followed by a consultative paper, *Ingredients for Success*, which invited comments from anyone with an interest in school meals (DfEE 1998).[5] Draft regulations were drawn up and issued for further consultation, with the result that, from 1 April 2001, nutritional standards for school lunches were set. In addition, LEAs and schools now have a duty to provide a paid meals service where *parents* want one. The regulations are based on the five food groups:

- fruit and vegetables
- starchy foods
- meat, fish and other non-dairy sources of protein
- milk and dairy foods
- foods containing fat and foods containing sugar

There are different requirements for different forms of schooling, related to the age of pupils. In primary schools, for instance, starchy foods cooked in oil must not be on offer more than three days a week. In secondary schools starchy foods cooked in fat or oil can be served daily—but an alternative starchy food not cooked in such a way has also to be available.

This review of past policies on school meals has shown the importance of the recognition that nutrition is crucial for the health of the population. Policies began with the realization that unless children get enough food they are unlikely to grow up at all, and certainly not as fit human beings. Given the evidence that this goal was being met during the 1970s, it could be argued there was a nutritional case for the policy change in the 1980s. There was evidence that children were so well nourished they were in a position to reject the food they were served. It is in this context that the debate on the adequacy of the *composition* of children's diets emerged. It was no longer appropriate to focus on the mere quantity of food being eaten by children.

Changes in Ruling the Population

Although we have noted the importance of the link between nutrition and health in the development of school meals policy, we cannot assume this was the sole motivating factor. Health has often served as a front for other policy objectives. In this case, the way that school meals policy has been formulated is illustrative of changes in government *per se* over the course of the twentieth century.

Beginnings

The introduction of school meals in 1906, rather than simply focusing on nutrition, can be seen as a measure to support the needs of industrialization and international competition (Thane 1996). Bauman (1998) points to the importance placed upon instilling a work ethic (implemented through the Poor Law) into the population during the nineteenth century. He states: "In that classic era of modern industrial society, work was simultaneously the pivot of individual life, social order and the survival capacity ('systemic reproduction') of society as a whole" (1998: 16). The compulsory education of the young was part of this drive to produce the disciplined workforce required for future industrial production. So, when it was discovered that some children were unable to take part in this due to lack of food, something had to be done. Hence the introduction of school meals can be seen as one part of the responses the state had reluctantly to endorse, in balancing the worst effects of the changes imposed on the population by industrialization (Bauman 1998).

According to Ivatts (1991), the introduction of school meals represented a significant ideological break with a past that had been characterized by a *laissez-faire* free market approach. The 1906 Education (Provision of Meals) Act is one example of increasing state intervention in the private lives of the population. However, it is important to note that this was a *permissive* legislation. There was no *obligation* to offer school "feeding" and it was left to local authority discretion whether to do so. Thus at this time the state is taking on a regulatory function, *enabling* the development of certain welfare services including school meals. In practice, this school meals policy affected relatively few children at the time and provided insufficient nutrition—so could have had little real impact on children's health status. Nevertheless, it could be seen as one of the measures indicative of an increasing state interest in the lives of its citizens.

Doyal (1979) has reinterpreted the apparent humanitarian developments that were taking place at this time as being, in reality, a series of attempts to rule the masses with a view to improving military and capitalist prospects—while also reducing the risk of social unrest among the urban poor.

Welfare state

The school meals policy that was part of the 1944 Education Act was in stark contrast to its predecessor. A nutritious lunch, typically consisting of meat and two vegetables, was to be available to every schoolchild in the country. It was envisaged that this would eventually be free of charge to all (Alexander 1944; see below), but in practice it was to remain means-tested. Even here, however, it may be questioned whether nutrition was the main motive.

Royle (1994) notes that the period following the Second World War signified a marked change in the style of government. The creation of the welfare state brought with it a vision of rights and entitlements that in turn gave rise to British notions of citizenship. William Beveridge's vision of the welfare state was one based on universal flat-rate contributions matched by universal flat-rate benefits in times of need. Provision had indeed to be universal as it was felt that anyone could fall on hard times (Thane 1996). Furthermore, the emphasis was to be on "survival with dignity" rather than just survival (Bauman 1998: 45). Collective and standardized provision was to be coordinated and directed by a strong central state. In such a climate there was much less scope for individual expression or local variation. This influenced the form of school meals policy: the provision of a standard type of meal, based on the latest knowledge in nutritional science, for every child.

The welfare state under question

The investigation by the DHSS (1973) identified the regular rejection of school food by pupils as extremely wasteful. These concerns happened to be raised at the start of stringent economic times, when severe pressures were being exerted on public expenditure, and when, indeed, the whole idea of the welfare state (not just in Britain but in Europe generally) was being called in question. These deliberations can be seen as paving the way for the reform of school meals policy that took place in 1980, under the banner of Thatcherism. This time, the main concern was certainly not nutrition.

Hirst (2000: 18) points to the emergence of *governance*[6] at this time, in response to "the growth of new public management strategies since the early 1980s". As public services became privatized there was a need to regulate these, by monitoring quality and adherence to contracts. The deregulation of school meals policy in 1980 can then be seen as a response to a changing world order, wherein government was attempting to match demands with, on its part, the would-be limited use of public funds.[7] Slater (1995) argues that this was an inevitable solution for a consumer society, where people are having increasingly high expectations of public services, yet there are finite resources to meet such demands.

New Labour

The latest government policy on school meals reinstated nutritional guidelines, yet has retained some features of choice. It could be argued that this policy reintroduces the importance of nutrition to the agenda. However, if we examine the process of policy formation, it appears that the new school meals policy is indicative of yet new strategies of governance. Before the implementation of this policy, a series of consultations took place, firstly on the consultative paper *Ingredients for Success* (DfEE 1998). This had invited comments from "all those with an interest in school meals" (1998: 3). On the basis of the 180 responses received from a range of interested parties (e.g. LEAs, organizations and individuals representing nutrition, diet and other health promotion interests, schools, governors, parents and others with education interests, and the food industry), "Draft Regulations", together with guidance for "Nutritional Standards for School Lunches" were issued for further consultation before the final regulations came into effect in April 2001.

Harrison and Mort refer to such public consultation efforts as "technologies of legitimation" (1998: 60). They argue that public participation offers a solution, in a context where there is concern over democracy due to lowered rates of participation in elections. By involving a greater constituency in the process of policy-making the government thus hopes to be able to legitimize its decisions none the less.

It would appear that school meals policy illustrates the way in which the present government seeks to govern people and to balance a number of demands and needs. The shift could be characterized as one from government to governance.[8] Still, however, the supposed target of school meals policy, i.e. the child, appears to have been marginalized in all these policy processes.

The State, the Family and Children

We have noted how there have been changes in school meals policy reflective of broader changes of approach to governing the population. Yet throughout this period children have been marginalized and their agency ignored, for all that school meals policy clearly affects children in a very direct way. Why is it that children themselves have not featured more directly? Part of the explanation for ignoring children in this context may be discovered in the relationship between the state and the family.

Children have tended not to feature to any extent in public policy-making processes, in their own right. They have been considered, on the one hand, predominantly as future adults and, on the other, as belonging to the private world of families, where the state does not tread. Indeed, Land and Parker argue that "[t]here is a widely held view that family life is, and should be, a private matter" (1978: 332).

Early twentieth century

The Bill to introduce school meals in 1906 was proposed by a Labour MP, but was not met with great enthusiasm. Indeed, there was consternation in parliamentary debates, where the Bill was opposed as being a threat to traditional family responsibilities (Ivatts 1991). There was concern that families might recklessly abandon any sense of responsibility for their offspring. Clearly, there was considerable caution when it came to usurping the responsibility of the family. Nevertheless, this policy does reflect the nature of reforms taking place at the time, when children were coming to be seen as material investments in national progress, in a fiercely competitive international environment (Hendrick 1990). So, although the school meals policy did not necessarily reflect a concern with children for their own sake, their future contribution to society as adults was of concern. In the main, however, families were still seen as the proper location for the protection and physical nurturing of children.

The privacy of the family was strengthened further during the interwar years, when psychological theories of child development became popular (Hendrick 1990). These confirmed that a stable family was important for the normal development of children. During the creation of the welfare state the family was defined as a nuclear family with a male breadwinner and a female homemaker (Royle 1994). Welfare was provided to the family unit and in this sense it was assumed that the welfare of the child was under control. Childhood had, as it were, come through the worst threats of industrialization, urbanization and war. Childhood was henceforth something to be enjoyed and treasured (Cox 1996).

Mid-century

Food rationing had been imposed nationally during the Second World War and this had ensured a minimum equality of food distribution to the population (Murcott 1994). This "imposition" was illustrative of a broader approach on the part of government. The school meals policy intended for all children followed just this model, with its standardized requirements and menus. But this measure can be seen as part of a wider development in universal support of the family, rather than as an intervention coming between parents and their children. For example, there was a booklet for parents outlining the 1944 Education Act (at the cost of 2s). In this parents were told that local authorities had a duty to provide school dinners at cost price. The same booklet also promised: "the Minister has announced that when the School Meals Service is fully developed, school meals will be provided free of charge as part of the educational system" (1944: 22). This illustrates that the government considered it important to relay information to parents, but clearly was not attempting to deal directly with children.

Hendrick (1990: 56) argues: "Childhood [*sic*] had been reconstructed on two levels, both of which had their origins in the inter-war period: as an individual citizen in a welfare democracy, and as a member of a family". They thus had a right to be brought up in a family and to be given a nutritious meal at school. However, it may be closer to the truth to describe them as the *children* of citizens. As Mayall (1996) observes, social policy discussions have tended to focus on children's needs rather than their rights. Children appear then to be the beneficiaries of an optimistic and adult vision of future society characteristic of modernism. Although children were seen as important for the future they were not included in their own right as children, rather as members of the family unit where the state was reluctant to tread.

The 1980s

The next school meals policy in 1980 was to paint a very different picture. Its implementation signals a shift in the vision of the child, from being a collective recipient of stipulated, standardized provision to an individual consumer capable of selecting from a range of alternatives. In the previous decade, concern had been raised by the DHSS about removing the entitlement to free milk, since it was felt to be unsafe to assume that parents would "accept responsibility hitherto discharged by the state" to provide milk (1973: 2). However, in the new relationship between the state and its citizens, "social security is not a function of the state alone. It is a partnership between the individual and the state" (DHSS 1985; cited in Drakeford 2000: 70). The school meals policy from 1980 therefore shifted responsibility firmly from the state to, if not the individual child, the child's family. According to Mayall (1996) it signalled the replacement of the education system's responsibility for children's diets with individualistic health education. Prout (2000: 301) argues that "[i]n the policy environment of the 1980s the family increasingly replaced the identification of young people as a group. The family became the government's preferred route to policy interventions."

"Welfare pluralism"

Nevertheless, it is not only the family that mediates between the state and children. In the case of school meals policy, various campaigning organization do so too: in that they advocate greater regulation and protection in the interests of children. The Child Poverty Action Group argues, on grounds of both health and equality, that children should be protected from the poverty of their families. It advocates an extension of free school meals to cover those from families in receipt of tax credits (*www.cpag.org.uk*). They are thus campaigning for intervention on behalf of children as a group and are suggesting a more public role for the protection of children. The issues thus raised concern children's present health status, their ability to learn, their future health status and concerns regarding the increasing inequality and poverty experienced by large numbers of children (Dowler *et al.* 2001). The arguments raised by such an organization may nevertheless present difficulties in a society where children who need the protection of the state have been constructed as belonging to "abnormal" families (Moss 2000). The state, in such circumstances, is understandably reluctant to intervene in families not so defined.

Meanwhile, another mediator between the state and the family is the market. Witness the role of advertisers directing themselves towards children (MacDonald 1998; Sustain 2001). The UK government has long resolved that it is up to parents to decide on the level of their children's exposure to advertising.[9] In Scandinavian countries, however, the state has decided to ban direct advertising to children and is thus intervening between the family and children in this respect (Qvortrup 1993).

The most recent school meals policy has responded to calls for the reintroduction of nutritional regulation. So are we seeing a new relationship between the state and the family? According to Driver and Martell (2002: 58) New Labour family policies express "concerns for the family's functions in inclusion of *children*" [emphasis in original]. Thus we are not necessarily seeing any greater interference between children and their families, but rather policies geared to reducing social exclusion for all concerned—not least by ensuring that children entitled to free school meals are now to be offered a healthier menu.

Nevertheless, the agency of children has still not been particularly acknowledged in the policy process. The consultation document (DfEE 1998: 3) invited comments from "all those with an interest in school meals, including pupils and their families", but it was not clear how children would gain access to this consultation procedure; and in the follow-up document comments from pupils are not identified.

Children's role as active agents has thus been confined to "end of the line" decisions, where they are able to assert influence in a context where caterers are competing with lunch boxes and, in the case of secondary school pupils, with catering establishments outside of school. Eating at school is clearly something central to children's experience, yet over which they have very little influence (Mayall 1994). Mayall found that, whereas children were involved in the home setting in the choice and preparation of food, no such involvement was in evidence at school. The relationship between children and food at school was limited to accepting or rejecting whatever was served up. If school meals policies were to accept children as active social agents they might well be invited to participate more visibly in this process.

Policies are often influenced by specific goals, informed by research evidence; yet they are also influenced at times by unexamined assumptions. James *et al.* (1998) point to two pervasive popular perceptions of childhood—the "evil" versus the "innocent" child. The former sees the child as potentially dangerous and out of control, and as such as a threat to social order. Children are thus in need of restraint in order for them to become useful citizens. The other view of childhood, by contrast, is of a condition imbued with happiness, which requires nurturing but also protection from the harshnesses of the adult world. Both of these perspectives can be contained and nurtured within the context of the family.

There is no evidence, as yet, as to which perspective is best favoured by current school meals policies; any more than there is evidence, as yet, of children being taken seriously, in this context, as a social group in their own right.

Notes

1. The most recent government policy covers England only. Wales now formulates its own version, as Scotland and Northern Ireland have always done.
2. The Poor Law of 1834 was established to provide relief to those who were destitute. It established workhouses for the "deserving" poor, but made these unattractive in order to deter the "undeserving" poor. The policy was intended to support the freedom of the market (for further discussion, see e.g. Thane 1996).
3. In 1979 a Conservative government came to power that drew on "New Right" ideology in its approach to policy. Its aim was to reduce public expenditure and taxes with the individualization of problems and privatization of responses being favoured (see e.g. Kavanagh 1987).
4. The Social Security Act radically reduced access to welfare among the most vulnerable of the population. Benefits became more discretionary, young people were excluded from entitlement and citizens were urged to insure for their own potential hardship through private insurance (see e.g. Drakeford 2000).
5. The current discussion relates to the policies for England alone.
6. Pierre identifies two meanings to governance: (a) "empirical manifestations of state adaptation to its external environment as it emerges in the late twentieth century", (b) "a conceptual or theoretical representation of co-ordination of social systems and . . . the role of the state in that process" (2000: 3). I refer to the former in this context and thus argue that school meals policy is a reflection of this process.
7. Alcock (1996) demonstrates that public expenditure continued to increase during the 1980s, hence the government managed, at best, a cut in the growth in public expenditure.
8. These terms are used in this context to describe the changes in the way nation states are run. Where governments previously used to assert power and control in a direct way over the affairs of the state including markets and its population, they are now having to adapt to a global context where the state no longer can do so, and consequently need to devise a range of strategies that maintain order in more indirect and devolved ways (see Pierre 2000 for further discussion).
9. The Food Standards Agency is launching research into the promotion of foods to children that specifically seeks to explore whether the advertising of foods that are high in fat, sugar and salt undermines healthy eating advice.

References

Alcock, P. (1996), *Social Policy in Britain: Themes and Issues*, Basingstoke: Macmillan Press.

Alexander, W. P. (1944), *The Education Act: A Parent's Guide*, London: HMSO.

Baggot, R. (2000), *Public Health: Policy and Politics*, Basingstoke: Palgrave.

Bauman, Z. (1998), *Work, Consumerism and the New Poor*, Buckingham: Open University Press.

Cole-Hamilton, I. with Dibb, S. and O'Rourke, J. (1991), *Fact Sheet. School Meals*, London: The Food Commission and Child Poverty Action Group.

Ulla Gustafsson

Cox, R. (1996), *Shaping Childhood*, London: Routledge.
DfEE (1997), *Excellence in Schools*, London: DfEE.
DfEE (1998), *Ingredients for Success*, London: DfEE.
DHSS (1973), *First Report by the Sub-committee on Nutritional Surveillance*, London: HMSO.
DHSS (1989), *The Diet of British School Children*, Report on Health and Social Subjects 36, London: HMSO.
Dowler, E. and Turner, S., with Dobson, B. (2001), *Poverty Bites: Food, Health and Poor Families*, London: Child Poverty Action Group.
Doyal, L., with Pennell, I. (1979), *The Political Economy of Health*, London: Pluto.
Drakeford, M. (2000), *Privatisation and Social Policy*, Harlow: Longman.
Driver, S., and Martell, L. (2002), New Labour, work and the family, *Social Policy and Administration*, 36, 1: 46–61.
Gregory, J. *et al.* (2000), *National Diet and Nutrition Survey: Young People Aged 4–18 Years*, vol. 1: *Findings*, London: Stationery Office.
Harrison, S. and Mort, M. (1998), Which champions, which people? Public and user involvement in health care as a technology of legitimation, *Social Policy and Administration*, 32, 1: 60–70.
Hendrick, H. (1990), Constructions and reconstructions of British childhood: an interpretative survey, 1800 to the present. In A. James and A. Prout (eds), *Constructing and Reconstructing Childhood*, London: Falmer Press.
Hirst, P. (2000), Democracy and governance. In J. Pierre (ed.), *Debating Governance: Authenticity, Steering, and Democracy*, Oxford: Oxford University Press.
Ivatts, J. (1991), Forward to the 1930s: the case of the school meals service. Unpublished paper, University of Surrey Roehampton.
James, A., Jenks, C. and Prout, A. (1998), *Theorising Childhood*, Cambridge: Polity Press.
Kavanagh, D. (1987), *Thatcherism and British Politics*, Oxford: Clarendon Press.
Land, H. and Parker, R. (1978), United Kingdom. In B. Kamerman and A. Kahn (eds), *Family Policy: Government and Families in Fourteen Countries*, New York: Columbia University Press.
Lupton, D. (1996), *Food, the Body and the Self*, London: Sage.
MacDonald, T. (1998), *Rethinking Health Promotion: A Global Approach*, London: Routledge.
Mayall, B. (1994), *Negotiating Health: Primary School Children at Home and School*, London: Cassell.
Mayall, B. (1996), *Children, Health and the Social Order*, Buckingham: Open University Press.
Moss, P. (2000), The "child in need" and the "rich child": discourse, constructions and practice, *Critical Social Policy*, 20, 2: 233–54.
Murcott, A. (1994), Food and nutrition in post-war Britain. In J. Obelkevich and P. Catterall (eds), *Understanding Post-war British Society*, London: Routledge.
Pierre, J. (2000), Introduction: understanding governance. In J. Pierre (ed.), *Debating Governance: Authenticity, Steering, and Democracy*, Oxford: Oxford University Press.
Prout, A. (2000), Children's participation: control and self-realisation in British late modernity, *Children and Society*, 14: 304–15.
Qvortrup, J. (ed.) (1993), *Childhood as a Social Phenomenon: Lessons from an International Project*, Vienna: European Centre.
Rose, R. and Falconer, P. (1992), Individual taste or collective decision? Public policy on school meals, *Journal of Social Policy*, 21, 3: 349–73.
Royle, E. (1994), Trends in post-war British social history. In J. Obelkevich and P. Catterall (eds), *Understanding Post-war British Society*, London: Routledge.

Sharp, I. (1992), *Nutritional Guidelines for School Meals. Report of an Expert Working Group*, London: Caroline Walker Trust.

Slater, B. (1995), The private sector and the NHS: redefining the welfare state, *Policy and Politics*, 23, 1: 17–30.

Sustain (2001), *Food Poverty: Policy Options for the New Millennium*, London: Sustain.

Thane, P. (1996), *Foundations of the Welfare State*, Harlow: Longman.

Webster, C. (1993), *Caring for Health: History and Diversity*, Buckingham: Open University Press.

White, J., Cole-Hamilton, I. and Dibb, S. (1992), *The Nutritional Case for School Meals*, London: School Meals Campaign.

9

Food and Poverty in Britain: Rights and Responsibilities

Elizabeth Dowler

Introduction

> Social surveys have been made elsewhere, but they have not been
> planned on identical lines. The results of such surveys do, however,
> show that large numbers of families are forced to exist below the eco-
> nomic level of sufficiency. It does appear that the nutritional and phys-
> ical condition of families is closely associated with financial status.
> (M'Gonigle and Kirby 1936: 274)

The debates about causes of, and responses to, poverty, as well as its consequences for individuals, families and society in terms of health, well-being
and productivity, will be familiar territory for student, academic and practi-
tioner alike in social policy. The role of food and nutrition, to some extent,
has been taken for granted, particularly since Seebohm Rowntree's seminal
study of poverty in York in 1899 (Rowntree 1901): nutritional science
informed the construction of the poverty line used to distinguish "primary"
from "secondary" poverty, and "food" remains one of the basic needs for
which welfare must provide. However, the nutritional contribution to the
definition and measurement of poverty has in practice been contentious, in
Britain[1] as well as elsewhere, throughout the century, and the construction
of the British welfare system largely bypassed issues of food availability and
access, beyond provision for specified groups likely to be particularly vulnerable physiologically (poor women, infants and children of school age). This
invisibility of food as a component of social policy, where it relates to poverty,
is to some extent a puzzle. It presumably derives from an unacknowledged—
and therefore largely unchallenged—assumption that food issues belong to
the private, domestic sphere, outside the jurisdiction of the state except
where responsibility has been accepted, as in provision of school meals
(where rules about what is served at what cost to recipients have come and
gone on the political agenda in the UK—see Gustafsson, this volume). This
paper examines these assumptions in reviewing the relationship between
food and poverty in Britain, and concomitant rights and responsibilities. It
draws on material and ideas elaborated in more detail elsewhere (Dowler
and Leather 2000; Dowler et al. 2001).

Food and Nutrition in Poverty Definitions

Poverty is a highly contested condition widely discussed in the national and international literature (e.g. Bradshaw and Sainsbury 2000; World Bank 2001; Mosley and Dowler in press). Broadly speaking, there are two main roles for food and nutrition: as components of a minimum cost of living index, and as part of the lived experience of poverty. Food as a basic human need has also been important in the past, particularly in development debates and activity in the 1970s, but in practice this function is subsumed in the former two. Critically, food as a human right is gaining considerable political currency in development discourse at the present time (e.g. ACC/SCN 1997, 1999; Maxwell 1999), although not that which relates to industrialized, rich countries.

Seebohm Rowntree was probably the first to use ideas about nutritional requirements in a systematic way to define a minimal subsistence cost of living or poverty line. He used this poverty line to separate people identified as poor (done visually, on a relative basis) into those who had insufficient income to purchase basic survival necessities, and those whose income was sufficient to buy basic necessities but who were unable so to do for other reasons (Veit-Wilson 1986). In his calculations Rowntree used the new science of nutrition to give important credence and apparent objectivity to his choice of "dietary", although he was also wary of setting too high a standard, which would negate his aim, which was to conduct a social survey of poverty on a scientific basis.

> Booth, in his book, spoke of the working people as being fairly well off, poor, very poor, but he didn't define poverty in scientific terms. The whole science of nutrition was in a very elementary state then, but I got the best information that was available. I [also] got a good deal of information from Professor Attwater in the United States [...] and I got two or three medical men in this country to help me. Furnished with this information, my next task was to fix upon a diet which would supply families of different sizes with the necessary nutriment [...] of course supplied in an infinite number of different ways. I decided to base my poverty line upon a dietary which supplied the necessary nutrient[s] but which was more austere than that provided in workhouses and prisons. I did this because I didn't want people to say, "Rowntree's crying for the moon." (Briggs 2000: 10; quoting a letter from B. S. Rowntree to D. Caradog Jones in 1952)

Not only, then, was this dietary basis for the poverty line economical and unattractive in the extreme, it was also a theoretical dietary, not based on what people actually purchased to eat, nor on how much such a diet actually cost, nor how it was eaten (what combinations of food). Its purpose was recognized as "merely physical efficiency", not to estimate a minimum income people could or would actually live on (Veit-Wilson 1994).

Despite these efforts at objectivity, Rowntree's poverty line and the estimates of proportions living in poverty came under severe criticism at the time from the right, particularly the Charity Organization Society (COS), who saw poverty as a moral failure arising from social inefficiency. The Bosanquets (Bernard and Helen) argued that "the pauper was failing in the most basic duty of citizenship", that of self-realization to provide for himself (*sic*) and his family (Bowpitt 2000: 25). They even objected to Rowntree's choice of dietary standard, maintaining that a general standard simply could not be applied in this fashion, since diets should be adapted to the individual. This assertion could be regarded as technically correct, in that reference standards or recommended levels of intake to maintain health are probability statements, which apply to populations rather than individuals. There will always be some who physiologically need fewer nutrients or less energy than others. However, an individual's dietary requirement is no basis for defining a minimum cost of living, and anyway, depends to some extent on the condition of well-being and physical work circumstances of the individual concerned. Requirements or reference standards are set for population groups; they can be constructed for different age groups and by gender or workload as required, but they cannot be used to make judgements about an individual's well-being, only its likelihood. More critically, those objecting to Rowntree's usage of requirement figures, while raising the issue of individuals vs. populations, in fact held to the view that "malnutrition is more often due to misdirected feeding than to underfeeding in the ordinary sense" (Bosanquet 1903: 324; cited in Bowpitt 2000); the matter of how requirements were used in practice seems to have been a red herring. Rowntree himself countered these claims of mismanagement and individual inefficiency; even those in "secondary" poverty (i.e. which was not due to earnings too low or intermittent to meet minimal needs) were not able to manage their apparently sufficient income because of extreme adverse circumstances (Rowntree 1901). But the fundamental disagreement remained between those who believed in an individualist moral degeneracy—linked to late nineteenth-century ideas of a "residuum"—and those who focused on structural causes of poverty and pauperism, and continued to resonate throughout the twentieth century and on into the twenty-first, in debates about the existence, definition, measurement of, and response to, poverty.

Food and nutrition, then, played an important role in providing the legitimation Rowntree sought at that time, and it chimed with contemporary anxieties about physical degeneracy of the basic stock of the nation. The remit of the 1904 Committee on Physical Deterioration was to review the means of producing men (*sic*) capable of both defending the empire and working productively to further it, and food and nutrition were essential components of the response (see Burnett 1979; Petty 1987, for further accounts). Throughout the first half of the twentieth century in Britain, anxieties about food and nutrition remained high in the public and policy agenda (Drummond *et al.* 1959) and as components of the experience and measurement of poverty. In the 1930s, for instance, there was much public and government debate about hunger, malnutrition, appropriate levels of living and the role of the state, and the scientific profession was again annexed to determine minimal living costs (Smith 1995).

A quite different approach to the subject was taken by Boyd Orr in his 1935 survey of the causes and extent of poverty (Boyd Orr 1936). Rowntree had defined a minimal subsistence level, because it was appropriate to his purposes, and he had used the then latest nutritional scientific knowledge, which was on macro-nutrients of protein, fat and carbohydrate. By the time Boyd Orr was planning his work, he was able to draw on what was known as the "newer knowledge of nutrition" (which largely referred to work on vitamins).[2] He employed what he called "*optimum* requirements" (my italics), based on the "physiological or ideal, viz., a state of well-being such that no improvement can be effected by a change in the diet" (Boyd Orr 1936: 12).[3] Furthermore, Boyd Orr was not interested in keeping the poverty line as low as possible; instead, he set out to measure the level of income below which people could not participate in the customary life of society, in this instance, in eating the kind of diet considered appropriate for health. He estimated the level of income needed as about 20–30 shillings per person, where 10 shillings per head was spent on food—about 39 per cent (Boyd Orr 1936). By contrast, the British Medical Association (BMA) had said in 1933 that "it could be done on 5s. 11d. for a man, 4s. 11d. for a woman, between 2s. 8d. and 5s. 4d. for a child and about 22s. for the standard family of a couple and three children" (Woolf 1946: 75). These differences in necessary income, which depend on the underlying paradigm and assumptions about, or measurement of, proportion of income spent on food, proved critical in the establishment of how much money a family needed to live on, and thus levels of social assistance and wage levels. At the time, the BMA view prevailed among professionals and policy-makers, in terms both of the paradigm and of the actual costs.

Food played a critical role in national well-being during the 1940s: the Second World War, and in rationing during the following decade (Drummond *et al.* 1959; Burnett 1979; Murcott 1994). The role of food and nutrition in the measurement and lived experience of poverty then largely disappeared from public and policy view, and scientific or social study, for much of the rest of the twentieth century. Walker and Church (1978) represent a fairly lone nutritional scientific perspective when they investigated food expenditure and nutritional outcomes for lone parents living on supplementary benefit in the mid-1970s. They used prevailing government standards for food requirements and child growth, and national data as well as their own, to show the theoretical impossibility for parents whose income was exclusively state benefits to purchase sufficient food for their children to grow properly. Their work was largely ignored in the social and scientific literature and, despite some effort by the Child Poverty Action Group and minimal response from the Department of Health and Social Security, by government. A scattering of other nutritionists, public health or social policy professionals continued to investigate the relationship between poverty and food (e.g. Lang *et al.* 1984; Cole-Hamilton and Lang 1986; Cohen *et al.* 1992; Leather 1996; Craig and Dowler 1997). There has been no national survey of nutrition and diet in low-income households since the Second World War, although in early 2002 the Food Standards Agency commissioned such a survey as part of its regular surveillance programme, to report in 2005.

However, a separate strand of research has developed from the "dietary costing" tradition, where a basket of goods is costed and the results compared with income or benefit levels (see NCC 1995; Dowler *et al.* 2001, for summaries). Sometimes this work takes a Family Budget Unit approach: a theoretical food basket is constructed from national survey data on food and nutrient intakes so as to meet reference levels for specified household types, and average mainstream prices are used to cost it (e.g. Nelson *et al.* 1993). Others have simply used a list of typical basic food items and costed them using prices in shops patronized by poor households (e.g. Consumers' Association 1997), or compared the costs in contrasting richer and poorer areas (e.g. Piachaud and Webb 1996). Some have drawn up the "basket" using the experience of those living in different social conditions—consensual budget standards (Middleton *et al.* 1994). These differences in methods reflect different underlying assumptions about the relationship between poverty and food, and produce different results in terms of costs of living. For instance, contrary to what might have been expected, the same basket of goods can cost more in areas where poor people live than in those where richer people live (sometimes even in different branches of the same retailer) (Donkin *et al.* 2000; Consumers' Association 1997). Whatever the methodology, however, the general results have been similar: those living on low wages or state benefits could not afford to purchase sufficient, appropriate food to meet healthy dietary guidelines or nutrient requirements laid down by government committees of experts. They have insufficient money, however well they budget, shop and prepare food.

A third strand of research is epitomized by Townsend, who took a different stance, ignoring food prices and income and looking instead at the role of food in the experience of relative deprivation. He argued that people are poor who "lack the types of diet, clothing, housing, household facilities and fuel, and [...] conditions, activities and facilities which are customary, or at least widely encouraged and approved, in the societies to which they belong" (Townsend 1979: 413). In his deprivation index subsequently constructed from Londoners' views of "necessities", Townsend included a dietary deprivation index (Townsend *et al.* 1987) based on normative expectations, and based around foods and meals, rather than nutrients; including (among others) having had at least one day in last fortnight with insufficient to eat; having no fresh meat or fish most days; having no fresh fruit most days. Mack and Lansley (1985) in the *Breadline Britain* survey also constructed a deprivation index based on whether or not respondents thought items were "necessities", and again, not being able to provide three meals a day for children or two for adults; not having fresh fruit; and not having a meat, fish or vegetarian dish every other day, were ranked as criteria of deprivation. Callan and colleagues (1993) also found respondents' views of "necessities" included food patterns, as did the recent Poverty and Social Exclusion Survey (Gordon *et al.* 2000), which extended the *Breadline Britain* approaches and used consensually defined necessities. In these studies there was no requirement that people must use/consume these things, nor how often; simply that people should be able to do so—they should have the resources (money, time) and access to express normative choices. Such deprivation standards, particularly the consensual versions, arguably inject a note of realism into debates about whether poverty exists and why. Significantly for the argument in this paper, consensual standards always rank food deprivation indices quite highly. The approaches are gaining significant international currency (World Bank 2001); Howard and her colleagues (2001) discuss their use in Britain in more detail, along with the implications for policy (although they do not comment much on the food element).

In the USA something of a similar approach has been used in that indicators of household food security, both as perceived by household members, and in terms of practice and behaviour (such as going without food, or types of food), have been incorporated into national nutritional surveys (Radimer *et al.* 1990) and estimates of poverty (Andrews *et al.* 2000). Household food security has not been measured in Britain until recently; the current Food Standards Agency survey will include a food security questionnaire. Such a questionnaire, while not drawing on consensually defined characteristics, does acknowledge the lived experience of households in poverty (Leather 1996; Dobson *et al.* 1994; Kempson *et al.* 1994). For instance, household members might be asked whether they ever run out of money for food; if so, how often, and what they do to obtain food; how often they have gone to bed hungry in the previous month, and whether that was from being unable to afford food or because of some other reason (such as trying to lose weight). Householders might also be asked whether or not they make use of free food provision, and if so, how often (see Riches, this volume). Surveys now also ask about distance to food shops and quality of local provision, range and price of goods available, and, for households with school-aged children, will ask about the experience and quality of meal provision. Thus food and nutritional concerns in poverty definition and measurement have moved some way from costing a minimal diet for subsistence to an acknowledgement of the realities of managing on low incomes and in physical areas of multiple deprivation. Space precludes discussion of evidence about the role of appropriate knowledge and skills in contributing to poverty; these are covered elsewhere in the literature (M'Gonigle and Kirby 1936; Leather 1996; Dobson *et al.* 1994; Dowler *et al.* 2001).

Role of Food and Nutrition in Poverty Analysis

Nutritional data (i.e. data on consumption of food constituents and their adequacy for child growth or adult production) clearly contribute to a materialist analysis of poverty in the calculation of a minimal cost of living. The figures obtained are seen as objective because they use scientific criteria of requirements for survival or health, rather than observing what people living on low incomes actually purchase, thus bypassing potential "human inefficiency". In practice, however, such objectivity is probably less rigorous than many would suppose; requirements or standards do not unequivocally separate sufficiency from insufficiency but indicate the likelihood of avoiding deficiency or (less often) achieving health, if a given amount is consumed. They are socially constructed for a given place and circumstance, rather than scientific constants (Dallison 1996). More important, there is no standard for

Elizabeth Dowler

sources of nutrients which is "objective"—no one eats a diet devised by a least-cost analysis programme, nor one costed at theoretical minimal prices. Indeed, the reliability of many costing exercises can often be challenged over the source of price/quantity data and their uprating over time. Rowntree used the average retail prices for food in York, whereas the 1933 BMA recommended diet with costings quoted above seemed to have been based on the lowest prices obtainable for the worst qualities of every item, and at a time when the food index was lower than at any time since the 1914–18 war (Woolf 1946). Contemporary survey sources show that the diet recommended (which bore little resemblance to what people actually ate) would, in fact, have to cost 10–20 per cent more than the BMA report claimed (Woolf 1946). More recently, the National Children's Home, in a 1991 food cost survey, used prices typical of shops which their clients, known to be poor, usually used (NCH 1991); partly because of this method they were accused of subjectivity and lacking scientific rigour, as it was claimed people could (in theory) buy their food more cheaply in markets.[4]

The approach by Boyd Orr described above, and that of the contemporary Family Budget Unit (Parker *et al.* 1998) is quite different: look at what level of income is necessary to meet scientific requirements, or measure what people have to spend to obtain basic goods. In other words, avoid "expert" assumptions about food prices, what commodities are available in which shops, and what proportion of income is spent on food; instead, look at what people living in the conditions actually manage to achieve. While this is more humane and realistic, the methodology can still ignore issues of who decides on the actual commodities and their quality included (e.g. "own brand" vs. branded goods vs. "low-cost") and in practice can ignore the social and cultural constraints of poverty, induced by family, geography and social exclusion (Dobson *et al.* 1994; Lang *et al.* 2001; Dowler *et al.* 2001).[5]

There is a further challenge to using a "least-cost-diet" approach: people obviously purchase (and consume) food, not nutrients as such. It is a worldwide, general observation that poorer households maximize the nutrients and energy they can obtain for as little cost as possible, and that richer households, while they spend more on food than poorer, spend a lower proportion of income to purchase calories and nutrients, thus buying less "efficiently". Yet even the poorest households do not appear to purchase to meet physiological requirements alone. In fact, surveys continually show they will try to satisfy cultural demands for taste or tradition in food type or preparation methods (Lipton 1982; Berhman 1988); furthermore, as income rises households tend to buy more expensive foods than hitherto, which are sometimes less calorie-dense than commodities bought previously, but which carry higher status (such as meat), or are more tasty (such as fruit). Berhman (1988) argues that these economic data demonstrate people seeking and purchasing increased *food variety* as income rises, as opposed to behaving as "nutrient utility optimizing agents" (my term). He claims this is evidence that variety of foodstuffs must in itself be a desirable aspect of life; variety is a trait or consumption good which people, even though poor, are prepared to purchase for its own sake. This is an interesting challenge to defining poverty. Current recommendations for a diet conducive to health in fact include reference to variety and to specific food commodities—e.g. in the UK, to eat a varied diet and to consume five or more portions of fruit and vegetables daily. There is as yet no official recognition of either the actual practice, or measurement of the ability to purchase a varied dietary base/sufficient fruit and vegetables, as indicators of poverty.

The UK government is currently consulting on how to measure child poverty (Department for Work and Pensions 2002). Four different approaches are discussed and assessed in the consultation document, and comments invited. Under consideration are relative, normative indicators of deprivation experience such as those described above, including being able to eat in the same way as others in society (meals, types of food), rather than income cut-offs derived from nutrient-based food basket costings. Examples are given of measures used in the USA, in other EU member states (Ireland in particular), as well as those used in current UK surveys, and the experience of using them is discussed in some detail. Whether or not the outcome for measuring child poverty in the future includes food indicators remains to be seen.

Consequences of Social Policy Having Ignored Food and Nutritional Issues

Despite some notable exceptions (e.g. Maurer and Sobal 1995; Riches 1997; Craig and Dowler 1997), social policy analysis and writing have tended to ignore food and nutritional issues until recently (Leat 1998; Lang *et al.* 2001). This has had profound consequences for those living in conditions of deprivation and need, in Britain as elsewhere, although levels of poverty and exclusion have been more extreme in Britain than in other OECD countries, and remain entrenched (Joseph Rowntree Foundation 1995; Howard *et al.* 2001). Nutritional conditions have been notably worse for those in the lowest income groups and/or living in areas of multiple deprivation: intake levels of vitamins and minerals, and consumption of vegetables and especially of fruit, are much lower, and consumption of white bread, processed meats and sugar are higher, in households whose members are poor, by various socio-economic indicators, than in those who are richer, and nutrient intakes are often below reference levels (Department of Health 1996; Leather 1996; Dowler *et al.* 2001). These conditions have worsened over time: among the poorest fifth of families, intakes of vitamin C have declined by 23 per cent and of β-carotene (vitamin A) by 47 per cent over the last 15 years (Leather 1996). Health status of adults and children is markedly lower, and mortality higher, among those in the lower socio-economic groups, however social or economic status is measured, with a difference in life expectancy of as much as 7 years (see Marmot and Wilkinson 1999; Graham 2001; Leon and Walt 2001, from a very large literature). Food and nutrition probably play a critical role in these health inequalities (James *et al.* 1997; Davey Smith and Brunner 1997; Dowler *et al.* 2001), one now partially acknowledged (Acheson 1998; Lang and Rayner 2001).

However, the long reach of ideas of "human inefficiency" remains: they are still cited by professionals and public alike; and the policy response of education, either in household management (budgeting, cooking) or nutritional science (healthy eating campaigns) is constantly produced. The issue becomes particularly acute when poverty lines based on nutritional science are implicit in levels of social assistance, as they are in the UK, where the principles of "less eligibility" seem to have been lost, or are no longer explicit. Governments are always trying to reduce public expenditure, and there is pressure on the state to set its minimal subsistence level as low as possible if it also triggers welfare payments, and to assert its sufficiency for food as for other goods.[6] In fact, it can be shown that, in the UK until recently, the amount of money individuals received as income support[7] was simply uprated from the levels established by the Beveridge Report in setting up the welfare state (Walker and Church 1978; Dowler and Leather 2000). The scales for benefit levels used the BMA calculations referred to above (an amount which had already been shown to be below what was needed), with a minimal price uprating for cost-of-living changes since 1933, and a prob- able underestimate of the cost of necessities other than food (i.e. an over- estimate of the proportion of income spent on food). The BMA scale in turn was directly descended from Rowntree's original primary poverty line—a calculation designed to be bare survival and to "shock the public" (Walker and Church 1978). Rowntree's later "human needs" standard (still not an optimum diet but approximating the International Labour Office's 1938 sec- ond level of "decency without comfort"; Woolf 1946), was ignored. Thus the welfare state, in its origins, enshrined the original Rowntree poverty level as that on which people ought to be able to live with prudent budgeting. Those who could not—and still cannot—were and are seen as inefficient or incom- petent (Walker and Church 1978; Rivers 1979). They are thus responsible for their own poor nutritional state; their conditions are not the responsibility of the state (Leather 1996).

In practice, it is difficult to live on state benefits for any length of time without getting into debt or cutting essential expenditure, or both (Cohen et al. 1992; Kempson et al. 1994). While this fact is fairly well recognized, the role of food is not. For many, spending on food is the only flexible budget item (Dobson et al. 1994; Kempson et al. 1994). Empirical, qualitative studies have shown people economize on food either by buying cheaper or different items (no fruit, fewer vegetables, cheaper processed meats), or by omitting meals altogether (they eat sandwiches or breakfast cereals, or nothing). Ingenuity in store-cupboard cooking increases, as does borrowing food or money for food (Leather 1996; Dowler et al. 2001, among many). A survey of lone parents' diets and budgeting in the early 1990s showed that those who had lived on income support for more than a year, especially those who lived in local authority-owned housing, had worse dietary patterns (with much less variety) and lower nutrient intakes, than those who were not in these circum- stances (Dowler and Calvert 1995). About a fifth of benefit claimants have money taken off their benefits before they actually receive them, or have to use pre-payment meters charging higher rates for fuel: this is to repay arrears owed to councils or privatized utility companies for social fund loans, council tax, rent, water or fuel bills. In the lone-parent survey, parents in these circumstances had nutrient intakes which were half those of the other par- ents, and well below the levels needed for health, even when corrected for smoking and cooking practices (Dowler and Calvert 1995; Dowler 1998). Benefit levels are lower than people need, but when even these low levels are reduced, people simply go without food; the survey findings were harsh, as were the certain consequences for the parents' health and well-being.

Furthermore, there is evidence of regional variation in basic living costs of rent, council tax, utilities (other than food) and domiciliary care: variations of more than £50 in housing costs, and up to £10 a week for other basics, were measured (Kempson and Bennett 1997). The researchers showed such price variations could absorb up to a fifth of benefit payments for claimants in identical circumstances, depending where they lived. Food price variations can also be quite marked; for instance, Piachaud and Webb (1996) calculated households on benefits would have to spend 25 per cent more of their income on food if they could not get to a large supermarket or street market. Similar findings were reported by the Consumers' Association (1997): 12 widely available basic foods cost in total 50 per cent more in local shops (£7.87) than in supermarkets (£5.17). Fresh produce was similar in price, but frozen foods, coffee and tea, bread and breakfast cereals, were twice the price in local shops. Such factors are not taken into account in levels of benefits or wages. Leather (1996), among others, has argued for the food element in benefit levels to be ring-fenced; for instance, when fines or mandatory deductions are made for debts or arrears, sufficient money to enable the household to purchase food must be left. Indeed, she and others have continually called for transparency in what benefit levels, and minimum wages (e.g. Morris *et al.* 2000), are supposed to cover, and in particular, how food needs are to be met.

However, monitoring the price of food in different shops and places is not simple. For instance, supermarkets target special offers at their store loyalty-card owners; prices can vary slightly in the same supermarkets to reflect local store sourcing and running costs (and therefore store size). In some areas, where shop provision is good, food availability can be quite reasonable; where small shops are run by Asian and other ethnic minorities, using family labour to keep down operating costs, prices can also be kept reasonably low (Dowler *et al.* 2001). In many places, however, food in local shops costs more than in large supermarkets. Such local price variations might be a small proportion of the cost of food for a household on average incomes and hardly noticeable. To those on low incomes, who spend small amounts of money on food, such variations can be critical: £5–10 difference in food costs could account for nearly a fifth of the weekly food bill for a family on benefits or minimum wages, who can spend a quarter or more of their budgets on food. These amounts can make the difference between having enough and going hungry, or not buying items such as fruit or even vegetables, because low-income households have very little flexibility in how they spend their money from week to week. They have to prioritize payments for rent, gas or electricity, not least because defaulting on these leads to arrears, fines, or even imprisonment. There is some evidence that local authorities are beginning to investigate the price and availability of key foods in areas of multiple deprivation, as part of regeneration activities (Dowler *et al.* forthcoming).

The relationship between food and poverty is complex; this paper has of necessity had to simplify much research and the implications for individuals, households, communities and policy response. It is easy to lose sight of these complexities, and to assume that if people are rehoused or live in areas subject to economic development, they will be able to eat better. However, two recent examples of social intervention and evaluative research illustrate further why food and nutritional issues need to be specifically addressed and monitored. A study in Newcastle of the effects of privatization and basic services restructuring investigated access to energy, telephones, banking and food retailing, in two marginalized neighbourhoods (Speak and Graham 2000). These areas and the people living in them had been targeted by regeneration activities, but even so, service providers had withdrawn. The residents were quite clear about how their health had worsened because of their restricted access to good-quality, affordable food and their difficulties in heating their homes properly. The worse the access to a service, the more it cost; few had bank accounts, which had implications for basic budgeting and access to affordable credit. The higher costs of using pre-payment meters, small food shops, public telephones or credit agencies, considerably exacerbated the difficulties of managing on a low income.

Secondly, recent longitudinal research on the impact of regeneration to combat social exclusion on low-income households in East London showed how complex such assessments need to be to capture the realities of people's experiences of living through major change. Again, these were changes specifically designed to help reduce deprivation, but the evidence was that the regeneration process itself increased the costs of non-substitutable items (such as rent, council tax and water) so that food expenditure, among others, was reduced and many households ended up more deeply in debt (Ambrose and MacDonald 2001: 86). The findings in this research are extraordinarily reminiscent of M'Gonigle and Kirby's (1936) findings in the mid-1930s, investigating a puzzling increased mortality rate observed in a slum population which had been rehoused in Stockton-on-Tees. Careful, detailed measurement of household expenditures and behaviour revealed that increases in rent and other costs of living had led inexorably to a marked decrease in food expenditure and quality of diet, with a profound effect on health. These findings from the two contemporary studies imply that all evaluations of regeneration intervention should include effects on household food expenditure and usage.

These studies of regeneration activities also highlight the impoverished access to essential goods and services. The spatial dimensions of poverty and policy response are coming on to the research and intervention agenda (e.g. Gordon *et al.* 2000; Pantazis and Gordon 2000) but the food dimension has only recently been recognized, despite considerable evidence (Department of Health 1996; Dowler *et al.* 2001; Lang *et al.* 2001). As described above, both the economic and locational elements of food access are important: the range of commodities available and their prices, in the kinds of shops people can reach or choose to patronize. The increasing polarization of income and deprivation in the UK has contributed to the concentration in food retailing, such that shops generally struggle to survive in inner cities and/or large local authority estates. To some extent discount operators fill this retail gap, offering very low prices on a limited product range, but in practice, large supermarkets have captured 70 per cent and more of average food expenditure, including fresh fruit and vegetables (Lang *et al.* 2001). As Barling and his colleagues show in this volume, recent modest policy shifts notwithstanding, the major food retailers continue to court the car owner; policy to address the needs of those who lack car access in inner cities and rural areas is often inadequate. Many of those who are poor are also unable to walk far or use public transport easily with heavy shopping, because of physical disability or having young children. The demise of post offices and banks in rural areas has been widely reported, yet the equal loss of shops is hardly mentioned. Those who are poor have increasingly been denied food access on both counts, and their losses seldom explicitly figure in regeneration activities.

Policy Responses to Food Poverty: Responsibilities vs. Rights

At the start of the new century there is increasing international policy recognition that food poverty, the opposite of food security, refers to the inability to acquire or consume an adequate quality or sufficient quantity of food in socially acceptable ways, or the uncertainty that one will be able to do so (Riches 1997; and Hussein, this volume). Access, availability and affordability are important dimensions of food security, but the food itself, and the ways in which it is obtained, have to be socially acceptable as well as nutritionally adequate: people should not have to beg in the streets or live off "free" food distributed via charitable outlets (see Riches, this volume). Food is more than a "bundle of nutrients": it represents an expression of who a person is and what they are worth, and is a focus for social exchange. Food is also, of course, a major contributor to health and well-being, both of which are compromised in households and communities living in poverty. Policy responses have to mirror these complexities in the relationship between food and poverty. In this paper I can only highlight some key issues, many of which are discussed in more detail elsewhere (Dowler *et al.* 2001; Watson 2001). As has been shown, food and nutrition have often been relegated to a sideline in regeneration or anti-poverty strategies; equally, the realities of life for those with too little money and living in areas of multiple need are often ignored by professionals running food and nutrition programmes. Food has been seen as an individualist affair; it is usually labelled under "lifestyle" rather than being seen as a basic entitlement. The underlying assumption behind much intervention remains as nutritional or housekeeping ignorance—that people do not know how to budget or cook properly. Policy response has been to try and teach people appropriate knowledge and skills, while avoiding inappropriate state interference with "food choice" in the private, domestic sphere, where intervention would undermine the family as a social institution (Leat 1998). In practice, policy solutions located in individual change have had only limited success (Lang *et al.* 1999; Dobson *et al.* 2000), not least because food poverty needs more fundamental and structural response.

The premise for policy intervention in food as a critical element in poverty has usually been either welfare support or the development of human capital

Elizabeth Dowler

(see Gustafsson, Riches and Hussein, this volume). Welfare is provided for those who have been unable to provide for themselves, or for whom the market has failed to supply the means of adequate living. Indeed, "welfare foods" is often the term used to refer to food distributed to people seen to be in special need, either because of their age (children) and/or their physiological state (such as pregnancy), or because they do not have enough money from work or a pension to feed themselves (benefit support claimants). In Britain, the Welfare Food Scheme, set up in 1940, was originally a universal provision to protect expectant mothers and children as part of the war effort, but was subsequently targeted to the economically vulnerable, defined by social security provision. One reason why mothers and babies are protected and fed is because they represent human capital. Children are future workers, who have to be healthy and strong, and able to take advantage of education; expectant mothers need to produce healthy children. All need food to be able to work productively. Yet as other authors in this volume argue, there is a widespread international recognition of access to sufficient, safe, appropriate food as a human right (see Hussein, Riches and Ojaba et al., this volume). A human rights framework imposes obligation on the state, not just recommended options, and carries with it civil and political rights, which must be implemented in practice, in national and European law. A rights framework also introduces accountability, and implies a normative basis to responses rather than that of a safety-net or emergency.

The human rights approach to food has not yet gained much currency in Britain, despite the resonance with normative poverty definitions. Some voluntary sector groups are picking up on social justice in relation to food, and some local primary care trust partnerships have used a rights approach (Killeen 1999; Aston-Mansfield 2001). However, there is, as yet, no duty on local authorities to ensure that affordable food is available in local shops, or that people have sufficient income to obtain food. It has simply been asserted that social assistance provides sufficient for people to eat (see e.g. note 6). A current campaign, *Food Justice*, involving a group of charities, MPs and some academics, is using the means of a Food Poverty Eradication Bill, to aim to secure a duty on government, in conjunction with local authorities, to draw up and implement an action plan to eradicate food poverty within 15 years.[8]

In practice, one route to persuade government at national and local levels to take more concerted action is to highlight the public health and social care costs of ignoring food and poverty. Such a strategy, of course, sidesteps the rights framework by appealing to enlightened social self-interest. The cost savings are potentially considerable; for instance, estimates from WHO put the "costs" of poor nutrition, obesity and low physical activity for Europe, calculated in Disability Adjusted Life Years (DALYs), as at 9.7 per cent, which compares to 9 per cent DALYs due to smoking, currently attracting much policy attention (WHO 2000). Some recent analysis suggests strategies to promote healthy eating and dietary change are among the most cost-effective of methods of preventing cardiovascular disease (Brunner et al. 2001), although such analyses cannot as yet take account of the specific problems and barriers facing low-income households, the most likely to experience these problems, nor of the specific costs in addressing them.

Inequalities in health and social exclusion are already on the political agenda in the UK, as elsewhere in Europe; to a lesser extent, the role of food in mediating those experiences is also mentioned (Acheson 1998; Department of Health 1999, 2000). However, to date most actual proposals for response still focus either on individual change (skills, cooking) or on community- and voluntary-led activities to effect wider changes. It is true that an increasing role is envisaged for partnership responses in area-based regeneration and development initiatives, and in promoting consumption of fruit and vegetables, particularly for areas of multiple deprivation.[9] Nonetheless, even partnerships pose a challenge in that food initiatives have to compete with mainstream health and/or economic initiatives, and again, all too readily fall at the hurdle of "there is no demand for healthy foods from low-income households". Local and community-based initiatives have an important role as part of a range of solutions to food and poverty, but the increasing amount of research evaluating their effectiveness and sustainability, shows how critically both depend on sustained rather than start-up funding, shared ownership between communities and professionals, and realistic, flexible time-frames and goals (e.g. McGlone *et al.* 1999; Dobson *et al.* 2000).

Finally, the location and coordination of "joined-up" policy response is unclear, for food poverty as for food and nutrition themselves (see Barling and colleagues, Millstone and van Zwanenberg, this volume). The Food Standards Agency (FSA), which employs a policy consultant specifically to work on the needs of, and communication with, low-income consumers, has commissioned a national survey of nutrition and diet in low-income households to inform policy response (see above) and initiated a modest new strand of research on low income and food. How the outcomes from this research will influence policy response is not yet apparent, although in common with the rest of government, the FSA demands a best-practice evidence base. FSA partnership with national organizations and local authorities, and improved strategies to involve people on low incomes in the policy-making processes, are currently also stressed.[10] The Department of Health has a number of food and nutrition initiatives which by default reach many low-income households and communities, if not specifically so labelled (Department of Health 2000; Dowler *et al.* 2001; *www.doh.gov.uk/fiveaday/index.htm*). The Department still has responsibility for Welfare Foods provision, which has been under review for some time (Dowler *et al.* 2001). The Department of Social Security (now Work and Pensions) has never had much of a food role other than in targeting foods to social assistance claimants. "Want" was one of Beveridge's "5 giants" to be addressed by the welfare state, but income through work (or, briefly, benefits) was the solution, along with subsidized prices for key, basic foods. The role of food subsidies in maintaining a minimal cost of living and thus keeping wages low is beyond the scope of this paper, as is the role of welfare foods in primarily supporting producers' rather than consumers' interests. However, it is clear that there is urgent need for more research on levels of income which are sufficient to keep households on low wages or benefits out of poverty, and to enable, for instance, parents on income support with school-aged dependants to feed their children during school holidays when there is no free school meal.

Elizabeth Dowler

Government and agencies dealing with indebtedness and its financial and legal consequences must recognize that there are severe costs to families when their incomes are insufficient to meet the food budget. These costs are in short-term misery and long-term bad health outcomes.

Conclusions

This paper has examined something of the past and contemporary roles food and nutrition have played in the definition, measurement and lived experience of poverty in Britain, and the resulting policy responses. Society expects that those who have little money will manage that money with care, budgeting to meet essential needs, particularly for children and other dependants. However, until recently, members of households with low incomes, whether benefit claimants or those earning very low wages, have in effect borne all the responsibilities with few recognized rights: they have had no say in how much money they earn or can claim, what they have to pay for basic necessities such as gas or fuel, what happens to the local shops, and what prices they have to pay for food, and how regeneration affects these everyday experiences of food. The struggle to feed a family has largely been private and invisible. John Boyd Orr concluded his study of food, health and income in 1936 thus: "If these findings be accepted . . . they raise important economic and political problems . . . one of the main difficulties in dealing with these problems is that they are not within the sphere of any single Department of State" (Boyd Orr 1936: 50). Sixty years on we still have no real policy framework for dealing with food, health and (low) income; the responsibility remains that of (poor) individuals and not of society as a whole, or the state.

Notes

1. In this paper I use "Britain" because I present no data on Northern Ireland and have less knowledge of poverty, food and state response. In practice, in the space available I mostly refer to English experience; information and discussion of Scottish issues can be obtained from the Scottish Community Diet Project: c/o SCC, Royal Exchange House, 100 Queen St, Glasgow G1 3DN, UK, *www.dietproject.org.uk*
2. This "newer knowledge" led to an almost exclusive focus on nutritional explanations during the 1920s and 1930s as causes of, and solutions to, major public health problems (Petty 1987). However, in contrast to the nineteenth-century approach, the emphasis was placed on individuals' response in choice of food items, or ability to manage a household budget. This shift was a reflection of the discovery of, and resulting intense research interest in, vitamins, and hence in "protective" foods. The cause of malnutrition came to be identified as ignorance of dietary "quality", rather than simply one of quantity of food which could be purchased (Rivers 1979).
3. Boyd Orr in fact used the Stiebling standards from the US Government Bureau of Home Economics: a level which "provide[d] a sufficiency, with a safety margin, of all essential dietary constituents" (Boyd Orr 1936: 12). This description suggests the level was probably not the optimum Boyd Orr hoped for, but similar to the present reference nutrient values: mean requirement plus two standard deviations, or sufficient to meet the needs of 97 per cent of the population.

4. For example, broadcast by Right Honourable Anne Widdecombe, MP, the then minister for social security on Radio 4, *Today*, on the morning of publication (DSS official subsequently, personal communication).
5. For instance, the Family Budget Unit work, excellent though it be, uses J. Sainsbury's and KwikSave prices; many poorer people have no choice but to shop in smaller retailers where prices are likely to be higher.
6. "My Lords, we do not believe there is any reason why people on income support should not be able to follow a normal, healthy diet . . . people tend to eat different diets whatever their income. Some quite well-off people eat inadequate diets. Plenty of food is available at reasonable cost and people can thus maintain a reasonable and sensible diet" (minister of state, Department of Social Security (Lord Mackay of Ardbrecknish), during debate on reductions in lone-parent benefit, House of Lords, 14 March 1996).
7. Income support is a means-tested minimum income benefit in the UK; it was formerly called supplementary benefit and before that, national assistance.
8. For further information contact Ron Bailey, 62 Bargery Road, London SE6 2LW. *ron-bailey@bargery-rd.fsnet.co.uk*
9. For instance, the Department of Health *Five-a-Day* Programme encourages local partners to apply to the New Opportunities Fund local initiatives grant programme, drawing on evidence-based guidance for setting up initiatives; see *http://www.doh.gov.uk/fiveaday/index.htm*
10. For the latest Food Standards Agency output on low income, see *www.food.gov.uk*

References

ACC/SCN (UN agency Administrative Coordinating Committee/Sub-Committee on Nutrition) 1997 and 1999 annual meetings focused on human rights to food. See website: *http://acc.unsystem.org/scn/* follow links to meetings or SCN News.

Acheson, D. (1998), *Independent Inquiry into Inequalities in Health Report*, London: Stationery Office.

Ambrose, P. and MacDonald, D. (2001), *For Richer, For Poorer? Counting the Costs of Regeneration in Stepney*, Health and Social Policy Research Centre, University of Brighton.

Andrews, M., Nord, M., Bickel, G. and Carson, S. (2000), *Household Food Security in the United States, 1999*, Food Assistance and Nutrition Research Report no. 8. From *http://www.ers.usda.gov/publications/fanrr8/* (accessed February 2002).

Aston-Mansfield (2001), *The Right to a Healthy Diet: Sustaining the Fight against Food Poverty*, London: Aston-Mansfield, for the London Borough of Newham and Newham NHS Primary Care Trust.

Berhman, J. (1988), *Nutrition and Incomes: Tightly Wedded or Loosely Meshed?* PEW/Cornell Lecture Series, Cornell Food and Nutrition Policy Program, Ithaca: Cornell University Press.

Bosanquet, H. (1903), The "Poverty Line", *Charity Organisation Review*: 9–23, 321–5. Cited in Bowpitt, G. (2000), Poverty and its early critics: the search for a value-free definition of the problem. In J. Bradshaw and R. Sainsbury (eds), *Getting the Measure of Poverty: the Early Legacy of Seebohm Rowntree*, Aldershot: Ashgate, pp. 23–38.

Bowpitt, G. (2000), Poverty and its early critics: the search for a value-free definition of the problem. In J. Bradshaw and R. Sainsbury (eds), *Getting the Measure of Poverty: the Early Legacy of Seebohm Rowntree*, Aldershot: Ashgate, pp. 23–38.

Boyd Orr, J. (1936), *Food Health and Income: Report on a Survey of Adequacy of Diet in Relation to Income*, London: Macmillan.

Bradshaw, J. and Sainsbury, R. (eds) (2000), vol. 1: *Getting the Measure of Poverty: the Early Legacy of Seebohm Rowntree*; vol. 2: *Researching Poverty*; vol. 3: *Experiencing Poverty*, Aldershot: Ashgate.

Briggs, A. (2000), Seebohm Rowntree's *Poverty: A Study of Town Life* in historical perspective. In J. Bradshaw and R. Sainsbury (eds), *Getting the Measure of Poverty: the Early Legacy of Seebohm Rowntree*, Aldershot: Ashgate, pp. 5–22.

Brunner, E., Cohen, D. and Toon, L. (2001), Cost effectiveness of cardiovascular disease prevention strategies: a perspective on EU food based dietary guidelines, *Public Health Nutrition*, 4, 2B: 711–15.

Burnett, J. (1979), *Plenty and Want: a Social History of Diet in England from 1815 to the Present Day*, London: Scolar Press.

Callan, T., Nolan, B. and Whelan, C. T. (1993), Resources, deprivation and the measurement of poverty, *Journal of Social Policy*, 22, 2: 141–72.

Cohen, R., Coxall, J., Craig, G. and Sadiq-Sangster, A. (1992), *Hardship Britain, Being Poor in the 1990s*, London: Child Poverty Action Group in association with Family Service Units.

Cole-Hamilton, I. and Lang, T. (1986), *Tightening Belts*, London: London Food Commission.

Consumers' Association (1997), A healthy diet: only all right for some? *Health Which?* October: 162–5. Also *The Food Divide: eating on a low income*, Policy Paper, October.

Craig, G. and Dowler, E. (1997), "Let them eat cake!" Poverty, hunger and the UK state. In G. Riches (ed.), *First World Hunger: Food Security and Welfare Politics*, Basingstoke: Macmillan Press, pp. 108–33.

Dallison, J. (1996), RDAs and DRVs: scientific constants or social constructs? The case of vitamin C. Unpublished PhD thesis, University of Sussex.

Davey Smith, G. and Brunner, E. (1997), Socio-economic differentials in health: the role of nutrition, *Proceedings of the Nutrition Society*, 56: 75–90.

Department of Health (1996), *Low Income, Food, Nutrition and Health: Strategies for Improvement*. Report from the Low Income Project Team to the Nutrition Task Force, London: Department of Health.

Department of Health (1999), *Improving Shopping Access*, Policy Action Team 13, London: Department of Health.

Department of Health (2000), *The National School Fruit Scheme*, London: Department of Health. *http://www.doh.gov.uk/schoolfruitscheme/*

Department for Work and Pensions (formerly the Department of Social Security) (2002), *Measuring Child Poverty: a Consultation Document*, London: DWP. *www.dwp.gov.uk*

Dobson, B., Beardsworth, A., Keil, T. and Walker, R. (1994), *Diet, Choice and Poverty: Social, Cultural and Nutritional Aspects of Food Consumption among Low Income Families*, London: Family Policy Studies Centre with the Joseph Rowntree Foundation.

Dobson, B., Kellard, K., with Talbot, D. (2000), *A Recipe for Success? An Evaluation of a Community Food Project*, University of Loughborough: Centre for Research in Social Policy.

Donkin, A. J. M., Dowler, E. A., Stevenson, S. J. and Turner, S. A. (2000), Mapping access to food in a deprived area: the development of price and availability indices, *Public Health Nutrition*, 3, 1: 31–8.

Dowler, E. (1998), Budgeting for food on a low income: the case of lone parents, *Food Policy*, 22, 5: 405–17.

Dowler, E. (2001), Inequalities in diet and physical activity in Europe, *Public Health Nutrition*, 4, 2B: 701–9.

Dowler, E. and Calvert, C. (1995), *Nutrition and Diet in Lone-parent Families in London*, London: Family Policy Studies Centre with the Joseph Rowntree Foundation.

Dowler, E. and Leather, S. (2000), "Spare some change for a bite to eat?" From primary poverty to social exclusion: the role of nutrition and food. In J. Bradshaw and R. Sainsbury (eds), *Experiencing Poverty*, Aldershot: Ashgate, pp. 200–18.

Dowler, E., Turner, S., with Dobson, B. (2001), *Poverty Bites: Food, Health and Poor Families*, London: Child Poverty Action Group.

Dowler, E., Blair, A., Donkin, A., Grundy, C. and Rex, D. (forthcoming), Mapping access to healthy food in Sandwell, *Urban Studies*.

Drummond, J. C., Wilbraham, A. and Hollingsworth, D. (1959), *The Englishman's Food: a History of Five Centuries of the English Diet*, 2nd edn, London: Jonathan Cape.

Gordon, D., Adelman, L., Ashworth, K., Bradshaw, J., Levitas, R., Middleton, S., Pantazis, C., Patsios, D., Payne, S., Townsend, P. and Williams, J. (2000), *Poverty and Social Exclusion in Britain*, York: Joseph Rowntree Foundation.

Graham, H. (ed.) (2001), *Understanding Health Inequalities*, Buckingham: Open University Press.

Howard, M., Garnham, A., Fimister, G. and Veit-Wilson, J. (2001), *Poverty: the Facts*, 4th edn, London: Child Poverty Action Group.

James, W. P. T., Nelson, M., Ralph, A. and Leather, S. (1997), The contribution of nutrition to inequalities in health, *British Medical Journal*, 314: 1545–9.

Joseph Rowntree Foundation (1995), *Inquiry into Income and Wealth*, vol. 1, York: Joseph Rowntree Foundation.

Kempson, E. and Bennett, F. (1997), *Local Living Costs*, London: Policy Studies Institute.

Kempson, E., Bryson, A. and Rowlingson, K. (1994), *Hard Times: How Poor Families Make Ends Meet*, London: Policy Studies Institute.

Killeen, D. (1999), *Food Security: a Challenge for Scotland*, Glasgow: Poverty Alliance.

Lang, T., Andrews, C., Bedale, C., Hannon, E. and Hulme, J. (1984), *Jam Tomorrow?* Manchester: Manchester Food Policy Unit.

Lang, T., Caraher, M., Dixon, P. and Carr-Hill, R. (1999), *The Contribution of Cooking to Health Inequalities*, London: Health Education Authority.

Lang, T. and Rayner, G. (eds) (2001), *Why Health is the Key to the Future of Food and Farming: Joint Submission to the Policy Commission on the Future of Food and Farming in the UK*, London: UK Public Health Association. *www.ukpha.org.uk*

Lang, T., Barling, D. and Caraher, M. (2001), Food, social policy and the environment: towards a new model. *Social Policy and Administration*, 35, 5: 538–58.

Leat, D. (1998), Food choice and the British system of formal and informal welfare provision: questions for research. In A. Murcott (ed.), *The Nation's Diet: the Social Science of Food Choice*, London: Longman.

Leather, S. (1996), *The Making of Modern Malnutrition: an Overview of Food Poverty in the UK*, London: Caroline Walker Trust.

Leon, D. and Walt, G. (eds) (2001), *Poverty, Inequality and Health: an International Perspective*, Oxford: Oxford University Press.

Lipton, M. (1982), *Poverty, Undernutrition and Hunger*, World Bank Staff Working Paper, Washington, DC: World Bank.

McGlone, P., Dobson, B., Dowler, E. and Nelson, M. (1999), *Food Projects and How They Work*, York: York Publishing for the Joseph Rowntree Foundation.

M'Gonigle, G. C. M. and Kirby, J. (1936), *Poverty and Public Health*, London: Victor Gollancz.

Mack, J. and Lansley, S. (1985), *Poor Britain*, London: George Allen and Unwin.

Marmot, M. and Wilkinson, R. G. (eds) (1999), *Social Determinants of Health*, Oxford: Oxford University Press.

Maurer, D. and Sobal, S. (eds) (1995), *Eating Agendas: Food and Nutrition as Social Problems*, New York: Aldine de Gruyter.

Elizabeth Dowler

Maxwell, S. (1999), *Solutions Outside the Box: Can we Finally Implement the Human Right to Food?* Briefing Paper, London: Overseas Development Institute. *www.odi.org.uk*

Middleton, S., Ashworth, K. and Walker, R. (1994), *Family Fortunes*, London: Child Poverty Action Group.

Morris, J., Donkin, A., Wonderling, D., Wilkinson, P. and Dowler, E. (2000), A minimum income for healthy living, *European Journal of Epidemiology and Community Health*, 54: 885–9.

Mosley, P. and Dowler, E. (eds) (in press), *Poverty and Social Exclusion in North and South*, London: Routledge.

Murcott, A. (1994), Food and nutrition in post-war Britain. In J. Obelkevich and P. Caterall (eds), *Understanding Post-war British Society*, London: Routledge.

NCC (ed.) (1995), *Budgeting for Food on Benefits: Budget Studies and their Application in Europe*, London: National Consumer Council.

NCH (1991), *NCH Poverty and Nutrition Survey (1991)*, London: National Children's Home.

Nelson, M., Mayer, A. M. and Manley, P. (1993), The food budget. In J. Bradshaw (ed.), *Budget Standards for the United Kingdom*, Aldershot: Avebury Press, pp. 35–64.

Pantazis, C. and Gordon, D. (eds) (2000), *Tackling Inequalities: Where Are We and What Can Be Done?* Bristol: Policy Press.

Parker, H. with Nelson, M., Oldfield, N., Dallison, J., Hutton, S., Paterakis, S., Sutherland, H. and Thirlwart, M. (1998), *Low Cost but Acceptable: a Minimum Income Standard for the UK*, Bristol: Policy Press and Zacchaeus Trust for the Family Budget Unit.

Petty, E. C. (1987), *The Impact of the Newer Knowledge of Nutrition: Nutrition Science and Nutrition Policy, 1900–1939*. Unpublished PhD thesis, University of London.

Piachaud, D. and Webb, J. (1996), *The Price of Food: Missing out on Mass Consumption*, Suntory and Toyota International Centre for Economics and Related Disciplines, London: London School of Economics.

Radimer, K. L., Olsen, C. M. and Campbell, C. C. (1990), Development of indicators to assess hunger, *Journal of Nutrition*, 120: 1544–8.

Riches, G. (ed.) (1997), *First World Hunger: Food Security and Welfare Politics*, Basingstoke: Macmillan Press.

Rivers, J. P. W. (1979), The profession of nutrition—an historical perspective, *Proceedings of the Nutrition Society*, 38: 225–31.

Rowntree, B. S. (1901), *Poverty: A Study of Town Life*, London: Macmillan.

Smith, D. (1995), The social construction of dietary standards: the British Medical Association–Ministry of Health Advisory Committee on Nutrition Report of 1934. In D. Maurer and J. Sobal (eds), *Eating Agendas: Food and Nutrition as Social Problems*, New York: Aldine de Gruyter, pp. 279–303.

Speak, S. and Graham, S. (2000), *Service not Included: Social Implications of Private Sector Service Restructuring in Marginalised Neighbourhoods*, Bristol: Policy Press for the Joseph Rowntree Foundation.

Townsend, P. (1979), *Poverty in the United Kingdom*, Harmondsworth: Penguin.

Townsend, P., Corrigan, P. and Kowarzik, U. (1987), *Poverty and Labour in London*, London: Low Pay Unit.

Veit-Wilson, J. H. (1986), Paradigms of poverty: a rehabilitation of B. S. Rowntree, *Journal of Social Policy*, 15, 1: 69–99.

Veit-Wilson, J. (1994), Condemned to deprivation? Beveridge's responsibility for the invisibility of poverty. In J. Hills, J. Ditch and H. Glennerster (eds), *Beveridge and Social Security: an International Perspective*, Oxford: Clarendon Press, pp. 97–117.

Walker, C. L. and Church, M. (1978), Poverty by administration: a review of supplementary benefits, nutrition and scale rates, *Journal of Human Nutrition*, 32: 5–18.

Watson, A. (2001), *Food Poverty: Policy Options for the New Millennium*, London: Sustain.

WHO (World Health Organization) (2000), *The Impact of Food and Nutrition on Public Health. Case for a Food and Nutrition Policy and Action Plan for the WHO European Region 2000–2005*, Food and Nutrition Policy Unit, Copenhagen: WHO Regional Office for Europe.

Woolf, B. (1946), Poverty lines and standards of living, *Proceedings of the Nutrition Society*, 5: 71–81.

World Bank (2001), *World Development Report 2000/2001: Attacking Poverty*, New York: Oxford University Press for the World Bank.

Index

Index

Index

Printed and bound by CPI Group (UK) Ltd, Croydon, CR0 4YY

09/06/2025

14686107-0005